Art : Process : Change

"Given the increasing interest in socially engaged art, this is a timely and inspiring book. It offers many insights into the process of making community art from the 1970s to the present through the work of a significant contributor to the field, and clearly explores the challenges facing artists who wish to collaborate with communities."

Beverly Naidus, University of Washington Tacoma, USA

"This clear, comprehensive study, combining history, theory and practice, reveals a critically astute insider hard at work in the field she helped pioneer."

Gregory Sholette, Queens College CUNY, USA

This book brings a practitioner's insight to bear on socially situated art practice through a first-hand glimpse into the development, organisation and delivery of art projects with social agendas. Issues examined include the artist's role in building creative frameworks, the relationship of collaboration to participation, management of collective input, and wider repercussions of the ways that projects are instigated, negotiated and funded. The book contributes to ongoing debates on ethics/aesthetics for art initiatives where process, product and social relations are integral to the mix, and addresses issues of practical functionality in relation to social outcome.

Loraine Leeson is Senior Lecturer at Middlesex University, UK, and was Senior Research Fellow at the University of Westminster, UK.

Routledge Advances in Art and Visual Studies

A full list of titles in this series is available at: www.routledge.com/series/RAVS

Recently published titles:

Looking Beyond Borderlines
North America's Frontier Imagination
Lee Rodney

Intersecting Art and Technology in Practice
Techne/Technique/Technology
Edited by Camille C Baker and Kate Sicchio

Wonder in Contemporary Artistic Practice
Edited by Christian Mieves and Irene Brown

W.J.T. Mitchell's Image Theory
Living Pictures
Edited by Krešimir Purgar

The Politics of Contemporary Art Biennials
Spectacles of Critique, Theory and Art
Panos Kompatsiaris

Contemporary Visual Culture and the Sublime
Edited by Temenuga Trifonova

Art, Animals, and Experience
Relationships to Canines and the Natural World
Elizabeth Sutton

What Drawing and Painting Really Mean
The Phenomenology of Image and Gesture
Paul Crowther

The Concept of the Animal and Modern Theories of Art
Roni Grén

The Aesthetics of Scientific Data Representation
More than Pretty Pictures
Edited by Lotte Philipsen and Rikke Schmidt Kjærgaard

Art : Process : Change
Inside a Socially Situated Practice
Loraine Leeson

Art : Process : Change
Inside a Socially Situated Practice

Loraine Leeson

Routledge
Taylor & Francis Group
LONDON AND NEW YORK

First published 2018 by Routledge

2 Park Square, Milton Park, Abingdon, Oxfordshire OX14 4RN
52 Vanderbilt Avenue, New York, NY 10017

Routledge is an imprint of the Taylor & Francis Group, an informa business

First issued in paperback 2019

Library of Congress Cataloging in Publication Data
Names: Leeson, Loraine, author.
Title: Art : process : change : inside a socially situated practice / by Loraine Leeson.
Description: New York : Routledge, 2017. |
Series: Routledge advances in art and visual studies |
Includes bibliographical references and index.
Identifiers: LCCN 2017021202 | ISBN 9781138670631 (alk. paper)
Subjects: LCSH: Leeson, Loraine—Themes, motives. | Artists and community—England—London—History—20th century. |
Artists and community—England—London—History—21st century.
Classification: LCC N6797.L43245 A35 2017 | DDC 701/.03—dc23
LC record available at https://lccn.loc.gov/2017021202

ISBN: 978-1-138-67063-1 (hbk)
ISBN: 978-0-367-33044-6 (pbk)

Typeset in Sabon
by Florence Production Ltd, Stoodleigh, Devon, UK

To Peter, for the creative years

Contents

Figures

Chapter 1

Chapter 2

Chapter 3

Chapter 4

Chapter 6

Chapter 7

Foreword

This important and timely book by Loraine Leeson covers a crucial period in the development of contemporary art practices. It seems like a long time since the English art world mantra was "art and politics don't mix" and that painting on canvas was the ruling hegemony. This was one of the first accusations against many artists such as myself who are slightly older than Loraine Leeson and Peter Dunn (Dunn is a long time collaborator who then and subsequently made his important contributions to the field), with Leeson going on to create innumerable key projects, which are sometimes miscategorised as "political" art. Of course there is no such animal—all art is economic, ideological and political in different proportions. This notion was part of a major struggle by artists such as Leeson during the radical rethinking of art and its practices in the seventies, although currently it is no longer necessary to eliminate overt or covert relations between art and politics. Art forms such as Abstract Expressionism, which claimed universal and timeless validity when I was a student, turn out to be neither timeless nor universal, but of a place and a time—the Jackson Pollock I saw at the Tate Gallery as a thirteen year old is not the Jackson Pollock we are seeing now.

From Hogarth to Dickens and Cruikshank, to the short WW2 propaganda film *Target For Tonight* and documentary *Night Train,* and even The Beatles song *Eleanor Rigby*, the documentary can be seen as a classic of English art, and a key element in Leeson's projects. Between the radicalism of the late sixties, particularly the important events of 1968 when I was part of the occupations in Hornsey and the London School of Economics, and the current situation with globalisation and the death of the avant-garde (and possibly of the great white male), there has been a complete revolution. The integration of politics/action and culture at this time has been seen in such slogans as "Beneath the paving stones, the beach", or "If there is no dancing at the revolution I'm not coming", or, from a different feminist perspective, "If I'm still expected to make the coffee it's not a revolution", and, of course, the classic "If u r not part of the solution u must b part of the problem".

I was first challenged with the assertion that there was no history of this kind of activity in art at my 1970 exhibition *Garbage Strike* at Sigi Krauss Gallery in Covent Garden. In my search for a historical trajectory I cited Wordsworth, a poet who I encountered through my education in my Cumbrian village, as well as other poets and writers of that time. The general perception of Wordsworth as a poet of landscape is very much mistaken however. In *The Country and the City,* Raymond Williams quotes: "although people know me as a poet, for every hour I spend writing poetry I spend twelve hours considering the economic and political condition of men".

In fact Wordsworth was criticised for his choice of subject matter, which was considered unsuitable for poetry since the convention had been to write about the Greek gods and mythologies. He however democratised both subject and language, and Leeson is following in this radical tradition. Shelley, too, in his poem *Queen Mab* criticised the judiciary, the monarchy and the structure of British politics. Despite this, *Queen Mab* was subsequently in the pockets of 20,000 Chartists in the great rallies of these forbears of the unions several years after Shelley's death. Similarly Emily Brontë in *Wuthering Heights* embraced notions on exclusion with race as an invisible presence, touching on exclusion, migration, gender and sexuality, while Mary Shelley's Frankenstein's monster reflected the anxiety and frustration of Victorian women—the "monster" being women. A number of intensely political thrusts have arguably been deliberately hidden by the British and other establishments, not necessarily in visual art but in English literature, the hegemonic art form in Britain, but have come through to serve as pointers to those of us who find the impulse to conflate art with politics.

Political issues coincided with new media in the late sixties/early seventies with the growing women's movement after Friedan[1] et al. Dagenham women's strike in 1968, and then the women's strike at Brannans in my home village in the North of England, which I made the subject of an exhibition at the ICA in 1972, were serious signals at a period in a London art world that was dominated by the twin solipsisms of abstract paintings and cool disengaged conceptual art and theory as practice. Of my own work, several people said it really wasn't art.

As Leeson describes however, the seventies developed into a time when the art/politics conflation began to gain some momentum among artists. While I exhibited *Strike* in 1972, followed by *Work, Wages and Prices* in 1974, Margaret Harrison, Kay Hunt and Mary Kelly created the *Women and Work* exhibition in 1975 at the South London Gallery, and following my *Material* show in New York in 1978, a new group formed Group Material. To see the work of Dunn and Leeson engaging with the trades union movement certainly helped to reduce my sense of isolation at that time. I also recognised how ways forward in this area were being interestingly and diversely developed in directions I could never have imagined at the beginning of the seventies when I thought *Strike* was my farewell to the art world.

Alongside the advance of feminism and these new art forms in the UK was the attempt to develop a public art that would reach outside the gallery and attempt a public conversation. This was reflected in the US, where a number of artists were displaying posters outside the gallery system. The labor unions in New York, for example, published and posted images of my Feldman show about Northern Ireland around New York, and when Jenny Holzer came to the UK in the mid seventies she fly posted ephemera around London. The US feminists were reluctant to move outside the gallery system, but rather introduced radical subjects within it. Their fight for part of the existing "pie" is exemplified by the way the Guerilla girls aimed to be shown in the New York Met. In the UK, feminists were attempting to set up their own alternative and parallel systems, such as the Women's Postal Art Group. Leeson was a major contributor to the notion that art should move outside the gallery, arguably completely, and negotiating this tricky area was one of Leeson's strengths; in fact, her early recognition of the problem was possibly crucial to her achievements. The activist arts group Not An Alternative recognised the importance of this stance when they wrote:

> Institutional liberation isn't about making institutions better, more inclusive, more participatory. It's about establishing politicised base camps from which ever more coordinated, elaborate, and effective campaigns against the capitalist state in all its racist, exploitative, extractivist, and colonising dimensions can be carried out. This takeover will not happen overnight.[2]

The collaborations with communities and the introduction of interdisciplinary practices show how far Leeson's practice has developed in this way. Her work is realised through direct engagement with communities, as in her most recent project, in which the notion of energy joins forces with community to address one of the world's most crucial issues. There are parallels to be drawn here with my early *Strike* project and also current work about nuclear power and Sellafield, since neither practice features artists "parachuted" into a community, but rather engaging directly with an issue, a location, and a group of people who are personally involved and directed.

Leeson's work in the public domain has taken us a long way from the inelegantly phrased "turd in the plaza" critique of disengaged public art practices of fifty years ago. In this book Leeson explicates this in a way I could not have imagined in 1969 and has brought to her observations on methodology a rigorous knowledge and practice that pictures the art of politics and the politics of art in an important and comprehensive manner. Her contribution to bringing communities and important contemporary issues together to engage with change still reflects her early ambition to "change the world", but has achieved a whole new perspective on what is possible.

Conrad Atkinson
Emeritus Professor University of California
Cumbria 2016

Notes

1. Betty Friedan's *The Feminine Mystique* (1963) is widely credited with sparking the beginning of second-wave feminism in the United States.
2. Not an Alternative, "Institutional Liberation" in *e-flux* online, No. 77, Nov 2016.

References

Not an Alternative, "Institutional Liberation" in *e-flux* online (No. 77, Nov 2016) www.e-flux.com/journal/77/76215/institutional-liberation

Raymond Williams, *The Country and the City* (Chatto and Windus: London, 1973).

Acknowledgements

It was the artist Ailbhe Murphy who first suggested I consider completing my PhD at the Interface Institute at the University of Ulster in 2007, a suggestion for which I will be eternally grateful. This was a significant step on the way to producing the book that I had been wanting to write for a very long time, and enabled me to develop my ideas in an environment that was rigorous, stimulating and supportive. Eternal thanks therefore to my supervisors Declan McGonagle and Kerstin Mey, who offered intellectual stimulus from their deep knowledge of the issues at hand, which never failed to be both challenging and empathetic. Kerstin Mey has continued as a mentor in this capacity and played a pivotal role in enabling me to see this project through to realisation, not least in her help with the final revision.

Heartfelt thanks to artist John Cockram for our many conversations in the early days of writing that helped me grapple with ideas, and particularly with methodologies. Also to Belinda Kidd, original administrator of the Docklands Community Poster Project and cSPACE board member, who lent her extensive knowledge of both the practice and myself to checking the manuscript and offering valuable advice. I am similarly indebted to Karen Merkel, media artist and longstanding creative collaborator, who provided valuable information on the community arts movement, while her thoughtful support and incisive mind have helped with some of the more difficult parts of the text.

Others have also given of their time to help me think through different aspects of the book, particularly Alberto Duman, my teaching "buddy" at Middlesex University, and Jean Lowe, one of the original members of the Joint Docklands Action Group. My sons Liam and Louis may not realise how much they have helped. They were teenagers when I started the process and, without the patient understanding shown to their mother who monopolised the family's computer and regularly failed to cook dinner, none of this would have been achieved. I am grateful for every instance they have listened to the television using headphones so as not to disturb me. As young men they remain equally supportive, also inspirational in the way each is realising their own creativity.

The book would not exist without the art practice, and so the greatest thanks goes to all those people with whom I have had the benefit of working over the last forty years—the artists, activists, teachers, architects, cultural workers, youth leaders, designers, programmers, scientists, engineers, academics, seniors, young people and children who have contributed to the work that forms its subject. Without them there would have been no one from whom to gain the knowledge that I am now privileged to pass on. Particular among these is Peter Dunn, with whom I shared half my creative life. That partnership made possible all the early work, which was also so personally transformational. I am especially grateful for our ongoing dialogue, his insightful understanding of critical theory coupled with practical ingenuity, and his unfailing ability to think outside the frame. His generosity in providing additions and amendments to the text as well as agreeing to the reproduction of images of our joint work is also much appreciated.

Conrad Atkinson and Margaret Harrison have been role models of political astuteness and integrity my whole working life. Their friendship and support has been a constant source of encouragement as well as a creative touchstone. I am most grateful to Conrad Atkinson for his Foreword to this volume, in which he reminds me of the place of my own practice within the UK's long history of cultural politics.

Thanks to John Nassari, who photographed the launch of *The Young Person's Guide to the Royal Docks*, and also to John Cockram, Graham Downes and Anne-Marie Pereira de Mello who appear in that photo. All were key players in that project. Rhiannon Lyons has kindly given permission to reproduce the character template that she created as a child for *VOLCO*, as have collaborators and participants from the *Active Energy* project, who have given photo permissions and so much more. These include engineers Toby Borland and Stephen Dodds, Minnie Hill of Northside Seniors and, last but not least, members of the Geezers Club—Ray Gipson, John Bevan, Dennis Banks, John Day, Brian Godfrey, Tony Basra and Rick Ayliffe, who appear in the photos in this book. I am equally indebted to the rest of the Geezers, particularly Ted Lewis who came up with the idea of developing tidal power, and for their energy and enthusiasm that has made this current project such a delight to work on.

Finally, my appreciation goes to the editors at Routledge, who have enabled me to turn the dream of this book into a reality.

Introduction

I simply wanted to change the world. That is not as outrageous as it sounds. Adulthood started for me in the early seventies when many in my generation rebelled against the conventional lives achieved by our parents and grandparents who had survived two world wars. Brought up in greater security, we challenged the establishment with an optimism underpinned by Marxist thought and eastern spirituality. With this new information we sought alternatives to individualism, the Cold War, capitalism, nuclear arms and radioactive waste, supported feminism and collectivism and recognised that, if enough people intent on making a more equitable and peaceful society joined together, the world would indeed change. Despite the enormous societal changes that have intervened, many decades on these principles are still not far from my core values.

Although immersion in art pre-dated my political awareness, the latter brought with it some recognition of the role of culture in society, reinforced by the radical practices of other artists together with the writings of critical thinkers such as Raymond Williams, who so influenced the Left in my formative years. Of particular significance was the working collaboration and personal relationship I developed with artist Peter Dunn from the early seventies. With each other's support and insight we were able to try out a practical re-thinking of how an art that was directly contributing to social change could be realised.

For the subsequent forty years, initially with Peter and then with others, I have been using my skills as an artist to explore ways of supporting communities engaged knowingly or implicitly in transforming society, resulting in the projects outlined in the first part of this book. While the work has been frequently described and its wider political context addressed, little has yet been written concerning the processes involved in its development and realisation, nor the means through which broad intention became enacted through the hands-on practicalities of production. I am therefore specifically focusing here on how methodologies of organisation and social interactions have addressed the work's wider cultural and social agenda, together with the roles of aesthetics and functionality in process, product and outcomes. The present climate of increased activism and a growing interest in socially engaged practice would seem to make this an appropriate moment to bring this information into the public domain so that hands-on experience can contribute to current debates around these issues. These pages therefore constitute a process of excavation into those regularly occurring procedures that have woven their way through the practice, starting from what is known through the process of active involvement, but infrequently articulated. The intuitive enactment of art that is realised through interaction with other people is of course not unlike any other creative process. "Gut" feelings, intuition and underlying, but sometimes barely conscious, evaluative reflection inform work in the public realm as much as they do in the studio. At the same time this work takes on board the thoughts and ideas of others, together with wider social or political considerations. I will be attempting to identify the specific nature of the creative process in relation to this kind of practice and to uncover some of those decisions and actions made "on the run", often in time-pressured situations, that can play a key role in the outcomes and wider social ramifications of the work. The nature of the collaborations and interactions that lie behind individual projects will also be examined, together with their specificity and significance. The issue of finance will be frequently addressed, both in terms of how and from where projects are funded, and the impact this has made on the way the work is developed and delivered. It is one of those many hidden issues that are often left unconsidered when looking only at the outcome of a work, although in my own experience it has required at least as much time and an equal amount of creativity as the artistic production.

By taking a long view I have been able to identify factors such as these and other themes that have emerged through constant re-use and re-appraisal. Rather than an argument of concepts, then, the starting point for the book is the work itself from which embedded knowledge and experience are extrapolated. If there is an argument or proposal to be made here, it is represented through the totality of the practice as described. This writing project in fact parallels the methods of the art practice, where products emerge after having being developed over time and through a continuum of ongoing dialogue. In this case interactions with colleagues through informal conversations, joint initiatives, conferences, books and articles, and not least the supervision process for the doctoral thesis that preceded this publication have brought the valuable experience of people with different knowledge and expertise to bear on my emerging thoughts. I should point out that the book is written from my own perspective as an arts practitioner in the UK, and therefore some of the contextual information may not be relevant to those living and working elsewhere in the world. I hope however that its main points will nevertheless come through and can serve as a useful point of reference to others wherever they are located.

A previous publication has also looked at my work in some detail. *Art for Change: Loraine Leeson, Works from 1975–2005* was a catalogue produced in 2005 by the Neue Gesellschaft für bildende Kunst to accompany a retrospective of my work in their Berlin gallery. It contained essays in English and German by key thinkers, curators, art historians and practitioners, including one by myself, that explored different aspects of the practice, accompanied by reproductions of the images. This former publication did not address the methodologies of the work however, and therefore does not duplicate or share the same intentions as the content of this book.

The first part of the book outlines the span of the work within its social and political contexts and sets out the material that is later to be interrogated in terms of issues and approaches. There is a chapter dedicated to each of four decades, within which projects are listed chronologically to identify the changing social and political environment of that time. This temporal layout also emphasises the processes and procedures through which the practice has evolved, and the way that the relationships underpinning each creative undertaking, together with the lessons learned from that experience, have laid the foundations for subsequent activity.

Chapter 1 begins with contextual information on how the "process art" of the sixties fed through to the activist and community art of the seventies, touching on the impact of Marxism and feminism. Early influences on my own practice are introduced here, including the commencement of the longstanding collaboration with Peter, followed by our first attempts to move the work from an institutional framework into the social sphere. Projects summarised include the *London/Berlin Series*, which involved interactive events conducted when Peter was a postgraduate at the Slade and I was on a scholarship year in Germany. Next I describe the challenges of the image and text work of *The Present Day Creates History*, shown in local libraries, a precursor to our first activist work using video, posters and exhibition in support of the Bethnal Green Hospital Campaign. The chapter ends with a description of the collaboration with health workers' unions on the East London Health Project, for which we produced "visual pamphlets" addressing the potential effects of the first round of government cuts on the National Health Service.

The next chapter offers background information on the development of the London Docklands in the eighties. It demonstrates how and why the Docklands Community Poster Project came into being and the principles on which it was founded, with a description of how community representatives collaborated with the project team to provide contextual information and steer the content of the artefacts produced. The work of this time included large-scale photo-murals with imagery created through montaged black and white photographs that changed to reveal unfolding narratives on the community's response to the development. Support in the form of graphics and ephemera was also given to specific campaigns, with travelling exhibitions created for display at meetings and festivals, culminating in a *Docklands Roadshow* that took the lessons of the London Docklands to other development zones in the UK and continental Europe. Notable initiatives of the campaign included the *People's Armadas to Parliament*, which saw thousands of people take to the river to publicise the issues and persuade parliamentarians to implement the changes outlined in the People's Charter for Docklands from day one of the Labour Party coming into power. The Docklands Community Poster Project also designed the *People's Plan for the Royal Docks*, an initiative led by local people and supported by the Greater London Council's Popular Planning Unit, which is still widely used as a model for community-led planning.

At the beginning of the nineties the Docklands Community Poster Project transformed into the Art of Change and Chapter 3 describes the practice I undertook through this organisation for the rest of this decade. Work was conducted from this time through discrete projects, many with schools, which aimed to address the impact that changes in the urban environment were having on people's quality of life and cultural identity. The first examples described, *West Meets East* and *Celebrating the Difference,* made use of the previously constructed photo-mural sites through work with secondary schools to explore issues of identity and diversity. *Between Family Lines* next combined the technologies of tape/slide and sound to critique a widespread return to "family values" that was at this time taking place across cultures. Commissions by the Tate and Art Gallery of Ontario followed in the form of *Awakenings, I.D and Momentos*, through which young people explored identity in response to works in the gallery collection. These projects made particular use of advances in digital imaging and the worldwide web, the latter progressed through *The Infinity Story*, undertaken with the whole cohort of a junior school. This project, with its primitive use of interactive technologies, was to lay the foundations for new work that made extensive use of the Internet for collective creativity.

Chapter 4 outlines work conducted through cSPACE, initially established at University of East London following the demise of the Art of Change at the turn of the millennium. This era was characterised by a more individualistic politics, while the social value of art finally became accepted, with artistic input incorporated into many government run schemes designed to counteract social exclusion. Projects of this time included *The Catch* public artwork, involving local children in a commission that supported the regeneration of Barking town centre. *VOLCO* was a decade long initiative that picked up on the previous experiments with the rapidly developing Internet, setting out to counteract lack of creativity in the school curriculum while introducing young minds to the idea that they could indeed create a new world. The mentoring scheme *Cascade* took place in tandem with this over a period of five years, involving three levels of education to address issues of local regeneration. In its last stages it culminated in an online guide to the Royal Docks produced by and for young people. This led to *The Young Person's Guide to East London*, which used the 2012 Olympics as an opportunity to involve, disseminate and value the knowledge and creative production of East London youth. Growing consciousness about the environment led to collaboration with a scientist on issues of biodiversity in the tidal Thames, as explored through *Lambeth Floating Marsh*, which created new habitats for micro-organisms in the urban reaches of that river, using pavement projections to attract the interest of passers by. The final project described is *Active Energy,* of eight years' duration and still ongoing at the time of writing. I describe the project's development and its many spin-offs as the self-named senior's group The Geezers strive to introduce renewable energy into their community supported by myself and as much other professional help as we can muster.

The last chapter in Part 1 observes and comments on approaches that have run through the work. I identify a process of "joining up" that has helped to facilitate the input of diverse sources of expertise to projects, and note how all the projects described have woven together elements of need, opportunity, research, skills, context and funding. I also pinpoint some key aspects of the artist's role, including the construction of organisational and material "frameworks" to facilitate the gathering of community experience, and the requirement to "hold" a project while disparate elements combine to produce sometimes surprising results. I observe how "staying true" to the input of each participant has proved important to the authenticity and social effectiveness of the work, as has ensuring that the "drivers" of the content are those with direct experience of the issues involved. The chapter ends with a comment on the personal and financial precarity of working in this field.

Having laid out the practice in some detail in Part 1, Part 2 then considers the methodologies that have been involved. Chapter 6 begins this process by focusing on particular issues relating to development, realisation and outcomes. After looking at how initial ideas and the impetus for a project are built up through collaboration and dialogue, it explores the visual and organisational structuring that enables different parties to interact, and through which the work can finally be realised. I go on to identify those processes required in participatory projects to capture, hold and combine multiple ideas, visual or otherwise, and demonstrate how these frameworks ultimately create a means for collective expression.

Practitioners and critics in this field of art are often interested in the "underside" of projects—the difficulties encountered, and the failures that are rarely discussed, as this is where much of the learning takes place. I therefore explore some of the challenges that have arisen and indicate the strategies employed to address them. I will show why collaborative projects require careful management and how minor difficulties can become amplified and potentially destructive, particularly where multiple partners are involved. In relation to this I indicate the relevance of Freire's "problem posing" approach and how it can be helpful to see a process of ongoing troubleshooting as an integral part of a project's realisation.

The next section on "outcomes and products" deals with the pragmatics of bringing a material or virtual output into being through collective endeavour. Here I highlight ways in which an arts project can provide a vehicle for addressing the diverse needs of partners, collaborators and participants, each with a different interest and stake in the work. The process/product continuum of this nature of work is then examined, together with the problematics of exhibiting process-based outputs, and the significance of a project's "afterlife", particularly in relation to its potential transferability and sustainability. Finally, I consider the role of evaluation both in relation to funding and policy, as well as those informal procedures that feed back into projects to inform progress and facilitate future development. This section ends with a critical look at notions of "good practice" as frequently used in institutional funding, commissioning and evaluation procedures, and a warning of how these can be of detriment to the very artistic innovation that is being sought.

Chapter 7 addresses some of the wider issues that are thrown up by the practice. Definitions of "collaboration" and "participation" are questioned using examples drawn from past projects to demonstrate how the interweaving of different relationships determines their evolution. I then look at the relevance of interdisciplinary working in relation to social change including the early influence of Joseph Beuys on my own work, noting the importance of understanding one's own discipline and referring particularly to Alana Jelinek's differentiation between art and activism. Here I also address the value of creating spaces, real or virtual, that facilitate interaction between people with different life experiences. A number of years ago I coined the phrase "dynamics of difference" to describe the creative energy produced by this process, and in relation to this I will consider how the practice has addressed issues of ethnic diversity and migration against a backdrop of increasingly imposed and institutionalised notions of multiculturalism. Identity was a central theme of the politics of the eighties and nineties, also reflected in my work of that era, and I will note a shift in the practice from a directly activist approach towards one that has increasingly taken on board issues of identity and recognition.

Education has always been regarded as a poor relation to culture by mainstream art institutions in the UK. As an art practitioner it has generally been a label to avoid due to its widespread institutional use as a repository where community-based work could be kept safely away from the mainstream. While I will return in Chapter 8 to look at this in relation to the wider issue of functionality in art, here I concentrate on the positive connections between creative production and learning. The educational value that can be derived from art projects that directly involve others, particularly the young, is potentially immense and much of my practice has addressed the educational agenda in a more direct way—albeit with a cultural and social rather than a pedagogic goal. Indeed it has frequently directly embraced the UK's restrictive

National Curriculum, and I will be discussing those aspects of my work since the nineties that have been conducted through schools and educational establishments. In this section I will also ask what happens when the spheres of cultural production and educational process collide, and relate the experience of some instances where the encompassing of both has been achieved.

Technology has underpinned all my work, incorporating photographic and montage techniques from analogue to digital. The rise of the Internet since the mid-nineties opened up new possibilities for collective interaction. Indeed, most of my projects in the new millennium have involved web sites and digital interactivity. I will look at both positive and negative outcomes of this on the work's social agenda, questioning whether the online involvement of larger numbers of participants has reduced the experience for each individual. This section will also consider the extent to which technologies have impacted on the nature of the work itself and shaped subsequent practice.

Although there are many artist-led group initiatives in the UK, the most common perception of the visual artist is still that of an autonomous producer. Early in the eighties I made a decision with Peter to create an organisation through which the practice could be better realised. I will re-visit that move, looking at my choice of working through an organisational base from that time to the present. Sifting through the benefits and problems of different company structures and related administrative frameworks, I will also identify the contribution to the work made by others involved in these organisations—trustees, advisory members, employees, freelance artists and other professionals. These issues connect directly to the matter of funding, and the next section is devoted to how projects have been financed, and the extent to which shifts in public funding practices have affected the work over time. Arts policy will also be considered in relation to the growing trend of "top-down" approaches to funding and commissioning by institutions and public agencies. I will assess the impact of this on specific projects, questioning if and how socially situated work with a different agenda to the mainstream might continue to survive.

The policies that drive public funding are closely related to the regeneration issues that have formed a constant to much of my practice, from the redevelopment of the London Docklands through to the building programmes associated with Thames Gateway and the London 2012 Olympics. Over recent decades artists and cultural agencies have been increasingly identified as having a role to play in urban regeneration. This has served to reinforce the institutionalisation of arts-led social outcomes while nevertheless expanding opportunities for artists through commissioned projects. I will ask whether such an environment can foster or even accommodate work that benefits people over commercial or institutional priorities, and identify some of the strategies I have developed for weaving a way through this minefield. Most importantly I will consider useful roles that art with a social agenda might continue to take in relation to large-scale development.

Consideration of social change itself concludes Chapter 7, with a look at the wider social impact that can be made through art and how this might be ascertained and understood. I mention the archiving function that art can carry, intentional or otherwise, and also relate some of the project strategies to Chantal Mouffe's concept of "new resistances" that are re-shaping society from the bottom up. I then regard more closely the notion of "giving voice" in terms of creating opportunity for the wider society to hear articulation of knowledge that rarely reaches the public domain, as well as the strategy of developing alternative models, as learned through the Docklands campaigning. Finally I consider if and how social change brought about through an arts project can be assessed, and if so, what kind of legacy a successful project can hope to achieve.

Chapter 8 is concerned with issues of aesthetics in relation to the field of socially situated practice, both in terms of its more traditional meaning of visual power, as well as those other "rules and principles" through which my own work has been realised. My first task is to "locate the aesthetic" in disparate projects, asking how it may best be considered, and to what end. In his first book *Conversation Pieces* Grant Kester usefully sited this field of work within a notion of "dialogical aesthetics", circumnavigating the formalist arguments put forward by Nicolas Bourriaud in *Relational Aesthetics*. While my own focus in this book is on artworks created through a dialogic process, I am also aware of the significance of their tangible outputs. I therefore explore the role of visual and imaginative resonance in this work, despite the fact that it operates within a different paradigm to the avant-garde approach to social engagement advocated by Claire Bishop in her 2006 article for *Artforum*.

This leads me to consider the issue of function in art as it pulls away from the thinking originating in the Enlightenment that placed artistic function wholly within the realm of the aesthetic. At that time it served to liberate art from the utilitarian focus of the impending Industrial Revolution, but continued to be held sacrosanct by the art world for centuries, and was still pervasive for most of my career. Despite the fact that in recent times practical function has become a regular feature of socially engaged art practice, even desirable, during my working life this aspect of the work was frequently denigrated and criticised for being more akin to education or social work. I therefore make the case for utility and why it has been such an important and necessary element of my projects, but also indicate the problems that can be caused when institutions or government agencies embrace this feature for their own ends.

The book culminates in consideration of the wider political and cultural context against which some community-based visual arts developed via public art into the more recently termed "social practice". Arts policies by the UK's various political parties as well as its Arts Councils are examined here, together with the more radical socialist strategies of a recently re-formed Labour Party and the potential for change in both social and arts policy in the event of a change of government at the next general election. "Socially engaged art" is now developing on a global scale, with a new widespread spirit of activism and significant critique of this field, although the latter to date stems mainly from the US. I outline how these initiatives have the potential to open up possibilities for art to take a renewed role in social change, so long as they can escape co-option. I end by laying out what is needed for the support and encouragement of an art of change without bringing about even greater institutional control of this sector, but also signal the challenges that may lie ahead in the light of the current move to the right in western politics.

When embarking on the research that eventually led to this book I was driven by a desire to develop my understanding of the processes underpinning community-based art against the larger intention of social change. I was also curious to discover where the practice was situated in relation to the "cultural democracy" debates of the eighties, the shifting ideologies of the nineties and the aesthetic considerations of social practice in the present. That journey has eventually brought me to somewhere familiar that I had not previously known, to discover that the value, validity and authority I sought were to be found within the practice itself, which only had to be interrogated to offer up its lessons. The following is the result of my desire to place these findings in the public domain so that new generations of artists will not have to "reinvent the wheel", but can instead take the best of the old and re-fashion with new strategies to help bring the power of art to the heart of social transformation.

References

Claire Bishop, "The Social Turn: Collaboration and Its Discontents" in *Artforum*, (February, 2006).

Nicolas Bourriaud, *Relational Aesthetics* (Dijon: Les Presses du Réel, 2002).

Paolo Freire, *Pedagogy of the Oppressed* (London: Penguin, 1970).

Alana Jelinek, *This is not Art: activism and other non-art* (London and New York: IB Tauris, 2013).

Grant Kester, *Conversation Pieces: Community and Communication in Modern Art* (Berkely, Los Angeles and London: University of California Press, 2004).

Carmen Mörsch, et al., *Art for Change: Loraine Leeson, Works from 1975–2005* (Berlin: NGBK, 2005).

Chantal Mouffe, *On the Political* (Oxford and New York: Routledge, 2005).

Part 1

Contexts and Case Studies

Part 1 outlines a series of collaborative and participatory art projects with communities realised over a period of forty years. To help differentiate the changing social and political conditions of the times and the way that these factors have informed the nature of the practice, the projects are grouped into decades, which in some cases also reflect the span of the organisations through which they were realised. Since no project arose from a vacuum, I have indicated the processes and procedures through which each has evolved, the relationships underpinning them, lessons learned from the experience and how each has laid the foundations for subsequent practice. I conclude with some comments in hindsight on structures, principles and methods that have run through the work as well as the precarious nature of the whole endeavour.

1 Seventies

In 1973, Lucy Lippard published *Six Years: Dematerialisation of the Art Object*, tracing the move from minimalism through conceptualism to "process art" from the late sixties to early seventies[1]. It marked a moment when post-modernist thought in the visual arts was becoming reflected through increasing interest in process over product and a proliferation of new art forms. Individual creative authorship came under question, as did the role of the artist in relation to society. Marxist theory, particularly Gramsci's notion of hegemony, informed the growth of activist art practice of this time. Reflecting back on that decade, *Beyond the Fragments* by Sheila Rowbotham, Lynne Segal and Hilary Wainwright helped identify this time as an era in which previously passive or angry individuals and groups in isolation, such as women, gays, blacks and youth, became militant and organised[2]. In *Community, Art and the State* Owen Kelly surveyed this period in terms of creative work with communities and identified three distinct types. The first was the creation of new and liberating forms of expression, as in the work of the Arts Lab (precursor to the London Institute of Contemporary Arts). The second was the movement of fine artists out of the gallery and onto the streets. The third was a "new kind" of political activist who believed creativity to be an essential tool in any kind of radical struggle[3].

The first of these models was characterised by individual artists, particularly in Europe, using the gallery as a public arena for political activism. Conrad Atkinson, for example, staged his *Strike at Brannan's* exhibition at the ICA in London in 1972 to document ongoing industrial action at a thermometer factory in Cumbria. Workers held meetings in the gallery and one outcome of this public event was the unionisation of the factory's London branch. There was also significant arts activism in Germany—Hans Haacke was busy exposing the financial workings of big business, while Klaus Staeck brought together art and activism in political posters. Perhaps most influential to my own practice was Joseph Beuys. Crossing traditional and organisational boundaries, he saw the artist as a key player in social transformation, establishing the Free International University as a framework for interdisciplinary interaction and, briefly, a real institution. I was fortunate to experience at first hand this combination of political, issue-based thinking with art and education through my early involvement with events connected to his initiatives. Caroline Tisdall, my Art History tutor at University of Reading, had worked closely with Beuys for many years, and through her I not only came to hear Beuys speak, but was also included in meetings and events where current issues were debated from an interdisciplinary perspective. These experiences were shared with Peter Dunn, a fellow Fine Art undergraduate with whom I began an ongoing collaboration. In 1977 we were invited to participate in a "discussion room" set up for debate on social issues established by Beuys at Documenta 6, where we were able to test our emerging practice in an international forum. These experiences, with their concepts of cultural production as a catalyst for change and new ideas generated by interdisciplinary collaboration, laid important foundations for our subsequent practices.

The work of these artists with political agendas was nevertheless gallery oriented, and another form of art that characterised this era proved similarly influential. "Cultural democracy"[4] was the philosophy that underpinned the Community Arts movement. It recognised cultural plurality and took the premise that everybody is creative and has the right to express their ideas through creative means. Among its primary concerns was the decentralisation of cultural resources, production and distribution, aiming to move cultural production from a system in which ideas and products were transmitted from centralising sources to one in which they would be produced and distributed from the many local and regional sources where they occurred. Emphasis was also placed on support for the subsequent federation or networking of these resources, although its central premise remained the empowerment of ordinary people and communities through the arts[5]. In comparison to the mainstream, this movement was highly organised and subject to self-examination, with much of its debate in the late seventies and early eighties taking place through the Association of Community Artists. Two key conferences were organised in the UK. *Friends and Allies* was held in Salisbury in 1983 and *Another Standard* in Sheffield in 1986, the latter paralleled by a US event *ImaginAction* in Boston Massachusetts the same year. The sector was successful in securing funding and gained recognition from both local government and the Arts Council of Great Britain. It was also largely responsible for influencing the way that art was funded through the Greater London Council following the election of a left Labour majority in 1981. In this seat of metropolitan government Community Arts gained its own sub-committee status with an increasing £1m annual budget, resulting in half a decade of prolific arts activity in the capital.

Feminism was a similarly growing force at this time. Conscious-raising groups were becoming more widespread, awareness of women's achievements was growing, and women felt increasingly supported in standing up for their rights as equal citizens both within and outside of the patriarchal establishment. From the perspective of the third millennium it is hard to fathom the extent of the limitations that continued to be placed on women in the home and workplace in that very recent historical period. These issues were both reflected in, and on occasion, led by the arts and one of the many creative initiatives that for me made enormous impact was the exhibition *Women and Work: A Document on the Division of Labour in Industry* by artists Margaret Harrison, Kay Hunt and Mary Kelly at South London Gallery following the introduction of the Equal Pay Act in 1975. Feminism remains an important driver for my work, both reinforcing and supporting key concerns and approaches. Although women's issues are not often represented directly in my practice, it has nevertheless always centred on some of feminism's key tenets, such as social and civil rights, redistribution and recognition, making visible, giving voice, a refusal to dwell on appearance, a striving for equality, identities explored from the inside out, and the creation of narratives that counter the dominant.

In the projects outlined below I trace the development of these ideas, many of which originated in that time. The process has been aided by an overview afforded by *Art for Change*, a retrospective exhibition and catalogue[6] of my collaborative work that was initiated, researched and staged by the Neue Gesellschaft für Bildende Kunst in Berlin in 2005. The organising team, led by the cultural academics and activists Carmen Mörsch and Katja Jedermann, was keen to contextualise the work in a way that is still rare in exhibitions of contemporary arts, and the experience prompted me to consider the practice as a totality, providing the groundwork for the survey of accumulated experience that follows here.

London/Berlin Series, 1975–76

With so many of my undergraduate influences coming from Germany, it followed that, on completion of my undergraduate studies, I applied to the British Council for a DAAD[7] scholarship, which took me to Berlin in the autumn of 1975.

I was not however prepared for the traditionalism of the institution in which I found myself. At that time the Hochschule der Künste trained student artists for six years under the same professor, mainly in highly conventional media with none of the debate or critique of which I had come in search, and that certainly manifested itself in subsequent years[8]. This was in contrast to the cultural activism of the seventies art school scene in the UK, and particularly my experience of the Slade School of Art in London, where Peter was undertaking graduate studies and I was an associate student. In response to these contrasting experiences, Peter and I began to work together on a series of simultaneous performances between the two universities. These events questioned the context of art, the role of the artist, the relation of the individual to the group and the nature of collective cultural action. Initially enacted through a series of telephone conversations and personally transported written instructions, the processes employed were precursor to the digital projects involving communications technologies of later years. There is no doubt that the assertions embodied in that work relating to the constraints of art institutions and the desire to work in a wider social sphere have continued to underpin my practice.

For the first performance Peter made a drawing of the "individual private space" of his London studio, while I worked with a group in Berlin to translate this into physical form. We used soil and charcoal on the floor of a communal workspace at the Hochschule der Künste to recreate the studio as a metaphor for a "contextual frame" and write out questions about the context of art activity originated by Peter in his studio, then debated these as a group. Our amendments to the original statements were phoned back to Peter, who in turn incorporated these new ideas into his design. Photographic and video documentation of these events were later taken to a group event at the Slade, where the issues were further developed through discussion. Finally all the material was brought back to Berlin for the German end of the debate. I had in the meantime been working on an addition to the exhibition and discussion that we planned to stage there that responded to my perceived isolation of the educational experience of students at the Hochschule der Künste. Knocking on the door of every studio in its vast neoclassical building, most of which were locked, I asked any students present to photograph the interior and write a comment on communication. These were then pasted onto a plan of the building, constituting another frame that brought to light interior spaces, and indeed whole departments, hitherto unknown to many of the students there, as well as common concerns on issues of communication.

This early attempt by Peter and myself at collaborative working had proved fruitful, particularly since the work itself was based on dialogue and interaction. From that time we continued to work together on projects or individually through organisations that we co-founded, until the late nineties. We saw our work neither

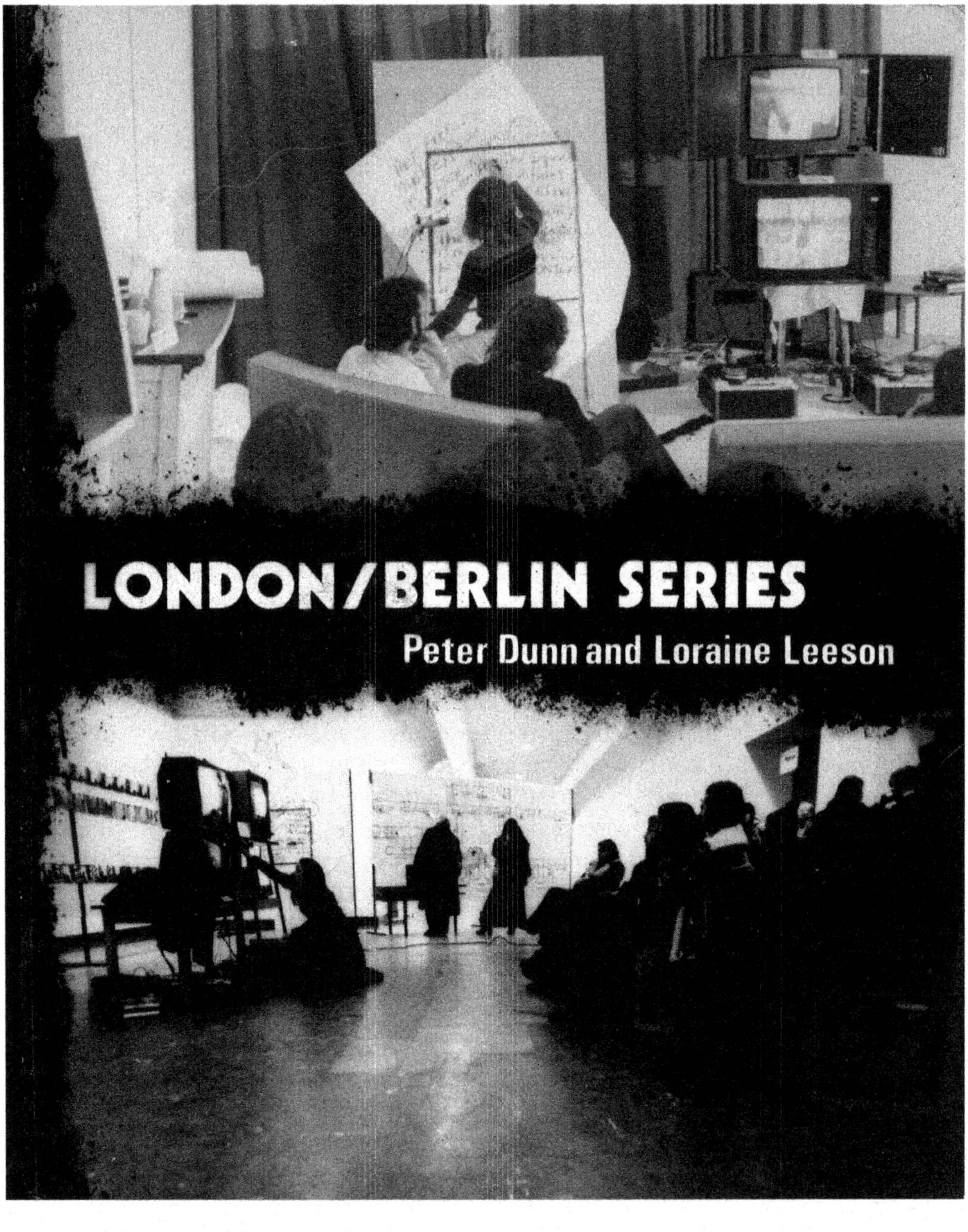

Figure 1.1 London Berlin Series book

© Peter Dunn and Loraine Leeson 1975–76. Hand-made book documenting a series of performances, video and installations between London and Berlin, questioning the context of art and role of the artist.

as community art, nor what was often at the time referred to as "gallery socialism", indicating those who "dipped into non-art contexts" using visual forms that were only comprehensible from an art world perspective. "Transitional practice" was a term that we often used to describe our position at that time, and indeed at this juncture we were in transition from working inside an institution to stepping out into the wider world, as we attempted to do in the next project.

The Present Day Creates History, 1976–77

The *London/Berlin Series* had questioned the role of art in society—indeed, had advocated breaking out of the institutional frame, though had not itself done so. To help us explore how we might take this next step and create a meaningful cultural intervention outside of a fine art context, we made a visit to UK artist Stuart Brisley, who was commencing an APG[9] placement in the "new town" of Peterlee in County Durham. He showed us the results of an early artist residency there by Victor Pasmore, which had resulted in sculpted mounds of communal lawns between the cuboid buildings. Brisley's desire was to do something that could engage more meaningfully with the needs of the new inhabitants who had been recently displaced from their mining village communities. He thus offered us a model of an artist working from within a community outwards, with social engagement as the starting point.

We chose to compare the development of the imposed urban development of Peterlee with a very different model, that of Ruislip, the suburb of London where I had lived in my teenage years. The aim was to expose the decision-making processes that underpinned each location, taking Brecht's perspective on the making of history through the actions of the present day. Our methodology was to uncover these processes through interviews and interaction with local residents, then to feed this material back through an exhibition in public venues where discussion could take place.

The exhibition, entitled *The Present Day Creates History*, comprised image and text derived from personal interview, family photographs, press cuttings, and local archives. Displayed in libraries and other public venues, it highlighted the social and political contexts that had framed the different development of each town, and indicated choices for the future. There was something missing, however. Although discussions accompanied the exhibition, we felt that meaningful connection with the local residents had somehow failed to take place, despite the fact that the material was gathered from local sources, and that one location was even my own home town, where I had personal history and local knowledge. People wanted to know why we were doing it. We had a sense of this ourselves, but were also not sure that this actually addressed the questions, or that we had sufficient grasp of the situation. The work had begun with a desire to shift people's perceptions and an understanding that as artists we were well positioned to operate in "peripheral" spaces and to facilitate dialogue and questioning unlikely to occur within institutions. Nevertheless, what did we think we were going to achieve in the minds of a handful of local residents who were puzzled as to why we were there at all? We noticed also that many people viewed the sepia toned images through a nostalgic lens, ignoring the text that we had designed to anchor them socially and politically. If we wanted to support social change did we not need to be less a drop in the ocean and more part of a groundswell? This was our first real lesson concerning collective action. The second was offered by a campaign to save an East London hospital from closure.

Bethnal Green Hospital Campaign, 1977–78

The seventies in Britain saw the first wave of cutbacks in the National Health Service, carried out initially by the Tories, then continued through the 1974 Labour government. As part of this policy, many small hospitals were closed. The Bethnal Green Hospital in East London served the local population as a community resource valued for its continuity of care and accessibility to local residents. In 1977, when the directive for closure came it was still working to capacity and it was clear that, once its facilities were withdrawn, patients would have nowhere to go except to join already over-long waiting lists for other hospitals. The staff therefore decided to "occupy" the hospital and a campaign was mounted to safeguard its future. The way that occupation worked was based on the duty of the health authority to pay staff salaries while patients remained at the hospital. When the administrators moved out, doctors, nurses and other staff therefore continued to perform their duties, general practitioners continued to refer patients, people attended the casualty department as normal and ambulance drivers continued to respond to emergency calls—and so the occupation took effect.

At that time Peter and I were sharing a Greater London Arts fellowship with a remit to set up and run film and video workshops in that area. Dan Jones[10], a local social worker, artist and member of the hospital's campaign committee, approached us with the offer of using the premises as one of our workshop locations to produce a video that could be used by the campaign. This seemed an opportunity to begin to use our practice as a means of supporting issues of relevance to local people.

Initially we attempted to produce a campaign video through the workshops as suggested. However it soon became apparent that process and product diverged in both intention and outcome. It is important in a workshop context that non-specialists are able to learn at their own pace, whereas a campaign video has to be produced rapidly and, to be effective, also needs to work aesthetically. We soon found ourselves editing out camera shake and other results of inexpert involvement, feeling torn between providing positive learning experiences for participants and the product that was needed. Eventually a reasonable outcome was produced in the form of the documentary *Emergency*, though at the same time we resolved to find a better working process.

The video being satisfactorily received, there was a further request for campaign posters. This time we found a more productive way of working through engaging directly with the campaign committee. By this means we produced the work ourselves but referred to campaign leaders regarding the meanings to be conveyed.

During the months of making the video and posters we became increasingly involved in the campaign itself, and had taken to photographically documenting events. It gradually became apparent that there was need for a more in-depth explanation of the issues for people entering the hospital. Drawing on our accumulated photographic documentation and working closely with campaign committee members, we therefore devised an exhibition for the hospital foyer to place the specific campaign within its wider social and political context, and to communicate this complex information in an accessible, though visually powerful, way. Referring to the work of artists such as John Heartfield and the Russian Constructivists[11], particularly Alexander Rodchenko and El Lissitsky, who we felt had in other times and places produced work with similar intention, we started to develop our use of photomontage

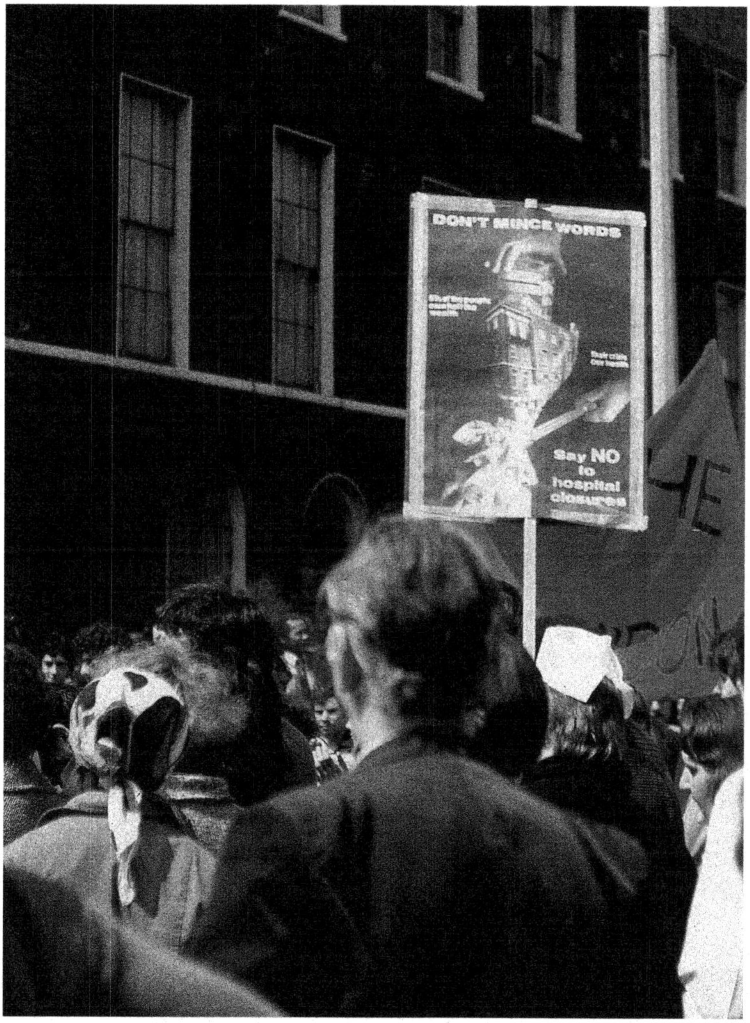

Figure 1.2 Poster in use at a demonstration

© Peter Dunn and Loraine Leeson, Campaign to Save Bethnal Green Hospital, 1978. A2 offset litho poster produced and distributed through the hospital campaign committee.

into an artistic and political tool while also addressing the image-text division of previous work.

While the exhibition fulfilled its purpose in the hospital, another opportunity emerged. Art critic Richard Cork had begun to curate an exhibition entitled *Art for Whom?* for London's Serpentine Gallery to reflect the growing interest in the potential "audience" for art beyond the gallery going public. He asked us to contribute the work we had produced for the hospital; however, Peter and I had great concerns about this, fearing that it might detract from the intended use of the materials. We nevertheless took the offer to the campaign committee and were surprised by their overwhelmingly positive response to go ahead, feeling that this further exposure would

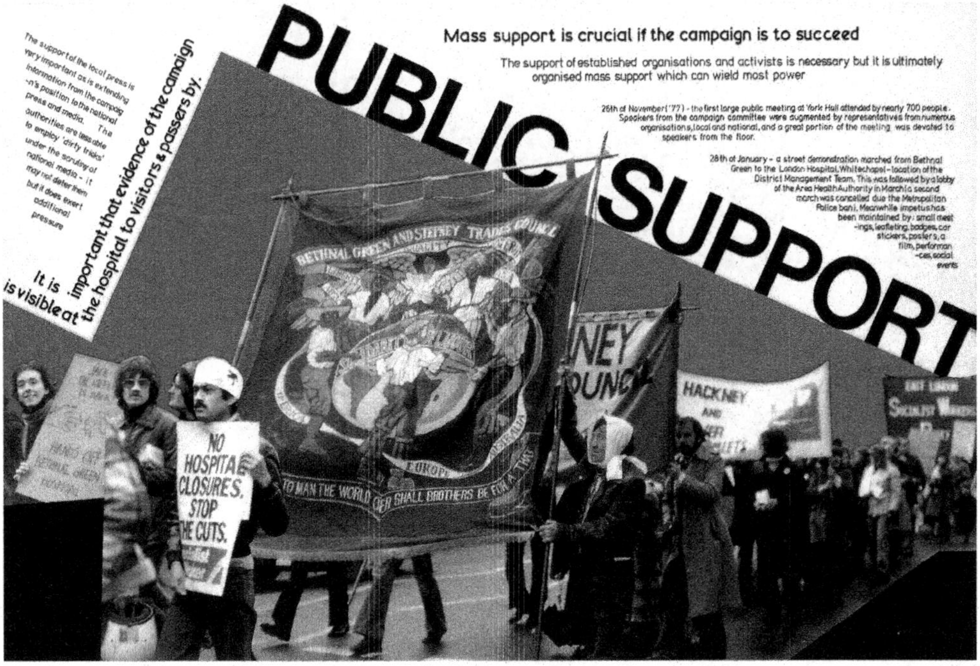

Figure 1.3 Public Support

© Peter Dunn and Loraine Leeson, Campaign to Save Bethnal Green Hospital, 1978. Sixth image from a sequence of exhibition panels displayed in Bethnal Green Hospital outlining the political decision-making behind its proposed closure. 2' × 3' (0.61m × 0.92m) photomontage.

greatly increase the spread of information about the issues. This gave us a different "take" on showing work in galleries and we have continued to embrace opportunities to exhibit documentation of our project work in this way. Keeping one foot in the art world seemed an important stance to take, since it enabled us to demonstrate that what we did was still art and should be considered as such, despite being produced outside of institutions. It also offered a means to liaise with other artists of like mind, and brought about our first personal encounters with Conrad Atkinson, Islington Schools Environmental Project, Public Art Workshop and Stephen Willats. Despite negative comments from the right wing press[12], the exhibition proved an effective tool for demonstrating that art was indeed a medium that could actively address issues affecting the lives of ordinary people.

East London Health Project, 1978–81

In 1978, the East London trades councils wished to disseminate information about health issues to the local population in light of the cuts being made to the National Health Service. They had a small amount of funding remaining from some recent campaigning, which they had originally intended to use for the production of leaflets. Our initial invitation to participate in the Bethnal Green Hospital campaign had come from local trades unionist and trades council member Dan Jones, who was also an artist and understood the role of art in social change. Appreciating the commitment and political understanding that he felt we had shown in our work for the hospital, he proposed that the trades councils take the risk of developing a new, visual approach to the broader campaigning. He instigated a small steering committee, which included representatives from Newham Trades Council, Tower Hamlets Health Campaign and the health workers' unions NALGO and NUPE. We worked with this group to determine a visual form most suited to its potential audience, and arrived at the idea of the "visual pamphlet"—essentially a poster containing information that could be used in health venues. This steering group provided us with an important learning experience regarding the power of collaboration. The role of each member was to share their specialist knowledge—the health representatives did not attempt to make aesthetic judgements, and we, as artists, did not assume expertise in the issues. The visuals that we produced from these discussions were evaluated by the group not so much on the basis of their appearance, but rather on their effectiveness in conveying meaning. This approach to collaboration proved highly successful, both in the way it resulted in a "multiplication" of skills and experience, and through the creative energy generated by the interaction. It completely contradicted the "design by committee" criticism often directed at collectively produced artwork of the time and provided a model for the structural foundations of our subsequent work in the London Docklands.

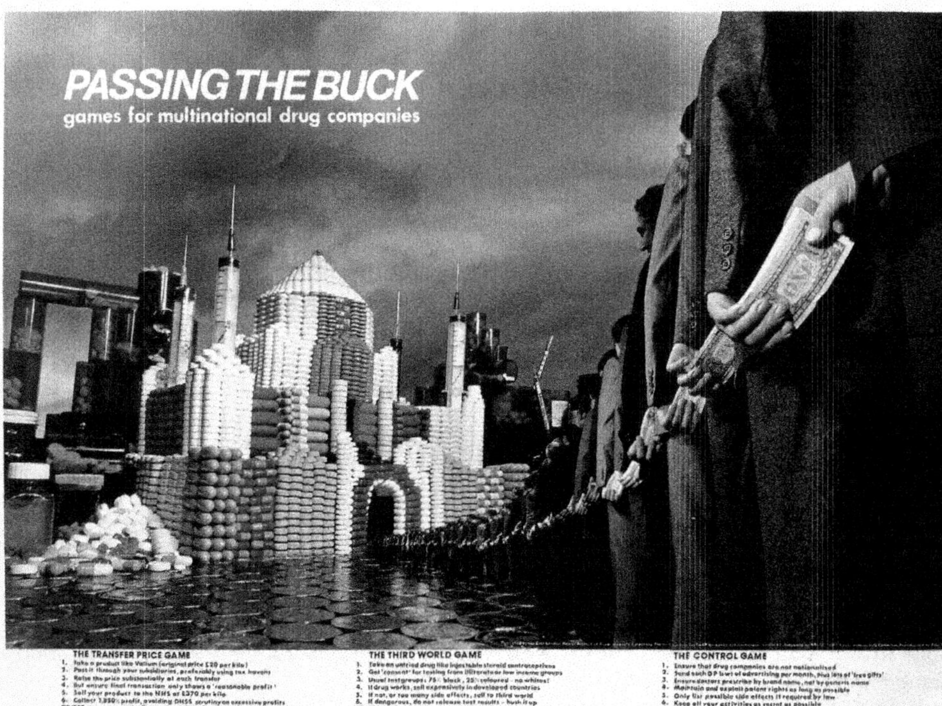

Figure 1.4 Passing the Buck: Games for Multinational Drug Companies

© Peter Dunn and Loraine Leeson, East London Health Project, 1979–80. Produced and distributed in conjunction with East London Trades Councils and health workers' unions. A2 poster.

Eight different posters were produced over the two years of the East London Health Project. These were widely distributed within the health sector, and also intervened in the art world through inclusion in such exhibitions as *Issue—Social Strategies by Women Artists* in 1980, curated by Lucy Lippard for the Institute of Contemporary Arts in London.

Notes

1. Lucy Lippard, *Six Years: The Dematerialisation of the Art Object, from 1966–1972*, London: Studio Vista, 1973.
2. Sheila Rowbotham, Lynn Segal, Hilary Wainwright, *Beyond the Fragments: Feminism and the of Socialism*, London: Merlin Press, 1980.
3. Owen Kelly, Community, *Art and the State*, London: Comedia, 1984.
4. "The ideas that constitute cultural democracy both enable and depend upon direct participation, and take as their aim the building and sustenance of a society in which people are free to come together to produce, distribute and receive the cultures they choose" (Merkel et al., 1986).
5. Karen Merkel et al., "Culture and Democracy: The Manifesto" in *Another Standard*, London: Comedia and Shelton Trust, 1986.
6. Carmen Mörsch et al., Art for Change—Loraine Leeson, Works from 1975–2005, Berlin: NGBK, 2005.
7. The Deutsche Akademische Austauschdienst in partnership with the British Council offered bursaries for postgraduate study.
8. Piloting of the Kulturpädagogische Arbeitsstelle für Weiterbildung, forerunner to the Institut für Kunst in Kontext, began in the same institution in 1976, the year I left Berlin. It was finally established in 1982.
9. The Artists Placement Group (APG 1966–1989, renamed Organisation and Imagination or O+I in 1989) was initiated by Barbara Steveni and John Latham. APG emerged from the idea that artists are a human resource underused by society, and placed artists in government, commercial and industrial organisations.
10. Dan Jones, key local activist, artist and campaigner for social justice in the London Borough of Tower Hamlets during the seventies and eighties later became Head of Education at Amnesty International UK.
11. A major exhibition of Russian constructivist art, Art in Revolution, had been staged at the Hayward Gallery in 1971.
12. Among these was an article in *The Times* by Bernard Levin entitled *This Poisoning of the Wells of Art* (London, 1978).

References

Owen Kelly, *Community, Art and the State* (London: Comedia, 1984).

Lucy Lippard, *Six Years: The Dematerialisation of the Art Object, from 1966–1972* (London: Studio Vista, 1973).

Karen Merkel et al., "Culture and Democracy: The Manifesto" in *Another Standard*, (London: Comedia and Shelton Trust, 1986).

Carmen Mörsch, et al., *Art for Change: Loraine Leeson, Works from 1975–2005* (Berlin: NGBK, 2005).

Sheila Rowbotham, Lynn Segal, Hilary Wainwright, *Beyond the Fragments: Feminism and the Making of Socialism* (London: Merlin Press, 1980).

2 Eighties

The area now known as the London Docklands extends eight miles downriver from Tower Bridge eastwards to the Royal Docks, and was described by its initial developers as the largest piece of real estate in Europe. It incorporated land used by the docks, warehouses and related industries as well as the housing and public amenities of the communities already living there. In this respect it differed in nature from other dockside areas in the UK, where development often only took place on defunct or derelict riverside sites. When the London Docklands Development Corporation (LDDC) moved into its Isle of Dogs offices in the early eighties, there were still local working docks, many small industries and a population of 56,000 people, mainly living in high-rise council tower blocks with poor amenities.

The people of Docklands have always been subject to the changing needs of trade routes, and from the 1850s onwards lived through major upheavals resulting from each successive rebuilding and extension of the docks. By the mid 1960s, having won rights in security of employment and decasualisation of labour, most of the dockswere closed. Once again the local working class population was at the mercy of the market. However this time their labour was not needed in the new "roll on/roll off" facilities, and the physical presence of their communities became both an inconvenience and an embarrassment. Keen to fulfil the new Thatcherite vision, the LDDC projected Docklands as a "virgin" site. Reg Ward, first Chief Executive of the LDDC, speaking at a local meeting in 1982 described the Docklands as "a blank canvas upon which we can paint the future".

Proximity to water was a key element in inflating land values and maximising profit. As luxury housing became a prominent feature of the development, a new politics of "the view" entered the frame. Those who had spent a large amount of money on their river vista did not want this marred by the sight of crumbling tenement blocks and unsightly council estates. Their case was powerfully stated in the theatre production *A View of the River,* written by East End playwright Alan Gilbey and professionally performed by the Half Moon Theatre with a cast of local people in the warehouses of Canary Wharf prior to its demolition.

Ironically it was to be the vast Canary Wharf office development that led to the eventual downfall of the LDDC. The ultimate in privatisation, the then tallest tower in Europe was financed from across the Atlantic. Planned into a scenario that had no current need for offices, an insufficient transport infrastructure and opposed by major voices in the City of London who had no desire to see London's financial centre move eastward, its developers failed to pre-let even one office space prior to the signing of the master build agreement. Once built, it took ten years for Canary Wharf to get off the ground, despite its skyward tendencies.

Docklands Community Poster Project

Peter and I co-founded the Docklands Community Poster Project in 1981 as a response to the concerns of East London communities over the extensive proposed re-development programme for this area. The newly elected Conservative government under Margaret Thatcher designated the land surrounding the working docks, from St Katherine's Dock east of Tower Bridge downriver to the Royal Docks, as an Urban Development Corporation. This effectively removed local control from an area crossing five London boroughs, with the aim of transferring it into private ownership. However this land, now the London Docklands, not only incorporated docks and warehouses but was also home and workplace to many thousands of people. Historically East London communities had been poor but politically active. In this case they were not against development, but wanted it to also meet their own needs. A struggle ensued.

The local trades council, as a result of our recent work around health issues in the area, asked Peter and myself to produce a poster alerting local people to what was to come. Following a period of consultation with tenants and action groups however, it soon became clear that the proposed poster was not enough. Posters were indeed wanted, but "large ones" to match the scale of the proposals, and design work to help with individual campaigns, documentation of the area before it changed and a record of each battle as it was fought. In addition, there was a need for easily accessible information that examined key issues such as housing and specific development sites in more depth.

With all this in mind, though with as yet no funding, we developed a plan that would deliver art and design work for these key areas. Most importantly, and based on experience gained through the East London Health Project, we created a steering committee. Tenants in the area were already federated into action groups for each locality and, since the proposed re-development of the Docklands, had also formed a representative Joint Docklands Action Group. The Docklands Community Poster Project organised itself along similar lines and representatives of each area met regularly to report on local developments, agree issues to be represented and consider the audience that the artwork should serve. A small amount of funding was eventually raised from the local boroughs and the regional arts board, finally matched by a significant grant from the new Labour controlled Greater London Council. The steering group became a community co-op, and staff[1] were employed to fulfil roles of administration, design and technical support. An arts project that began as a request for a poster eventually became the cultural arm of an extraordinary campaigning community over a period of ten years, while the images produced during the course of the project became the currency via which information about the extraordinary events in Docklands was disseminated across the world.

The Photo-murals

Large-scale posters were the first aspect of the work to be developed in response to the action groups' request. The Docklands Community Poster Project steering group considered carefully who the main audience for these should be—whether to direct their messages to the developers, explain issues to outsiders, or primarily to disseminate information among the Docklands communities themselves. It was decided that

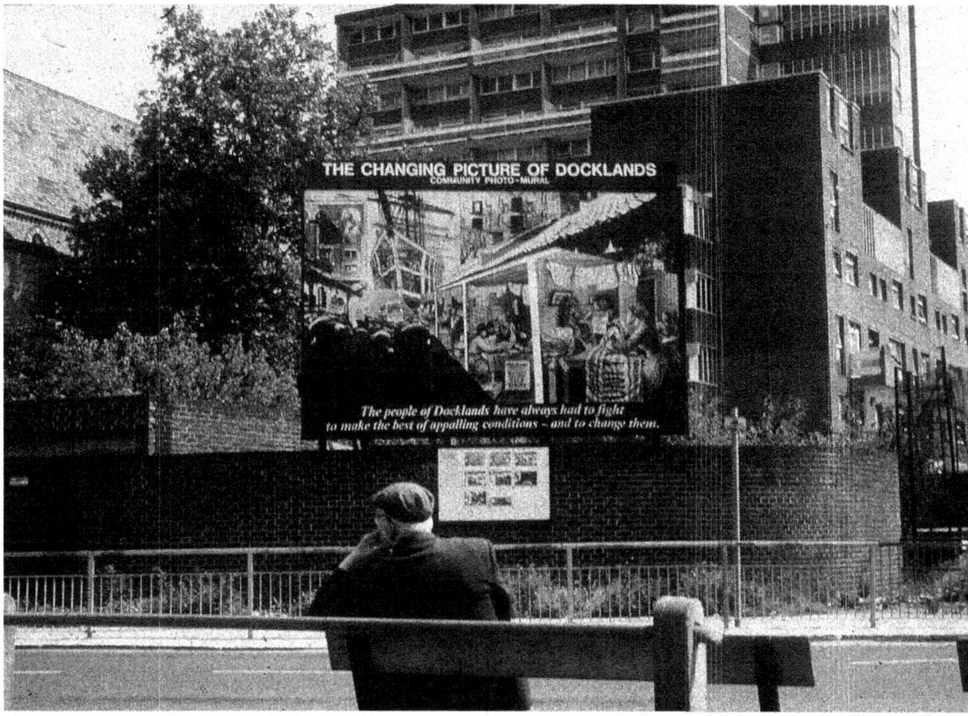

Figure 2.1 Photo-mural in situ, Wapping

Photo © Peter Dunn and Loraine Leeson, Docklands Community Poster Project, 1985. One of eight 18' × 12' (5.49m × 3.66m) photo-murals constructed in and around the London Docklands.

the latter group were the most important. Most local people were unaware of what was going on, although familiar with the miles of corrugated iron then surrounding what was left of the docks, and all too aware that they had been left stranded in poor housing with few facilities.

The siting of these images was also important. Commercial billboards, aimed at communicating a simple brand name, were often situated in locations where they could best attract the attention of passing motorists. However, since the information was aimed at local people, it was decided that the posters should be located where they could be seen over time by pedestrians. To this end we decided to contract the building of our own structures. The first was constructed opposite a health centre in Wapping, then over subsequent years with further funding from the Greater London Council (GLC), we built seven more in and around the Docklands area. Some were temporary, though at any one time six sites were in operation.

The images themselves were developed with these multiple billboards in mind. They were designed to change gradually through replacement of individual sections, and develop a narrative rather like a slow motion animation. In practical terms this meant the images could be transferred from one site to another, enabling the story of the Docklands to unfold through time and space. The name "photo-mural" was first used to describe this work by critic Richard Cork, and then coined by Alan Tomkins, cultural activist and Arts Policy Officer for the Greater London Council. Since then

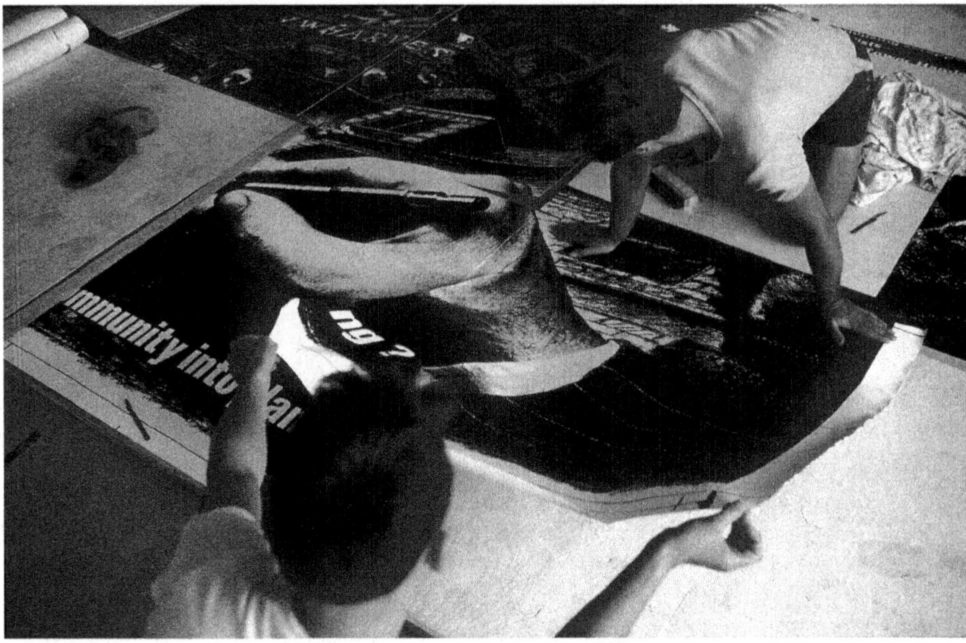

Figure 2.2 Pasting up

Photo © Peter Dunn and Loraine Leeson Docklands Community Poster Project, circa 1982. Enlarged sections of re-photographed photomontage were pasted onto plywood panels before hand colouring and varnishing, then manually screwed to the photo-mural backing boards.

it has become a generic descriptor for this art form, although inspiration for this format had in fact originally derived from Chinese wall posters, which had brought information to the people during the Cultural Revolution.

The project steering group initially met on a monthly basis to feed back on issues of the campaigning, action that was needed, siting of the photo-mural structures and to identify the messages to be conveyed. As artists we then worked to represent these themes, bringing imagery back to the group to check how well it conveyed its meaning as we had done in the East London Health Project, while the visual representation itself remained entirely our own. This process of decision-making and co-operation enabled a combination of different skills and experience to be focused on the work while creating a hub of creative energy that sustained the project throughout its ten-year duration and laid the foundations for much subsequent collaborative work.

First Photo-mural Sequence

The first sequence of photo-murals dealt with the issue at the forefront of local people's minds. What was going on behind their backs? Years of consultation by the Labour led boroughs had been rejected by the newly appointed LDDC in favour of the practical enactment of Thatcherite policy. Our photo-mural sequence followed the nature and concerns of the campaigning, commencing with a question and then considering the scenario that people could see being enacted around them. "Big money

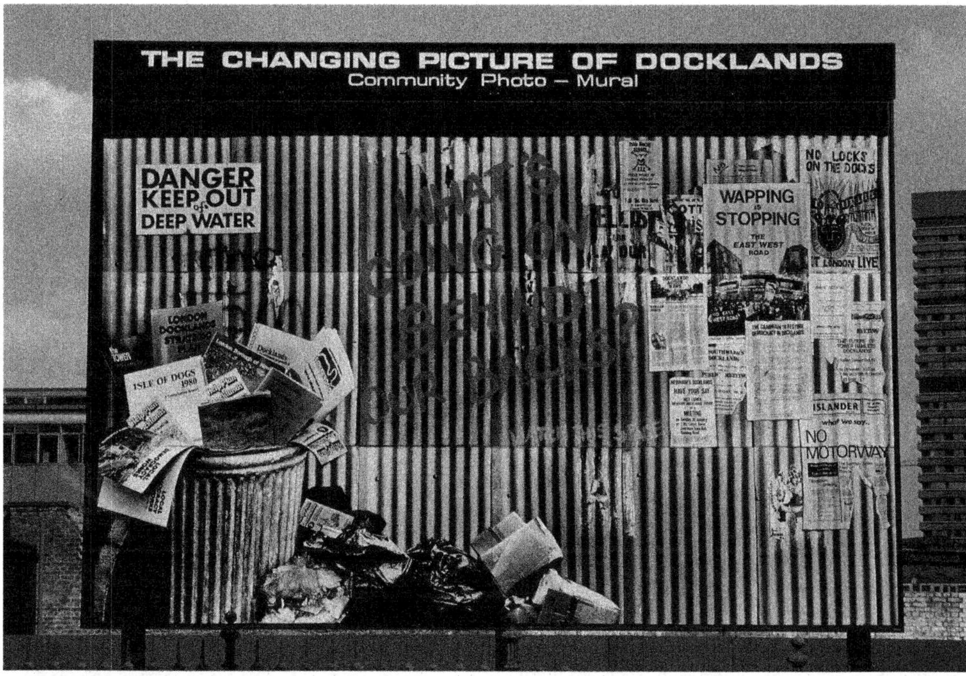

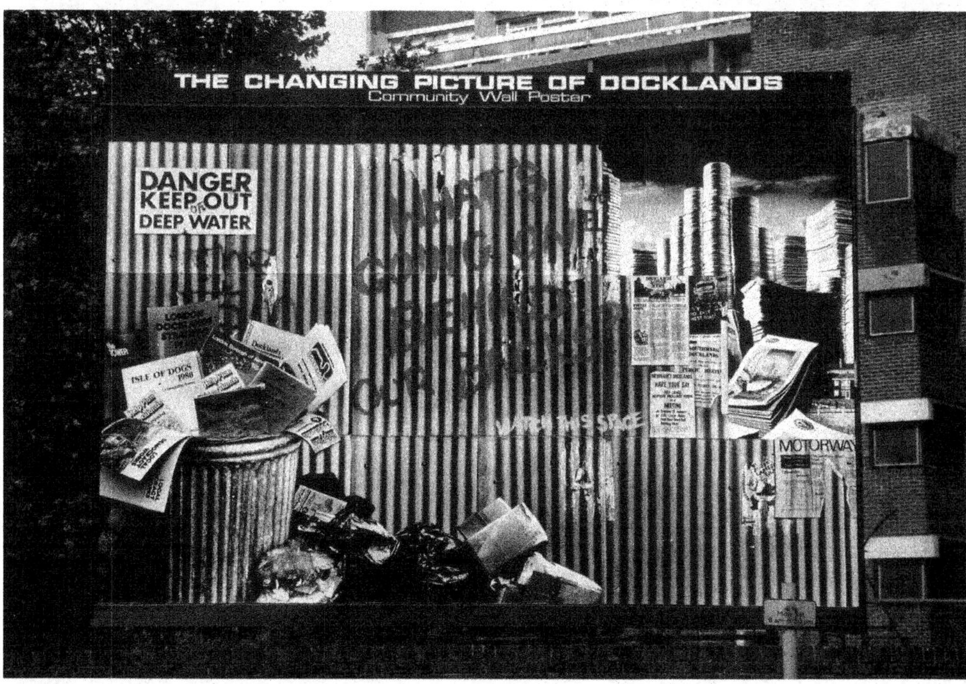

Figures 2.3–2.10 First Photo-mural Sequence

© Peter Dunn and Loraine Leeson, Docklands Community Poster Project, 1981–84. A series of eight 18' × 12' (5.49m × 3.66m) photo-murals exploring issues surrounding the re-development of the London Docklands from the viewpoint of local communities.

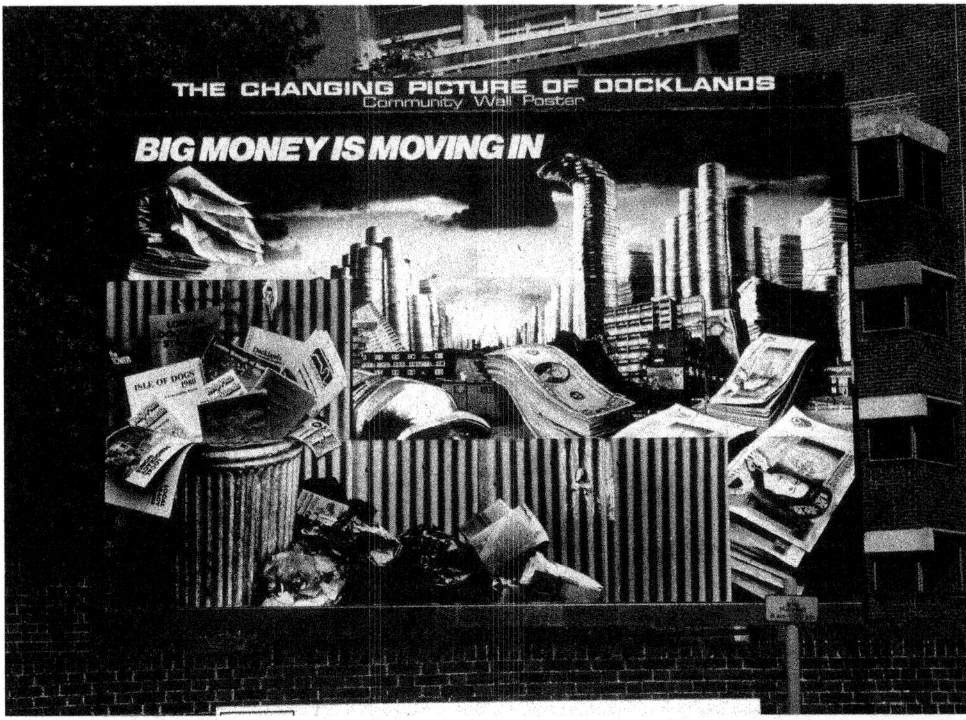

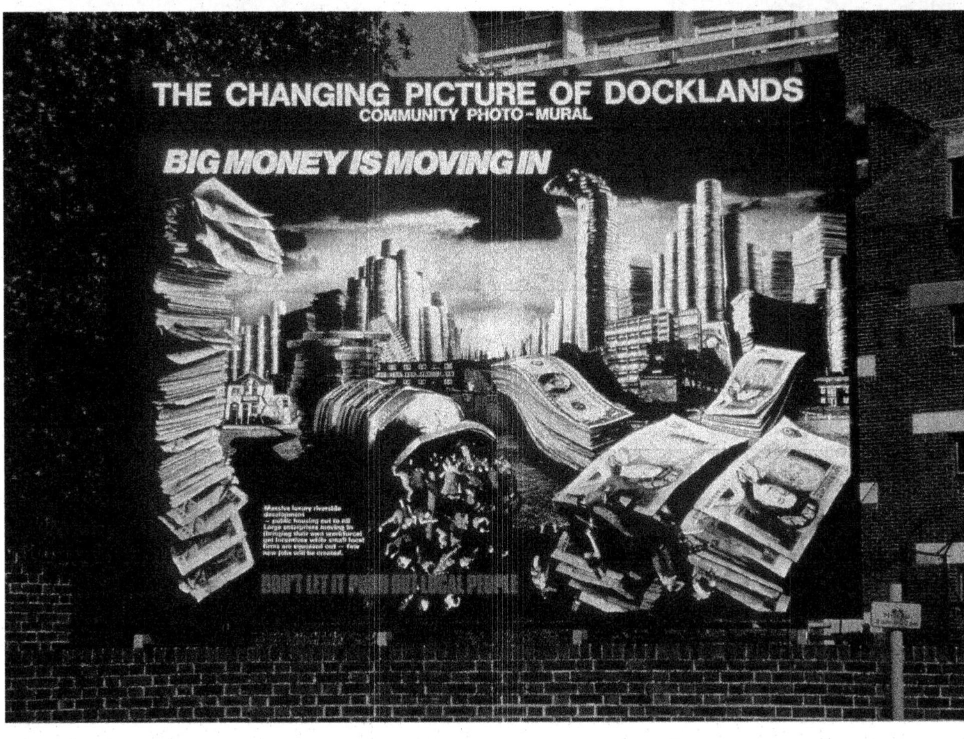

Figures 2.3–2.10 Continued

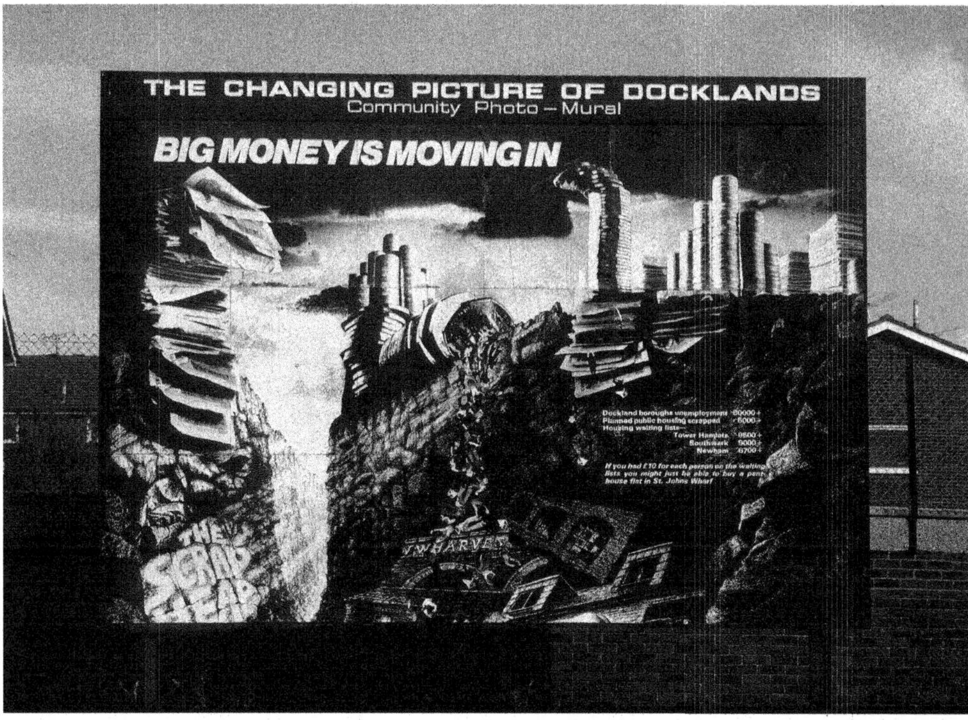

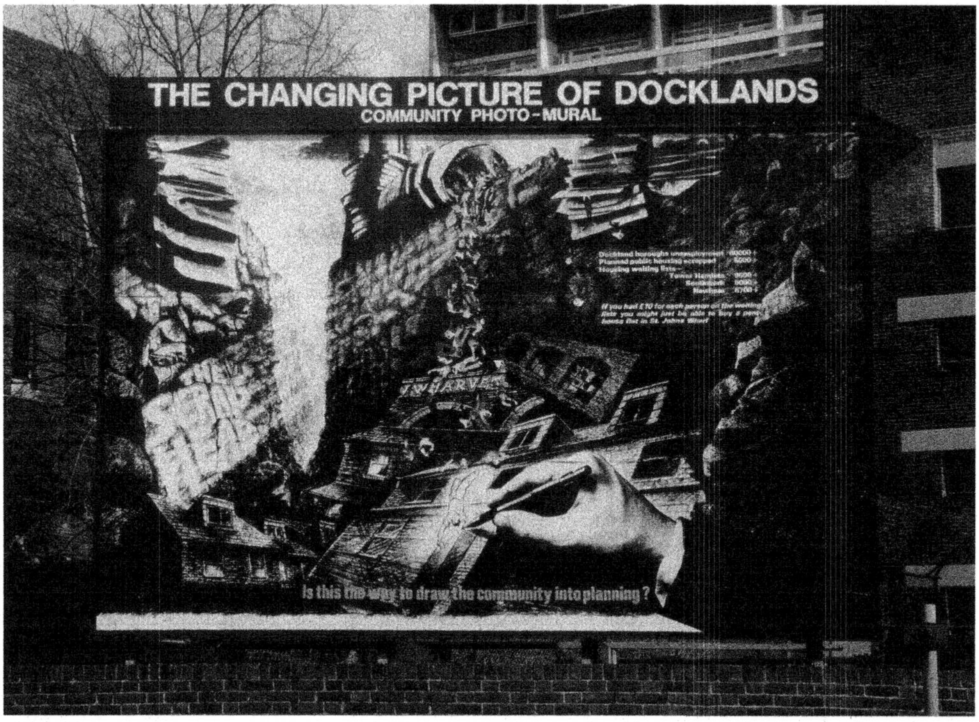

Figures 2.3–2.10 Continued

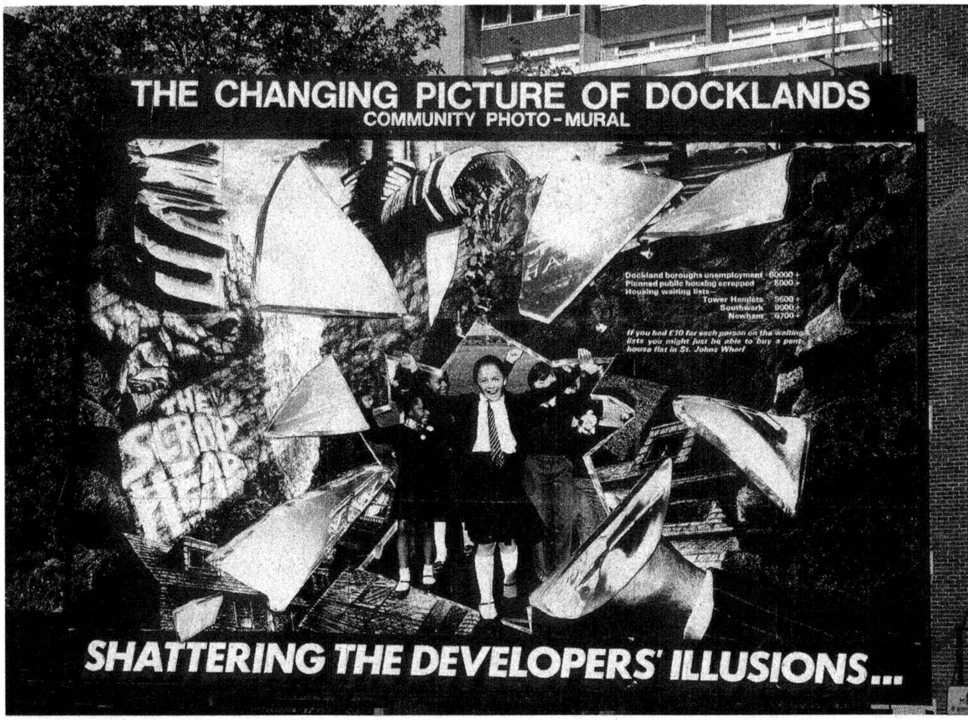

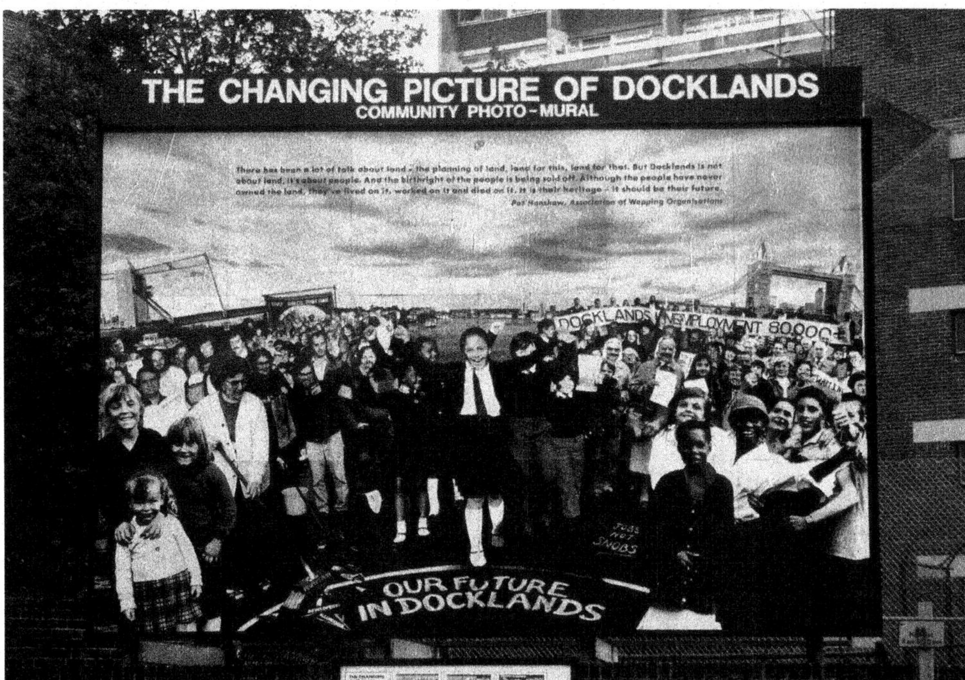

Figures 2.3–2.10 Continued

is moving in and is pushing out local people," explained one activist at a public meeting, so naming the next image of the sequence. Either Peter or I attended the meetings of every campaigning group during that period to familiarise ourselves with the issues. At these events activists were often heard to express their ideas through visual metaphor, and these frequently provided inspiration for the imagery. The visual representation of these issues that we produced also followed the development of ideas. For example, although fear of being thrown "on the scrap heap" was clearly expressed, local response to our first draft of the image depicting this was indignant. The "scrap heap" was seen as the developers' design on Docklands, not where the communities saw themselves. As a result this image sequence unfolded to reveal that this scenario truly was a "design" and not a reality. The nature of the campaigning itself was transforming and found new strength in a pro-active approach.

The final image in the sequence included a proclamation by the chair of the Association of Wapping Organisations:

> There has been a lot of talk about land, land for this, land for that. But Docklands is not about land, it's about people. And the birthright of the people is being sold off. Although the people have never owned the land, they've lived on it, worked on it, died on it. It is their heritage—it should be their future[2].

The image constituted a portrait of those concerned in the Docklands campaigning together with documentation of recent events. Referencing the relationship of portraiture to land ownership in eighteenth-century painting[3], it foregrounded the central characters against the landscape within which this drama was being enacted, and reflected the new strength through solidarity being developed by the campaigning communities.

Housing Sequence

Of all the issues affecting those living in the Docklands, housing was the most fundamental to people's lives, and the steering group felt it warranted a photo-mural sequence of its own. However it was difficult to portray the current housing conditions of the area without a context to explain the historical events that formed them and it was decided that housing and history should be combined. This led to an immediate difficulty of representation, since, although visual material for current issues was readily available from the project's own archives, historical material was imbued with the ideology of the context that led to its recording. For example, most photos of the housing of the area had been taken to promote reform–to bring better conditions to the poor and destitute. However those depicted as victims in the photographs were no less than the forerunners of the resilient and highly organised East Londoners of the present, the very people who had fought against the odds and forged the qualities of community cohesion of which East Londoners remain so justly proud.

We deployed two strategies to address these issues. The first was the use of drawing as a counterpoint to photography. Peter had first applied his drawing skills to deal with some of the complex issues surrounding the "scrap heap" image. The drawn imagery was able to convey a reality that remained invisible in the photography of the earlier period, and the engravings of Gustav Doré's *London: a Pilgrimage* provided

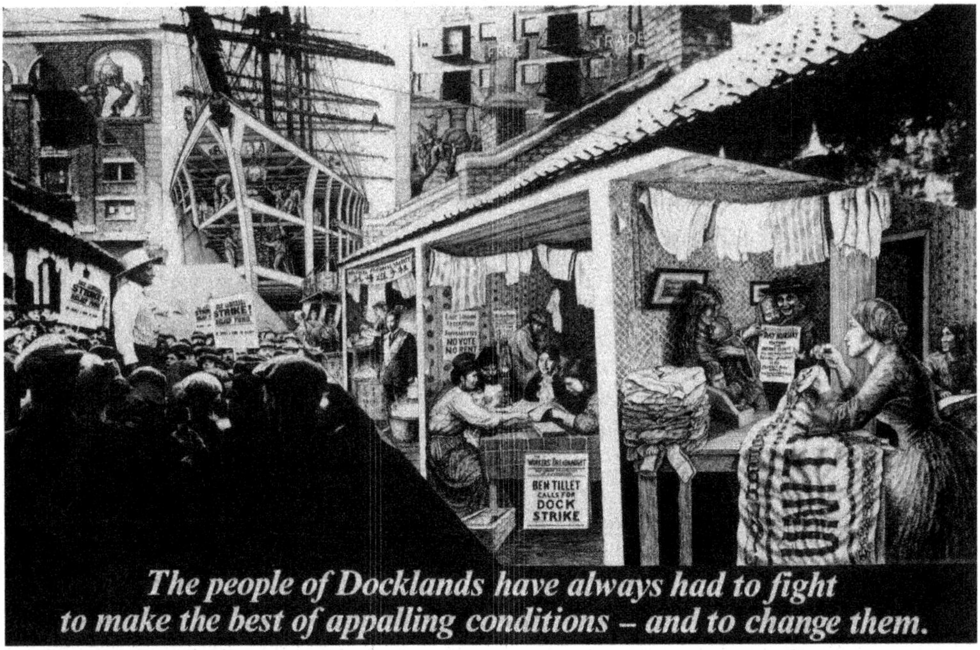

Figure 2.11 Housing 3

© Peter Dunn and Loraine Leeson, Docklands Community Poster Project, 1984–86. Third image from the second sequence of photo-murals dealing with issues behind lack of adequate housing for local people. 18' × 12' (5.49m × 3.66m) photo-mural.

technique and inspiration for this, Peter therefore combined photographic montage and drawing using black, white and sepia to reveal layers of reality. The second strategy concerned use of text. We had learned to keep text to a minimum in such work, understanding from earlier experience that imagery could be more readily assimilated while also capable of holding more layers of meaning than words. Some text was nevertheless often necessary to ground the images, and needed careful construction. A caption was therefore developed for this historical material that acknowledged the role of East Londoners in not only surviving, but also in changing their lot—a hallmark of both their past and present struggles: “The people of Docklands have always had to fight to make the best of appalling conditions—and to change them”.

Campaigns

Docklands campaigning was co-ordinated by the Joint Docklands Action Group, in turn managed by representatives of the different riverside neighbourhoods. This covered a substantial area however, and each location would initiate its own campaigns around specific issues. Our initial consultation with these local groups had resulted in repeated requests for a photographic record of the actions taking place, and constituted one of our organisation’s central activities. There were many initiatives during this period, the most significant being the *People’s Armadas to Parliament* and the *People’s Plan for the Royal Docks* both described below. However, also in constant progress were smaller campaigns that we documented to create a negative archive of material for publicity, publication and an ongoing record of events.

One of these was the East West Road campaign of the early eighties, which had been created in opposition to a proposal for a trunk road to cut through the centre of Wapping, one that would effectively take the heart out of this close-knit community. Early one morning, led by many of Wapping's elderly residents, people marched in an unending stream across a pedestrian crossing on the Highway, the main throughway for heavy vehicles north of the Thames to the east of Tower Bridge. Highly organised and using walkie-talkies to co-ordinate events, demonstrators successfully blocked the road for several hours, forcing heavy traffic down through streets along the designated path of the new trunk road. Traffic soon came to a halt, and was held there long enough to give the press the opportunity to document events and the community to tell their side of the story, which had hitherto failed to be taken into account. The East West road was never built.

Towards the end of the eighties moves were made by the LDDC to create a massive office development along Canary Wharf on the Isle of Dogs, a peninsula of the Thames riverside turned into an island by the docks cutting right through this narrow stretch of land. There was serious local concern that the Canary Wharf development would bring few resources and many disadvantages to the Island's communities, and the developers were able to demonstrate little practical benefit for residents. In addition, there was no significant lack of office space in the capital, the location lacked transport and other infrastructure needed for the estimated high volume of commuters, and key voices in the city were speaking out against plans to re-locate London's financial centre to this Docklands site.

A campaign was therefore launched by the Island's communities in response to these plans. One event, instigated and organised by local residents, was particularly interesting in that the method through which they chose to relay their message was entirely cultural. Following several years of campaigning through the arts in Docklands, it serves as an example of the shift in approach that occurred over this period, since the demonstration that was organised found its power of presentation in symbolic forms and creation of the photo opportunity tableau, and required only documentation and banners from the Docklands Community Poster Project. Community activist Peter Wade led a funeral procession dressed as an undertaker, accompanied by the local vicar and others carrying black banners that bore the names of the housing estates they represented. A coffin, representing the death of the Island, was wheeled on a carriage between them, and laid to rest at the Canary Wharf site.

A later event protesting the proposed closure of the Mudchute Farm was enacted at the instigation of the Canary Wharf development. The new plans for this area included the proposed destruction of the much loved Mudchute, a working urban farm, riding centre, public amenity and educational resource. It had been created, financed and run successfully for many years entirely through local effort and as such embodied many of the values dear to Island residents. This was to be closed and its animals destroyed, while the Canary Wharf office development, so unneeded and unpopular that even the City of London failed to give it support, was being forced through. This proved the last straw for many local people and an event hosted by the LDDC to celebrate the signing of the master build agreement for Canary Wharf provided a fitting public context for expression of local feeling. A champagne reception was held in the open air along the dock overlooking the Canary Wharf site. As the

Governor of the Bank of England stood up to deliver his speech, a whistle blew. From the tops of the warehouses bordering the dock, banners were unfurled proclaiming the ongoing nature of the Docklands struggle. A van drew up, its rear doors opened, and beehives from the Mudchute farm placed at each side of the flower decked podium and their lids removed. More was to come. A herd of sheep emerged from the van and veered towards the podium, where they began eating the flowers. When security guards started to pursue the sheep, someone called, "You're driving them into the dock!", after which the guards chose not to risk the animals' lives. The development corporation had organised national press coverage for their event. Needless to say, the Mudchute Farm was not closed.

The People's Armadas to Parliament

The Armadas serve as one of the best examples of the use of cultural campaigning during this period, as well as the collaboration that took place between local, professional, statutory and voluntary groups. During the campaigning of the eighties, representatives of both the Joint Docklands Action Group (JDAG) and Docklands Community Poster Project would attend the different meetings of the federated tenant and action groups around the Docklands area, in addition to inviting representatives to their own meetings. A comment was made at one such event that it was time to take another petition to parliament to challenge the imposition of the government appointed LDDC, which had effectively removed powers from the democratically elected local authorities.

Another delegate pointed out that, since both Docklands and parliament were situated on the river, this offered a potential route for delivery of the petition. Someone else spoke up to say that he was a lighterman in Wapping, and owned a barge—an appropriate means of transport for such a journey. There was a further proposal that this barge could be decorated. The idea was taken up by JDAG and introduced at the meetings of other Dockland groups, and in this way grew from a petition to a major event. People from each Docklands location wanted to take part, so the hiring of pleasure cruisers was proposed. There were also plans for what such a large number of people could do when they arrived at parliament. The Greater London Council were approached, and they provided funding for the event together with use of Jubilee Gardens close to the pier opposite parliament where the pleasure boats could discharge their passengers.

Delegates from JDAG and North Southwark Community Development Group organised the event, while the Docklands Community Poster Project co-ordinated East London arts groups to provide imagery, design and publicity. The main barge was decorated with a large banner, for which I created an image that was to become the emblem of the community fight back. This was a dragon in the shape of the river as it runs through Docklands, the beast of myth and legend, a force of the underworld, and a symbol of action against repression. The symbol caught the imagination of local groups and a wealth of ephemera was generated—t-shirts, mugs, letter headings, badges, balloons, and posters.

The Basement Arts Workshop printed neighbourhood banners for the barge and pleasure boats. However, first the main vessel had to be prepared. This was co-ordinated by Cultural Partnerships[4], who worked with young people to re-paint the entire vessel, hoist the banners, ensure their safety on the voyage and provide tannoy and music. A thousand people took to the river and sailed to parliament broadcasting their message, accompanied by music and songs. It was a moving moment to hear the Armada's progression up river, cheered on by crowds identifiable by their banners and balloons in the blue and red of the dragon banner, which had come to symbolise the Docklands fightback. At Jubilee Gardens more music, dancing and banners welcomed those who disembarked at an event that combined arts festival with political rally. Ken Livingstone, Leader of the Greater London Council, made a welcoming speech, and members of the Labour shadow cabinet were asked to explain how they would address the issues affecting the people of Docklands from day one of coming to power. Each politician was presented with a copy of the *People's Charter for Docklands*, reminding them of their pledge.

Three *People's Armadas to Parliament* took place from 1984 to 1986. By this time a host of poems and songs had been written about the issues and at the second and subsequent armadas Cultural Partnerships co-ordinated a barge of musicians, whose sound heralded its progression upriver. Their pyrotechnics expertise ensured that the flotilla of boats that circled at North Woolwich by the LDDC offices did so to the sound of cannon fire. These were emotionally moving events involving thousands of people from different generations and backgrounds who would not have otherwise participated in political campaigning, but who continued to do so in an unprecedented way. Labour and Liberal politicians continued to speak in support of the Docklands communities. Miners' leaders from the UK strike of 1984–85 held

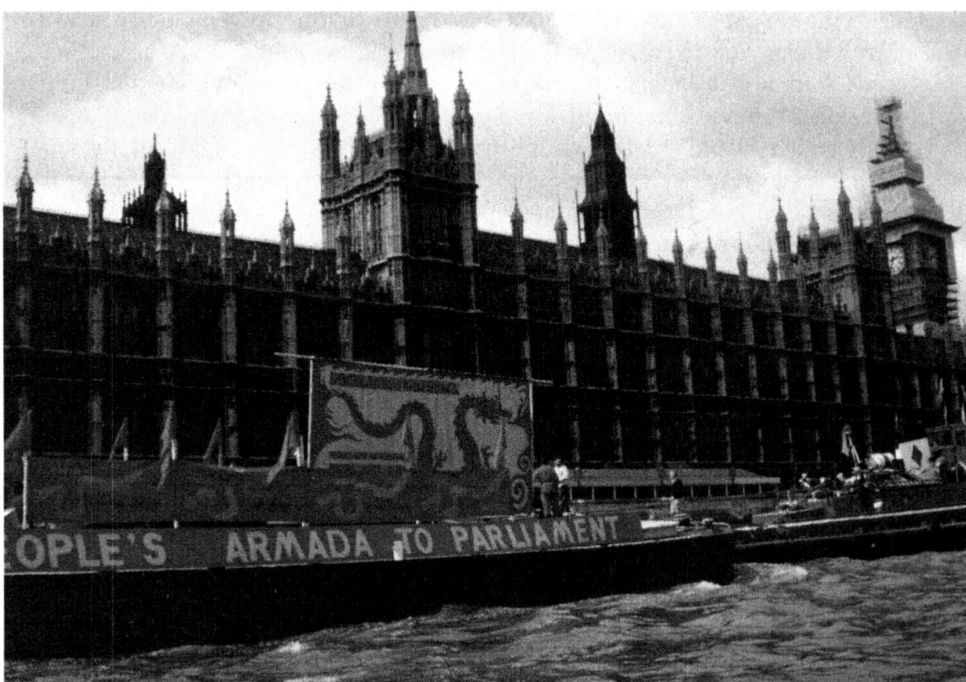

Figure 2.12 The first People's Armada arrives at Parliament

Photo © Peter Dunn and Loraine Leeson, Docklands Community Poster Project, 1984.

meetings with the Docklands groups, and launched a campaign entitled *Don't let the Mines go the same way as the Docks*. Impressed with the Docklands dragon, they created their own "pit dragon" as a massive carnival costume worn by young people, which accompanied the Armada celebrations.

Although events such as this were not able on their own to create the major shift in political focus that only a change in government would bring, much was achieved on the way. The Armadas also marked a shift from activism to pro-activism in the Docklands political campaigning, an approach that became a hallmark of this movement. This would be further developed through such initiatives as the *People's Plan for the Royal Docks*, and much later form the key strategy underpinning projects such as *VOLCO* and the Young Person's Guides. It also marked a moment for ourselves as artists where our cultural interventions had moved from the margins to the centre of an agenda of resistance.

The People's Plan for the Royal Docks

Initial redevelopment issues in the Docklands began at the western end of the designated land. The easterly lying Royal Docks remained largely untouched throughout the eighties. However, plans for one major development in this area were put into motion—a new airport for London, the runway for which would use the stretch of land between these docks and surrounding areas for airport buildings and parking. As with all LDDC initiatives within the development zone, local people had not been consulted. The area was renowned for its lack of amenities, jobs and transport, while most residents were squeezed into shabby tower blocks in urgent need of rebuilding. An airport would meet none of these needs, save for a few jobs for ground staff and cleaners, and would certainly not be providing the kind of transportation so urgently required.

As in the other Docklands areas, Silvertown residents were highly organised—a necessity for survival in such challenging conditions—with tough campaigners from all generations. On hearing of the development corporation's plans for the airport, the activists of this area created their own organisation, the People's Plan Centre, which operated from a local shop staffed by volunteers. They approached the Greater London Councils' new Popular Planning Unit for support. This unit employed key political strategists on its staff, including Sheila Rowbotham and Hilary Wainwright, co-authors of *Beyond the Fragments: Feminism and the Making of Socialism*, which had previously made such impact among my peers who had been working somewhere between the women's movement and male-dominated left. They took on the Royal Docks case, helping the People's Plan Centre to conduct their own research and consultation, access expert input and draw up a comprehensive document[5]. This detailed how the same area of land could meet local needs, including those of housing, childcare, the elderly, shopping facilities, transport, leisure and recreation, education and health. The Plan addressed the means through which this approach would create jobs and boost the economy while providing the local resources so urgently needed. JDAG was of course involved, while the Docklands Community Poster Project designed posters, helped stage events, provided a shop sign, promotional board for the centre and design work for the published plan, which was distributed by Newham council to every home in the area. There was no comparison between the social benefits of the airport proposal and those of the People's Plan, and Silvertown residents were successful in forcing the issue to public enquiry. This recognised the value of their plan, particularly in relation to the generation of local jobs. It nevertheless also acknowledged that control for development was held by the LDDC, and the airport went ahead.

Docklands Roadshow

The LDDC was only the second urban development corporation to be established by the Thatcher government following their return to power in 1979. It was regarded as a test bed where conservative policies could be enacted without recourse to local democratic processes. Requiring a special act of parliament and after much deliberation, it was finally passed through both parliamentary houses in 1980. New Urban Development Corporations were being set up all over the country, and as the London re-development progressed, the communities of Docklands decided to send a warning and the benefit of their campaigning experience to others facing a similar situation.

We had already produced a number of exhibitions to offer further detail on issues raised in the photo-mural and campaign work. These were created as laminated panels designed to fit onto a set of lightweight screens and could be rapidly assembled for use in meetings, festivals and events. Late in the eighties these were brought together with half-size versions of the photo-murals, photographs, posters, banners, leaflets, articles, plans and other documents produced during the course of the Docklands campaigning to form the *Docklands Roadshow*. A package was offered to other locations where development corporations were due to be imposed, so that an exhibition of the work of the Docklands Community Poster Project, accompanied by speakers including community activists and professionals, could be hired to bring relevant advice and information from a community perspective to other locations. The *Docklands Roadshow* in various combinations toured locally and nationally, and also took the Docklands experience abroad to Amsterdam and Berlin.

Notes

1. Docklands Community Poster Project staff comprised lead artists/co-ordinators Peter Dunn and Loraine Leeson, graphic designer Sandra Buchanan, administrators Belinda Kidd and Roberta Evans, with other input from Sonia Boyce, Sara McGuinness, Tony Minnion, Keith Piper and Donald Rodney.
2. From an address to a Docklands meeting by Pat Hanshaw, Chair of the Association of Wapping Organisations, circa 1983.
3. In *Ways of Seeing* (1972) John Berger examines the link between portraiture and property in *Mr and Mrs Andrews* by Gainsborough 1727–1788.
4. Graham Downes of Hackney based arts organisation Cultural Partnerships coordinated preparation of the barge, undertaken with staff and volunteers of that organisation. He accompanied it on Armadas and provided pyrotechnics for its later voyages.
5. The concept of an alternative plan as an effective oppositional tool was introduced to the campaigning communities in Docklands by Hilary Wainwright, who had witnessed the alternative plans drawn up by the shop stewards' combine at Lucas Aerospace, some ten years previously.

3 Nineties

The left Labour controlled Greater London Council of the early eighties proved too popular for Margaret Thatcher's ultra right wing government. Following failure to block many of its policies, the government resorted to the only means remaining to stop them, which was to remove from the whole country the tier of government it represented. It took several years to achieve, but in 1985 a Local Government Act was passed to abolish the Greater London Council and six other Metropolitan County Councils. As a result of this, funding that had supported so many community based initiatives in London gradually came to an end.

Although the Docklands Community Poster Project managed to continue a version of its original programme for the rest of that decade with monies from other sources, its scope gradually diminished. Following three terms of Thatcherism, most of the land in Docklands had been sold to private developers, with little left that could be used for social purposes. Despite many battles won in the process and some of the land put to good use, the war had effectively been lost. It was time to re-group and look at what could still be achieved.

The Art of Change

By the beginning of the nineties we had been working for ten years around issues of planning and development. Although the loss of our main source of funding was serious, we also welcomed the opportunity of a shift in emphasis. This disruption in its own way offered a chance to address other issues relating to the many changes that were happening in London's East End, and the impact these were having on local communities. The organisation was lucky to retain half of its former funding, which now came through the regional arts board. The remaining shortfall was addressed through a plan to raise money on individual projects, and expand the now diminished staff team[1]. Salaries and income for the organisation were to be covered by the funds they generated. While these strategies were never entirely effective, they did keep the organisation afloat for a further decade and allowed us to produce work through many different, separately funded projects while still retaining our common theme. I co-directed the organisation with Peter, although we now only seldom work together on creative projects. The new emphasis nevertheless opened up a range of collaborative partners with whom we could now engage, plus possibilities for new types of approaches. We re-named the organisation The Art of Change.

By 1995 National Lottery funding had been introduced and resulted in a burgeoning of public art in the UK. However, following an initial spate of unpopular commissions, community consultation and other means of involving local people began to be particularly encouraged. This opened up a potential new source of support for organisations such as The Art of Change, which already had a track record of community involvement. As a result Peter and I carried out several Lottery funded consultancies and public art strategies as well as projects resulting in public artworks, frequently supplementing this income with applications to trusts, foundations and public bodies. Particularly important to me at this time were the opportunities that came up to work with young people, coupled with the innovations being made throughout the nineties in digital technology.

I had started my artistic life in the seventies using photography, film and video as part of a fine art practice. The subsequent collaboration with Peter had led to the development of photomontage as a working process, with the "cut and paste" techniques used in our early poster and exhibition work around health issues becoming expanded into complex montaged imagery for the Docklands photo-murals. All incorporated a filmic use of narrative and sequence. During the nineties, imaging software, which Peter in particular keenly explored, introduced the possibility of combining photographs and other artwork with more sophistication, while scanning and digital photography created greater flexibility and new ways of working with source material. This became particularly pertinent in work with schools, where pupils were able to make artwork in a size or medium appropriate to their classroom context, which could also positively bring in teachers' own skills. As the Internet and communications technologies became more widespread, these opened up alternative ways of working with groups. The web offered interaction in terms of both communication and narrative, plus a virtual domain for the public siting of process and product.

The collaborative relationships developed with activist groups in the seventies and eighties significantly informed the new work with young people. They had expertise of a different kind and their direct local knowledge and lived experience made them valuable partners in identifying issues of relevance to a wider public. This age group also had imagination in abundance, together with a stake in the future. Whether the engagement was with infants or teenagers, I found that the collaborative approach taken with the Docklands activists was still appropriate, and that the project processes previously employed could be adapted to ensure good communication of their ideas and expertise. In the work with the young participants you could still say that we were working in our own ways towards a shared goal to which each brought different skills and knowledge, even though our needs and aspirations regarding process and outcome were different.

* * *

During this time I was involved in a number of other groups and initiatives in East London. Those who have worked in collectives or co-operative know that the interaction in these types of organisation is not always easy, and so during the late eighties I trained in conflict resolution as a means of better understanding and managing the dynamics of these more democratic structures. Through this I came to understand that conflict was frequently sparked when differences collided, and it was the fear that accompanied this clash, rather than the differences themselves, that often caused the problems. I learned about the beneficial role of "safe spaces" where diverse ideas could be expressed; that underlying needs, once uncovered, may not necessarily be at odds; and that creativity can be the most useful means to achieve a positive outcome when all other procedures fail. Above all I discovered that, when the differences that lead to the conflict are able to come together without fear, and underlying needs are addressed, new ideas frequently result. In fact, as I began to discover, the greater the difference the greater the possibility for innovation. The notion of "active listening" experienced in this training also confirmed the importance of an approach that had already proved invaluable in situations where others held the expertise and information required for the content and context of the work—an attitude of "not knowing" is central to any creative endeavour, and all the more essential when working with other people. The training in "conflict transformation", as I came to see it, enabled me to approach potentially difficult situations with the confidence that I not only had the skills to address issues as they arose, but that this negotiation of difference was itself the stuff of which the best work was made. All this fed into the collaborative work begun at The Art of Change and further developed through cSPACE. Key to the multi-collaborations of the later work was recognition of the possibilities that could result from involving numerous different parties with diverse interests, all realised through the same project.

The production of publicly accessible outcomes remained essential for the work's remit of social change, and projects with schools in the early nineties initially made use of the billboards originally constructed for the Docklands Community Poster Project. At the same time it became clear that benefit to participants escalated if their work fed into a publicly valued, collective outcome of professional quality that clearly embodied their own ideas. Outputs had to be of good aesthetic value and functionality while at the same time irrefutably embodying their ideas and input. Recognising that one of my roles as an artist in this work was to enable these factors to co-exist, I began to create structures that allowed the power of participants' ideas to come through without being diminished by their lack of skill. Both aesthetic and organisational, these frameworks offered boundaries while also facilitating production processes. They ranged from the physical borders and production techniques of *West Meets East* and *Celebrating the Difference* described below, to the digital montages and structured visuals of the later web projects such as *I.D* and *Infinity Story*. The case studies below identify some of these frameworks and processes, to which I will also return in Part 2 to identify underlying themes.

West Meets East, 1992

My first project with young people was instigated through a commission by Central Foundation School in Bow, East London, at a time when we were offering re-use of the Docklands Community Poster Project billboard sites to other local organisations for creative purposes. The school had attempted to devise its own project on the theme of the Docklands, and it was only when that failed that they invited The Art of Change to take over the work. I recognised that the teenage participants were not at all interested in this issue and decided, in collaboration with their art teacher who had not previously been consulted, that participants should determine what was of importance to them. The students were following a vocational course at sixth form level and had transferred from schools across the borough. The cultural make-up of this course differed from year to year and on this occasion most attending were

Bangladeshi girls. I felt acutely aware of my position as a white middle class Englishwoman leading a group with such different life experiences, but came to recognise that an appropriate approach would be not unlike the way we had negotiated class differences with the Docklands communities. My role needed to be to listen and allow those with whom I was working to speak for themselves. Discovering what these young people had to say was nevertheless a challenge in itself. Some had only recently arrived in the country, some spoke no English, and none took readily to brainstorming as a means of developing ideas. Under these circumstances it seemed most useful to make the focus of the work the young people's own experience, so they could identify what was pertinent to them. This did nevertheless require the teacher and me to devise some creative strategies to enable this to happen.

On examining the girls' portfolios I discovered that some students had not previously studied art, although all had worked with fabrics or embroidery. The teacher's specialism was also textiles. As a way of bringing our respective skills together I began by asking participants to bring to school images and objects that expressed something about who they felt themselves to be. These initial collages combining fabric and photographic imagery were relatively loose and functioned as a means of exploring ideas and materials. Next, a very "structured" exercise highlighted specific ideas and helped to identify design possibilities. The process of combining ideas where choice was limitless into a structured framework clearly worked. The resulting A4 designs were stunning, and together indicated an emerging theme, that of the experience of living in two cultures.

This project introduced me to the importance of the collaborative relationship with the teacher. It also demonstrated how, as with any teamwork, early clarification of roles and responsibilities would better enable each to contribute their particular expertise. The teacher, Ros Thunder, had particular skills, including knowledge of how to facilitate decision-making through visual means. On one occasion for example, pupils were sent home with small card "windows" to place over something they considered important and draw the contents. These drawings were then duplicated many times over to form the borders of their montaged images. Moving from individual designs to a shared work was not easy, however. I had assumed that elements from some of the process work could be combined to create the main image of the photo-mural, though it soon became clear that this would not work. The border was the most straightforward element so I drew up a template for the final artwork based on the imagery produced thus far and Ros worked with participants to translate this into fabric using embroidery and quilting. The central images on each side of the border were taken from drawings of scenes remembered from Bangladeshi village life that some of the students had made for the first part of the project. The corners related to images selected by the pupils to describe their experience of life in the UK. All of these were embroidered and between them were sewn fabric lino prints of imagery created using the card "windows". The inner border was constructed from embroidered words in English and Bengali, selected by the group from sets of words that had been chosen individually with the help of their language support teachers. However, while a satisfactory border could be constructed from materials generated through an incremental process, these did not work at all for the main image in the way I had hoped. Since that time I have recognised this situation of feeling "stuck" when a key creative element cannot be resolved in this way and seems to call for what I have come to think of as a "multiplicatory" rather than an "additive" approach. It also marks the moment where the artist has to move beyond the role of facilitator.

In this case the shared central image was the most challenging. Visually and aesthetically it needed to take on a unified and symbolic function in contrast to the fragmented and accumulative quality of the border. Since one-to-one conversation had proved the most effective means of verbal communication within the group, I talked to the students individually about the content of their initial montages. Out of this a concept began to emerge from repeated anecdotes of how each was grappling with their identity as a London teenager while living within traditional Bangladeshi family values. The struggle of each seemed characterised by the attempt to assimilate both these identities rather than to be wholly within one. An idea emerged of using one of the many sewing machines that filled the classroom to join fabric representing the two cultures. This became modified through an initial photographic shoot[2] in the classroom, which gave us an idea of how the final image might look, although it was still not quite right. One day I arrived to find that the students had all done *mendhi* designs for hand paintings. Having experienced the first photo shoot, they had decided between them that joining the fabric together was symbolic of a marriage of cultures, and *mendhi* hand painting as used by a bride at a marriage ceremony would therefore be appropriate. The design in the final artwork does not use the traditional henna, however. The girls apparently made these designs on their hands quite regularly at school using nail varnish, which could be wiped off before going home so as not to be seen by their parents. The hand design in the final image is therefore made from nail varnish.

Finally the artwork was copied and enlarged—the first photographic print in full colour that we had been able to produce for use on a billboard. Reflecting the early stage of that technology, it had to be covered by an ultra-violet acrylic filter to prevent fading. However when the photo-mural was recreated two years later for display in Barcelona, inkjet printing onto vinyl overcame that problem and from that time presented a more durable solution to photo-mural production.

While the format of the main output of this project was pre-determined, the route to achieve this was necessarily an organic one and embodied many learning experiences that served to underpin future practice. Not only was I introduced to new processes of collaboration and participation, but the inappropriateness of class discussions for this group forced me to identify other means for the visual development of ideas. I also glimpsed the power of chosen objects and imagery to access layers of meanings for participants without excluding those less confident or proficient in language. All these devices continued to be employed in Art of Change projects as well as in later work, particularly *VOLCO*. *West Meets East* perhaps most significantly offered an introduction to the necessity of "structuring" in both a visually and organisational way, to allow shared meaning to emerge. The reaction of participants to seeing their ideas sited in public demonstrated the potential of this aspect of the work to enhance the self-recognition of their ability to act on the world—a theme that would become central to *Awakenings*, then *VOLCO* and *The Young Person's Guides* many years later.

With hindsight, the decision in this project to move from the issue-based work of the eighties to a focus on participant identities also embodied the shift from the politics of distribution, which underpinned the Docklands project, to one of recognition, which was to characterise the work of The Art of Change over the following decade.

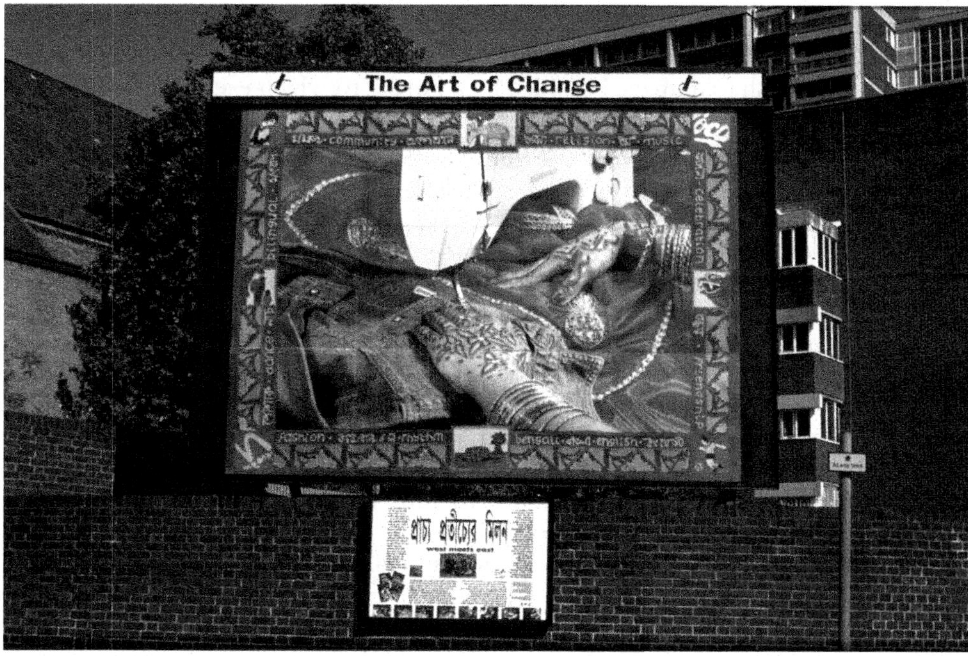

Figure 3.1 *West Meets East* in situ at Wapping Lane, London E1

© Loraine Leeson, 1992. Photo-mural produced with teenage girls and teacher from Central Foundation School. Fabric and photographic montage displayed as a 16' × 12' (4.88m × 3.66m) photo-mural. Below the billboard was an explanatory display panel.

Celebrating the Difference, 1993–94

West Meets East proved so popular locally that we produced an exhibition documenting its making to tour schools and community centres. At that time the ultra right wing British National Party was proposing candidates for local council elections on the Isle of Dogs in the London Borough of Tower Hamlets. Riots were breaking out and unrest in this area was featured regularly in the news. On seeing the *West Meets East* exhibition the Head of Art at the Island's secondary school asked The Art of Change to run a similar project, this time on the theme of anti-racism. I felt concerned, however, that addressing this subject directly could result in the polarisation of participants, so re-focused the project on the notion of difference, allowing it to act as a "safe space" where individuals could interact without conflict. It nevertheless required sensitive management. Unlike the *West Meets East* group, the secondary school class taking part was racially mixed; racism was rife in the school and there were regular classroom scuffles. The Head of Art was an excellent teacher, however, with a well managed class, and such a project seemed possible. I started with a similar approach to *West Meets East*, whereby pupils produced collages that allowed each to express who they felt themselves to be. This was important as a means of creating an opportunity for the expression of sometimes fragile identities, and no element was criticised so long as it did not denigrate anyone else. This idea of offering participants the licence to represent themselves in whatever identity they wished became a theme further developed through later projects, and ultimately through the fantasy characters of *VOLCO*.

The device of a shared image bounded by a border to which each could contribute again proved useful. This time the surrounding images were drawn from collages, reproduced with the help of the teacher through various printing techniques. Advances in technology had occurred since the previous project and I used Photoshop to construct a "border of difference" that would combine imagery produced by each participant. The concept for the centre image was again developed through one-to-one conversations. I asked each pupil, "If in ten years' time you could live anywhere in the world, where would it be?". Almost without exception each replied that they would remain on the Isle of Dogs. As if the nightly news broadcast of racial hatred and unrest did not exist, the comments of the young people insisted that this was a positive place to be, with good social networks, and not one participant referred negatively to the existence of other ethnic groups. For the central image, as in *West Meets East,* I took one of their means of production, this time an art room paint palette, and used digital imaging to add the outline shape of the river surrounding the Isle of Dogs. This picked up the various colours as it traversed the blocks of paint, ending not in a muddy multiculturalism, but rather a rainbow, where the vibrancy of the colours was accentuated by their coexistence. At the same

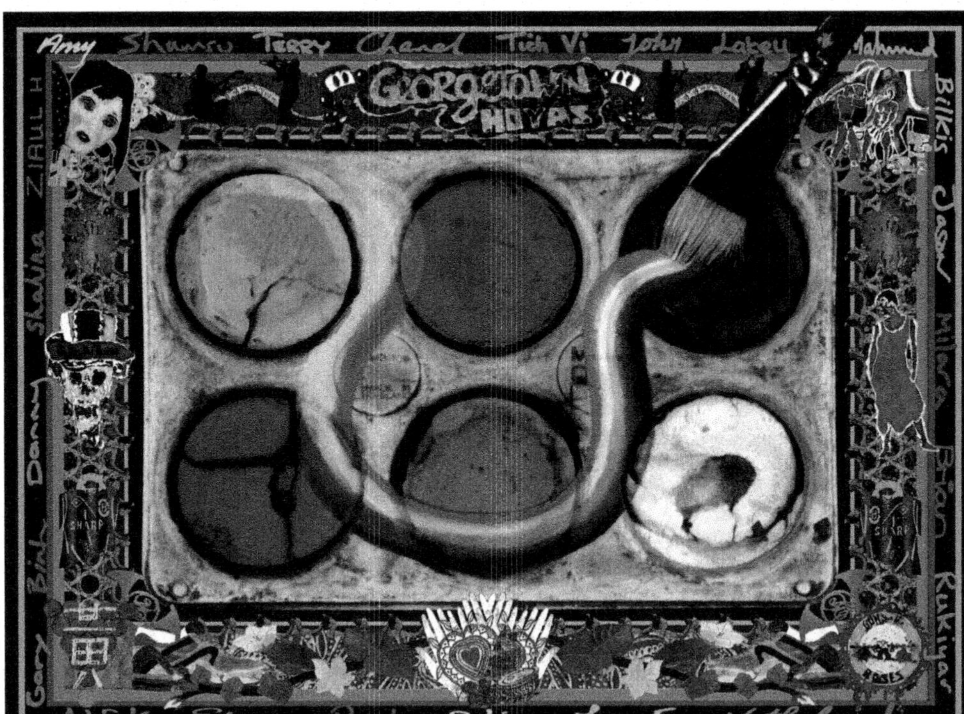

Figure 3.2 Celebrating the Difference

© Loraine Leeson, 1993–94. Photo-mural produced with teachers and pupils from George Green's School, Isle of Dogs, 16' × 12' (4.88m × 3.66m) digital montage displayed as a vinyl photo-mural.

time a poster being used in local elections to counter British National Party publicity came to light. It depicted a similar "rainbow river" with the caption *Celebrate the Difference*. The leader of that campaign was a teacher in the same school and with her blessing the young people named their photo-mural *Celebrating the Difference*. At its launch campaign members gave out rainbow ribbons they had used in the recent council elections, where the nationalist candidates had been successfully defeated.

While the project could only play a small part in addressing such serious social rifts, the participants were certainly proud of their joint creation. To themselves, their friends and families, the image they had made, translated into a photo-mural and prominent in the midst of their community, was clearly very pleasing. Its resonance resulted not only from a carefully structured combination of their different contributions, but emanated at source from the very nature of their differences. The public siting allowed them to witness themselves making a visually powerful statement back into their community, and it began to consolidate my own thoughts regarding the role of aesthetics at the service of social change.

Between Family Lines, 1994

Not all Art of Change projects were with young people. *Between Family Lines* was a collaboration with media practitioner Karen Merkel, previously Chair of the Association of Community Artists. The prominence of collaborative working had already begun to influence public funding, and we took the opportunity to apply for grant aid for this purpose from the London Arts Board to enable us to work together on a new project. Although our practices employed different media and working contexts, Karen and I shared a broad approach to work and politics and both as a matter of course worked collaboratively with community or activist groups. Furthermore, Karen had connections with Women Against Fundamentalism, an organisation that had come together following the fatwa on Salman Rushdie[3]. The group comprised women from different cultures who were concerned that a return to "family values" was taking place across cultures and forcing women back into the home. 1994 was the UK's Year of the Family and movement towards absolute beliefs was being encouraged in many different religious quarters.

Members of Women Against Fundamentalism were keen for creative material to use in their educational work, and to address this need Karen and I arrived at the format of a four-projector tape slide production[4], advanced technology for this time, which could also be translated into video. The group put us in touch with women from five different cultural backgrounds, who had all suffered through fundamentalism or orthodoxy, some in extreme circumstances. Each had, against the odds, managed to make a new life for themselves that rejected fundamentalism, yet retained their culture. We interviewed these women and heard stories of extraordinary courage, then asked for any songs, poems or visual artifacts that evoked the transition they had made in their life. While Karen made recordings, I photographed the objects or images they chose, making over a thousand 35mm transparencies with a small copy stand that I carried with me to the women's homes or meeting places. We focused on the watershed in each of their lives and the ways each woman had managed to navigate sometimes seemingly hopeless situations. In addition to the tape/slide production a set of exhibition panels were produced to sum up each woman's story.

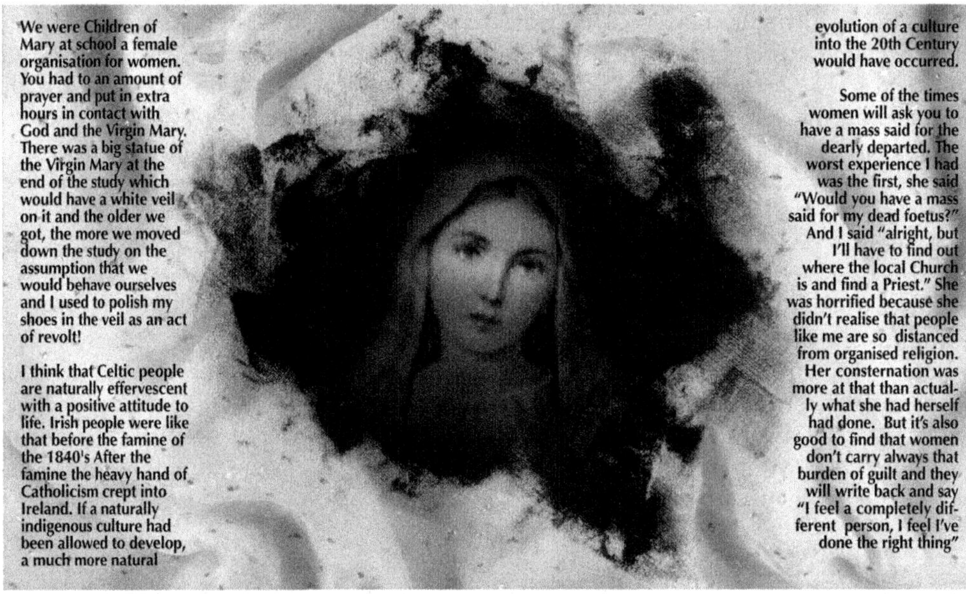

Figure 3.3 Ann from *Between Family Lines* exhibition

© Loraine Leeson, 1994. Digital montage from a sequence of five exhibition panels produced as part of a collaborative project with Karen Merkel and Women Against Fundamentalism.

The exhibition and audio-visual production then toured London, accompanied by discussions led by Women Against Fundamentalism, before being translated into video for its ongoing work.

Awakenings, 1995–96

During the mid nineties Colin Grigg, Head of Young Visitors' Programmes at Tate Millbank, was keen to expand the gallery's educational work beyond the limits of its gallery tours and day-long workshops. He felt that the collection had the potential to serve communities beyond the existing gallery-going public, and as such paved the way for the Tate's now extensive community programming. He invited five organisations, including The Art of Change, to initiate projects beyond the confines of the gallery. Peter and I chose to work together and to involve the Isle of Dogs secondary school where *Celebrating the Difference* had taken place. The commission fee itself covered little of the time needed for community-based work, so we used this as match funding to attract further finance that would cover a year's worth of activities.

Our initial concern was how these young people might relate to the Tate's collection in a way that was meaningful and empowering for them. It was important that the approach should be less about appreciating works of art and more about using them as source material to feed their own imaginations. We felt that if the young people put themselves into the place of the artists, the collection could become material through which they might then visualise possibilities for themselves. Thus the initial working title for the project came to be *Changing Places*. The teacher involved wanted the work to fulfill National Curriculum[5] requirements, which included copying works of art, and so this was also built into the project.

The project started with the young people being introduced to the Tate by gallery staff, and our instruction to them was by the end of the day to simply choose a work they liked, knowing that this would help trigger the hoped for identification process. Participants copied their chosen paintings in the classroom, selecting one item in the artwork to change in a way that would reflect their personal identity. This process began individually, then developed into small group work on a larger scale with a variety of media. This time only the formal structure of the work was retained and the iconography re-cast in terms of how they saw themselves, their cultures and their environment.

Peter later wrote about the project in an article we produced for the CAA Journal[6], describing how Stanley Spencer's monumental *Resurrection, Cookham* was chosen for the final phase of the project. He noted that its attraction stemmed from its representation of a "moment of rebirth" set in an unspecified future. Throughout the history of western art the Christian notion of resurrection has been used to explore contemporary values, both as critique and an embodiment of aspiration. Practically speaking, its scale and matrix of discrete elements meant that all those involved in the project—pupils, teachers, artists, and Tate personnel—could be included. The painting is of course also a celebration of starting a new life[7]. Replacing its Christian roots with the personal experience of the young people involved, poised at the beginning of their new life as adults, *Awakenings* was chosen as the title for the final work.

Spencer's work also revolves around a celebration of a place, Cookham, and its local narratives[8]. Brecht is purported to have said that all the great issues of human experience are enacted upon local stages. This idea related not only to Spencer's Cookham, but also to the sense of place that the Isle of Dogs seemed to generate for the young people living there. There were other interesting similarities, since both places are situated on the River Thames. Cookham, to the west of London, is an island created by irrigation and navigation channels during the agrarian revolution, where rural English village life was threatened by encroaching industry. The Isle of Dogs, in East London, is similarly an island created through industrialisation and the building of the docks. During the nineties the residents of this urban community were also under threat, this time from a post-industrial climate of unemployment combined with the physical and social dislocation of major redevelopment and the racially divisive tactics of British National Party campaigning.

The centre section of the painting depicts African figures rising out of baked earth in what looks like a boat, bearing mysterious objects, which may be interpreted as "precious gifts" from Africa. Spencer's brother in law, also featured in the painting, was an anthropologist and mounted one of the first exhibitions of African Art in Britain[9]. We interpreted this as important cultural influences and asked pupils to identify some knowledge or wisdom passed through their families that brought information and insight from elsewhere, and to identify an object associated with this. For all those involved, *Awakenings* became a celebration of another fusion, a remaking of "Englishness" as a variegated richness of cultural difference.

Working in pairs and small groups, students were taken through a process of imaginatively rethinking different aspects of the painting in their own terms: what their families or relatives would do with their body if they died; how their family

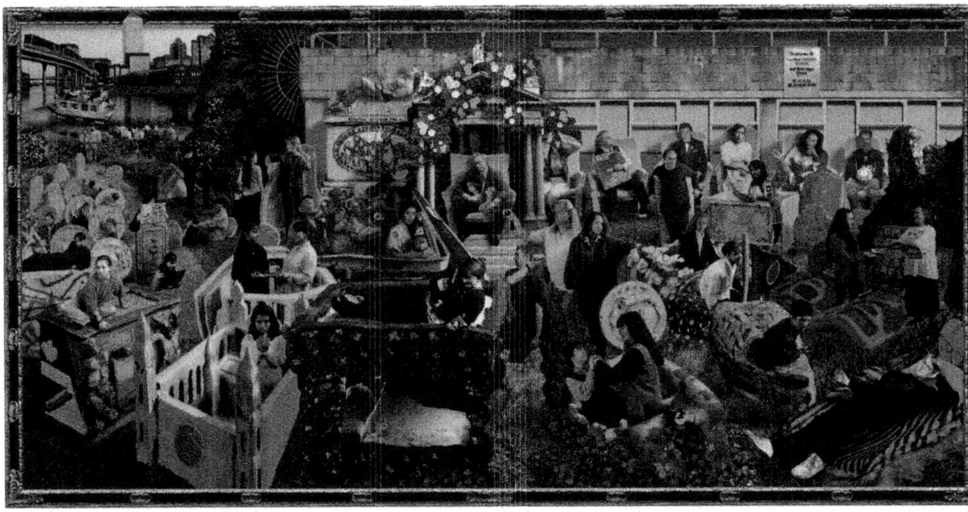

Figure 3.4 Awakenings—after Stanley Spencer's *Resurrection, Cookham*

© Peter Dunn and Loraine Leeson, The Art of Change, 1995–6. Digital montage displayed as a 13' × 7' (3.96m × 2.13m) Cibachrome print.

might commemorate their life; by what images they would choose to be remembered; the first thing they would choose to do if they came back to life; to where they would like to return to feel most "at home". Drawing on the specialist skills of one of the teachers, clay was used to re-make the paintings, tombs and commemorative plaques, with batik for the foliage and textures. A temporary photographic studio was set up in the school where participants took their own portraits using a squeeze-ball trigger. The final work was compiled on computer using an early version of Photoshop.

Awakenings was finally displayed as a large photographic print at the Tate Gallery, with examples of work in progress and some of Spencer's working drawings. Spencer's daughters also attended the opening. A key moment, however, was when the young participants arrived. Although they had visited the gallery before and knew that this was the destination for their work, they seemed astounded. "What's it doing there?" asked one pupil, "It's ours!" The gap between the personal creativity and social standing of these young people's ideas became bridged though the public viewing of the artwork. In this situation the gallery itself fulfilled the function of the public space that brought the young people's perceptions to wider attention, while at the same time delivering a message back to participants that what they had to offer was of the highest quality and of value to society. *Awakenings* now hangs on permanent display in Tower Hamlets town hall, at the entrance to the Isle of Dogs.

The Infinity Story, 1997

Two commissions followed this work, taking a similar approach to *Awakenings* but created as web site projects: *I.D*, with designer Henry Iles, and *Momentos* with Peter. *I.D* was the first web project commissioned by the Tate, aiming to involve London teenagers in a response to its John Singer Sargent exhibition. This led to the commissioning of *Momentos* by the Art Gallery of Ontario, who were wishing to involve teenagers in the exhibition of the nineteenth-century "father of Canadian painting" Cornelius Krieghof. Both projects were approached in a similar way to *Awakenings*, avoiding "appreciation" of the art and instead utilising the work of these established artists as a catalyst to encourage the young people to develop ideas about their own identities and futures. Although these projects made some creative use of the web, I was nevertheless concerned that the limited understanding of Internet technologies on behalf of the commissioning institutions was restricting the scope of what could be achieved. Emerging web technology seemed to hold the potential to expand both process and product in collective work and I was also interested in the opportunity to involve much larger numbers of participants. I particularly wished to explore whether personal contributions could still be allied to coherent collective expression when those numbers increased. There was a great deal of talk about use of the Internet for exchange of information. However I was more curious about the extent to which it could serve as a site of creative production, and whether the web could act as a "safe space" where the differences of many collaborating partners could come together and create something new.

These interests in the technology were combined with concerns about how statutory education was failing to tap into its potential. At that time I was mother to two young children and a school governor, and had observed how the National Grid for Learning[10] was introducing computers into schools with little initial training for teachers, and even less support or encouragement for exploration of its learning potential. This was also a time when the effects of standardisation and target setting, which had come to characterise the wider economy, had begun to undermine creativity in education through frequent inspections and testing[11]. Since only Maths, English and Science were originally tested, primary schools began to put less emphasis on other subjects and in some cases art was relegated to a few weeks at the end of the summer after tests had taken place, or dropped altogether. Warnings that creativity was being drained from the curriculum and threatening to undermine the country's future economic development eventually led to the commissioning of Ken Robinson's groundbreaking report *All Our Futures—Creativity and Culture in Education,* which demonstrated the key role played by creative expression and engagement in children's development[12]. It was on the cusp of this shift, when cross-curricular project work was again being encouraged and the importance of creativity to education just beginning to be recognised, that I developed the idea for *The Infinity Story.* As I later wrote in *Rising East,* it would be a way of giving a glimpse to a whole school—pupils and teachers—of some of the excitement and potential of digital interactivity. At the same time they would be engaged in exciting and purposeful endeavour towards a collective outcome[13].

An artist colleague Camille Dorney had begun an interactive story on her web site, and this seemed an ideal format for working with children. The two of us set about adapting the process for a creative writing project in which the whole school community could participate. The result was an imaginative, non-linear illustrated story developed from a theme collectively chosen by all the children in Godwin Junior school. Its structure followed the shape of a three-dimensional tree. A "trunk" contained the beginning of the story and characterisations, and from here the narrative branched off in all directions as the children added or developed different aspects. Camille worked with small groups and, starting with the youngest class of seven year olds, the project worked its way through the school up to the top classes of pupils aged eleven, with three days of production per group. As the project reached each new class, children would decide whether to continue an existing strand of narrative, or begin a new one. The final product, comprising forty thousand words written by over three hundred pupils, incorporated many different branches, a number of which sub-divided again and again. In addition there were histories or "roots" for the original characters. The story could be accessed as a whole or in part, the reader creating their own version by the way they chose to move through it. The narrative therefore changed according to the audience, more in keeping with an oral tradition of story telling than the printed word. Sadly, as technologies move on, it is no longer online, although the experience it generated had ongoing effect.

The Infinity Story's key lessons were in the unexpected and unplanned outcomes that emerged through its ability to transform the personal experiences of many participants into a collective entity. Children honed in on those aspects of the story that they found most intriguing, and built on certain themes again and again. In this sense the characters and themes that emerged are more "archetypes" than stereotypes. The narrative reflected and illuminated, sometimes surprisingly, preoccupations of the age group of its creators. The plot centres on an East End family seen through the eyes of six children when their parents depart for a round the world holiday, leaving them in the hands of a mad babysitter. The parents' role seems to be characterised by their absence, and they are quickly despatched again whenever they make an appearance. Their function appears to be of a benevolent background presence, and fulfilment of the children's fantasies on their endless journeyings. By contrast, the babysitter is a continuing (and "disgusting") presence in the children's lives. Whenever she is sent away, it is only to be promptly returned. By turns witch, sorceress, clearly sexual, she is also the inept childminder and carer of the family. She lives in a locked room at the top of the house, the starting point of many mysterious adventures. The eating of the inedible, smells, the dual forces of dirtiness and cleanliness, return again and again. The story seems to create a vessel for the children's hopes, desires, anxieties and experiences, conscious and unconscious. Collective identities also come through. The family at the centre of the story is an uncanny representation of the school community. As the story arrived into its new class, one child asked "How could there be West Indian triplets with white brothers and sisters in a family called "the Patels", with a white Mum and a brown-skinned Dad?" Responses from the other children in the class included: "Perhaps it isn't their real Dad/perhaps they are all adopted/perhaps some of them are fostered/my parents and I all have different skin colours."

Whether through its online location, bizarre humour or collective nature, the story seemed to provide the "safe space" for joint creative endeavour that I had been seeking. Difficult issues from either actual or perceived life experiences were expressed and explored, initiated by individuals and then taken up by their peers. Following a description of the childminder's tragic childhood, for example, we hear how she managed to obtain a flat through a homeless people's organisation, "tidied herself up and got a job as a childminder". Bunny the mother, trapped in Dominica looking after someone else's children, was suddenly put on a plane and brought home, only to be sent off again by another of the story's young authors. It seemed that one child could solve what another could not, and in this way participants were able to indirectly support each other, examine options and ultimately problem-solve together. If three hundred children could collectively write a coherent story, I began to wonder what would happen if even larger numbers were to invent a new world. *The Infinity Story* thus paved the way for *VOLCO*, which added to the mix online dialogue between children with diverse life experiences and drew further on my knowledge of conflict transformation with an aim to foster understanding across difference.

The Art of Change embodied a decade of participatory and collaborative projects embracing public art, education, digital interactivity and a growing interest in sustainability. It came to an end at the turn of the millennium following a change in policy by the London Arts Board, which for ten years had provided our principal source of funding. This new era was also marked by a decision by Peter and myself to go our separate ways, both professionally and personally.

Notes

1. Designer Dini Lallah was taken on to develop work for the voluntary sector and Bob Harris, a Labour councillor in the London Borough of Greenwich, was employed as business development officer to fundraise and explore new opportunities for the work.
2. The photography was undertaken by Peter using a medium format camera.
3. Salman Rushdie's novel *The Satanic Verses* published in 1988 had led to protests from Muslims in several countries, some of which were violent. Faced with death threats and a fatwa issued by Ayatollah Khomeini, Rushdie spent nearly a decade underground, appearing only occasionally in public.
4. Technology and expertise was provided by photographer Andy Golding of University of Westminster, the only media professional I have ever encountered who used the medium of tape-slide in this innovative way.
5. I since learned to incorporate National Curriculum outcomes, which teachers were under increasing pressure to deliver, into schools' projects from the outset. If a project fell outside of these, it would receive considerably less time and attention. With an approach that took multiple needs and interest into account, adding in these requirements seemed a small price to pay for teachers' energy and focus, as well as the excitement of the young people doing an arts project instead of their usual lessons.
6. The following paragraphs are derived, in part, from an article entitled "The Aesthetics of Collaboration" published by Peter and myself in CAA Art Journal, Vol.56, Issue1,1997, available online: http://caa.tandfonline.com/toc/rcaj20/56/1?nav=tocList
7. The Resurrection was regarded by Spencer as his Primavera or Allegory of Spring as in Botticelli's fifteenth-century painting of that name, both artistically and as a celebration of his new life as a married man. His new wife appears prominently several times in the painting.
8. Most of Spencer's paintings of this period (1920s–1930s), whether a "resurrection" or some other significant historic/spiritual theme, were depicted in specific recognisable places in or around the village of Cookham. Spencer believed there was a kind of parallel spiritual Cookham that could not be corrupted by the ordinary passages of time. It was for him the embodiment of place.
9. The Tate put the Spencer curator at the project's disposal, who furnished much useful information about the artist and painting we were to re-interpret.
10. The National Grid for Learning was introduced by government in 1997 as a means of bringing school technology into the twenty-first century. Its goal was to bring information and communications technologies into everyday use in teaching and learning. Scrapped in 2006, its greatest effect had been to ensure that all schools were equipped with computer hardware, although it largely failed to introduce new ways of learning through the technology.
11. The Standard Assessment Tasks (SATs) were introduced as part of the National Curriculum to assess children's attainment at regular stages throughout primary and secondary education. This was really a tool for assessing school standards rather than for pupil benefit and became widely blamed for introducing unnecessary stress into young people's learning.

12. Ken Robinson, *All Our Futures—Creativity and Culture in Education*, Suffolk: DFeS, 1999.
13. Loraine Leeson, "To Infinity and Beyond: New Technologies, Arts and Education" in *Rising East Vol. 2 No 3*, Cambridge: Cambridge University Press, 1999, pp. 136–142.

References

Peter Dunn and Loraine Leeson, "The Aesthetics of Collaboration" in *Art Journal* Vol. 56, No.1, Ed. Grant Kester, pp. 26–37 (New York: CAA, 1997).

Loraine Leeson, "To Infinity and Beyond: New Technologies, Arts and Education" in *Rising East* Vol. 2 No. 3 (Cambridge: Cambridge University Press, 1999).

Ken Robinson, *All Our Futures—Creativity and Culture in Education* (Suffolk: Department for Education and Science, 1999).

4 The New Millennium

Shifts in the social, cultural and economic climate taking place during the nineties began to impact on how the practice could be managed and delivered. The London Arts Board had re-categorised The Art of Change as "public" rather than "visual" art. It then changed its public art policy so that only agencies could receive finance, and as a production organisation we therefore lost our funding. As background to this, the Arts Council of England was reorganising itself into a centralised institution. One of its new strategies was introduction of "Grants for the Arts", which amalgamated all of their funding programmes, but no longer offered any mechanism for small organisations to bid for revenue funding. With this important source of income gone, all the work including research, development and fundraising had to be supported through project money alone. I have heard this referred to by policy makers as improving the "efficiency" of organisations, encouraging sustainability and ensuring that the majority of resources went to participants. In practice it simply meant that preparatory work was unfunded, increasing the strain and insecurity of artists and diverting valuable creativity into the attempt to make project funds cover areas of expenditure for which they were not intended.

This was also the time of "New Labour" government led by prime minister Tony Blair, and a move to the middle ground of the political spectrum. The administration's attempts to counter "social exclusion" led to finance for projects that they considered as meeting the needs of those sectors of society designated as underprivileged, but this was mainly designed for the public sector and large institutions. Cultural institutions were now also in the sway of the target economy, resulting in content, creativity and participant experience being subsumed into numbers and target outcomes, while the notion of accreditation overtook opportunities for "informal" learning through the arts. There was funding available therefore, but it had to be carefully negotiated and managed to ensure that the agenda for a creative project remained one's own. While the value of community-based public art had been taken on board by government departments and regeneration agencies, these institutions used the arts largely as a social panacea within what were essentially top-down processes of urban redevelopment. Arts funding also became an increasingly constraining force, directing artists to follow bureaucratically determined "good practice" rather than supporting artist- and community-led initiatives developed through organic engagement with local issues and contexts.

The changing social and political context itself called for different ways of working. The earlier practice of the seventies and eighties had taken place against a backdrop of grass roots social organisation in the UK that failed to survive into the new millennium. Activist art became a more complex activity in this more fragmented society where popular political organisation tended to group around single issues. For the young at this time there was little belief in a future world that could be changed for the better through collective action.

cSPACE

Working via an organisation rather than as an individual was the method through which I had realised my practice since the establishment of the Docklands Community Poster Project in the eighties. Although it is still a relatively uncommon mode of operation for artists, it offered advantages for conducting large-scale projects including greater opportunities for fundraising, structures for employment and the support of a board of trustees. However, establishing and running a new organisation without regular funding was not easy. Peter and I had split our practice into two new organisations, and while he set up ART.e, I chose to re-locate my work in a university environment. This enabled me to keep overheads down while the university benefited from the contribution to its research and public engagement profile.

At the millennium, I moved my practice to University of East London and by 2002 had founded cSPACE, which has provided the infrastructure through which I continue to develop and manage projects, overseen by a small board of trustees[1]. Its initial base at the university's Docklands campus provided the continuity of a working environment by the docks in the heart of the London Thames Gateway regeneration zone. The higher education context also provided access to research and potential collaborative partners, and the opportunity to involve students in projects. While based there cSPACE was successful in some sizeable bids for public money as well as match funding from local trusts and foundations. The projects outlined below indicate how the task of finding support for this work wove its way through opportunity and circumstance. The increasing insecurity of this process once led me to describe it as "walking on ice floes", but it enabled the practice to continue for a further eleven years in the face of an impending economic crisis that had a knock-on effect for the arts.

The Catch, 1997–2002

I was not in the habit of bidding for public art commissions. However, at one particularly lean period of The Art of Change it had seemed expedient to do so. With regeneration imminent, the London Borough of Barking and Dagenham invited proposals for a gateway public artwork for the town centre that would reflect its heritage and also involve workshops and other activities with young people. My submission won that competition, despite proposing a scheme that would cost twice the sum offered. This was in 1997, but it took the planning department several years to raise the balance of funds and the new millennium was well underway by the time the project was realised. During this time the commissioners discarded the idea of community involvement and it was not until the project was nearing completion and a new officer in place that I was able to persuade them of the value of this approach. The borough finally supported the involvement of local children just a few weeks before installation of the sculpture.

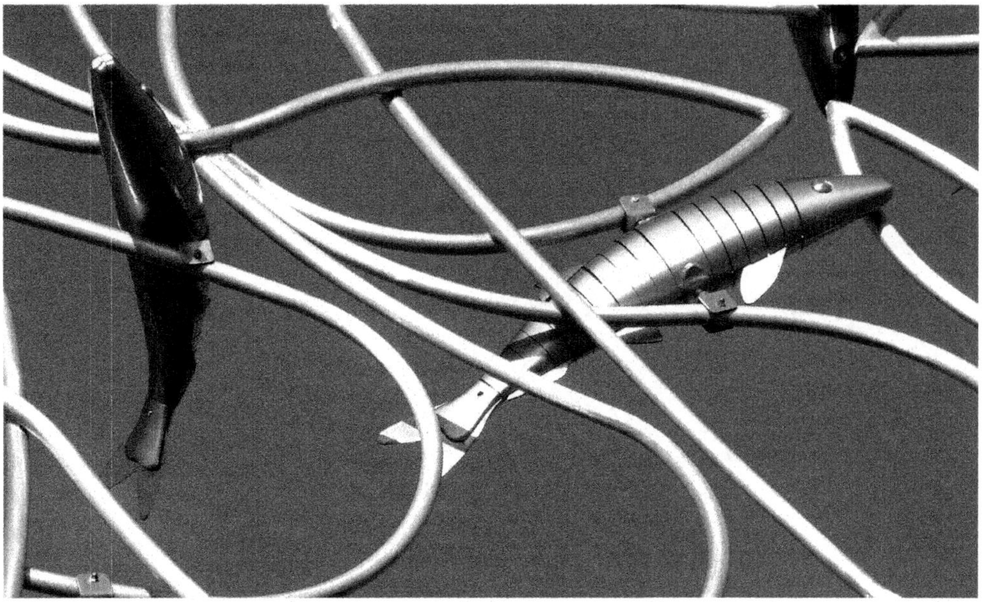

Figure 4.1 The Catch—detail

Photo: © Loraine Leeson, 2002. From a public artwork in Barking produced in collaboration with Anne Thorne Architects.

The Catch was launched in 2002 on the Fanshawe Avenue roundabout, close to Barking town centre. Its theme reflected Barking's historic fishing industry as well as its Saxon heritage, but, more importantly, was conceived as an image to inspire children and young people in their ideas and wishes for the future. Its concept was based on a children's rhyme:

> Where are you going, and what do you wish?
> The old moon asked the three.
> We have come to fish for the herring fish
> That live in this beautiful sea;
> Nets of silver and gold have we . . .[2]

I invited architect Anne Thorne to join me on the project. Our work had great affinity and we had already worked together on several occasions. Her input was major in realising this ambitious steel structure with moving parts that was also to stand ten metres high. The sculpture represented two nets, interlaced with fish, being cast upwards and outwards with the force of a wave. The structure of the nets derived from Celtic knotwork depicted on the stonework in the ruins of a local abbey and was constructed from rolled aluminium to create the "nets of silver" of the rhyme, while the fish interweaving the nets were constructed from resin and rubber[3] to achieve a sense of movement. The children finally involved were from a local junior school close to the site, and over three hundred participated by making a fish of their own together with a wish for the future of their community, which appeared on *The Catch* website together with information about the artwork and its references. Graduate

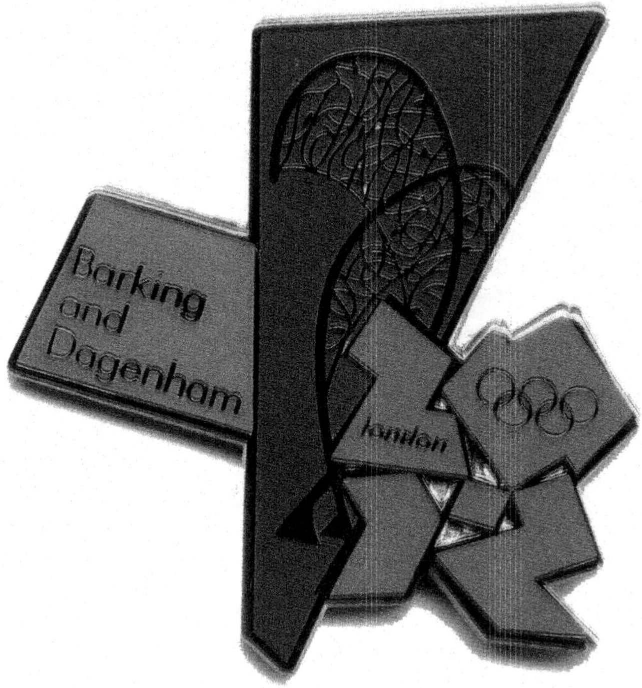

Figure 4.2 The Catch—Olympic pin badge

Photo: © Loraine Leeson, 2012. The public artwork was chosen by local people to be their London Olympic Landmark.

students from the University of East London and local sixth formers helped run the workshops as part of the first *Cascade* mentoring programme described below, and the artwork's launch at the town hall was accompanied by an exhibition of the children's work. At the opening ceremony the children presented to the mayor their ideas for the future, bound into a Book of Wishes, as their contribution to Barking's regeneration strategy.

Prior to the London Olympics local people had an opportunity to vote for their borough's London 2012 Landmark[4]. Despite the many major public artworks that had been commissioned for that borough in the interim, Barking residents chose *The Catch*. This was undoubtedly due to the sense of ownership engendered by the children's involvement, minimal though this had been considering the scale of the project. It could have been so much more if the borough's planning department had understood the importance of this kind of community involvement to their own priorities, and recognised that this would have been more beneficial if intrinsic rather than an add-on to a public artwork.

VOLCO, 1999–2009

VOLCO stood for an evolving Virtual Online Co-Operative environment, a planet in cyberspace constructed by children and young people, who communicated online to make links across geographic and cultural divides. Work on the pilot project began in 1999 following completion of *The Infinity Story* to further develop the potential that had emerged from this earlier use of the Internet. The aim was to create an artwork with a life of its own that would evolve according to the children's ideas and also embed a creative approach to Internet technologies in schools. To achieve this I took the principle of the "structuring" devices of earlier projects such as *West Meets East* and *Awakenings* to provide a web-based framework that would ultimately require minimal direct creative input from myself. I was interested in establishing a system where, having set the parameters, I would be able to simply observe what emerged. This project constituted a further "safe space" for the coming together of differences, as in *The Infinity Story*. Since this approach had previously worked well with children in the school where I planned to pilot the project, I wondered if it could bridge even greater gulfs in life experience than has previously been the case.

By the time this project began the range of communications opportunities offered by the Internet had grown and young people were increasingly making use of chat rooms and multi user domains to explore their identities through online interaction. One problem with these communications, however, seemed to be that participants sometimes never left the virtual worlds, so that the experience gained would fail to translate into their lives. In *Life on the Screen* Sherry Turkle raised the possibility of a time when the real and the virtual could be made "permeable", so that each could enrich and expand the other[5], and this is what I attempted to achieve with *VOLCO*. My plan was to again combine the ideas of hundreds of young people into the creation of a new collective entity, this time to create a new world. Participants would interact online as Volcans, but at the end of the project have opportunity to meet each other in the "virtual" flesh, using the new video conferencing technology of the time. Following the project's pilot run between the school in East London and another in North Carolina, the children were indeed excited to meet each other. At the same time they were surprised and delighted to find out that, despite writing in the same language, there were also differences, since the real children they encountered were far from their expectations. As one child from North Carolina expressed, "We expected all the children in London to be white and speak like the Queen". The joy with which they discovered these differences after involvement in the project contrasted with the partnering of schools through the Internet that I had witnessed as a governor, where children were asked to simply correspond with others who they did not know. The sharing of creativity and ideas on this virtual planet seemed to be able to achieve a bond that pre-empted the fear of stereotyped difference.

The project also set out to address the new developing concepts for education as outlined in the Robinson report, which called for the concept of creativity to become intrinsic to education[6]. As much as *VOLCO* was an attempt to bring the process of exploring identity experienced on the Internet back into the real world, it also set out to bring the learning potential and excitement of these virtual environments into the classroom. Children loved doing it because of its combination of creativity and technology. At the same time addressing National Curriculum outputs together with the new requirement of using computer technologies in nearly every subject area ensured a similar welcome from teachers. If a planet is to be invented, then all aspects of life, and therefore many disciplines, can be covered. A study of the project undertaken by teachers in 2004[7] identified eleven different subjects in the UK's Key Stage 2 (junior) curriculum that could be in part delivered through *VOLCO*. Making the project attractive to schools in this way ensured that large numbers of children

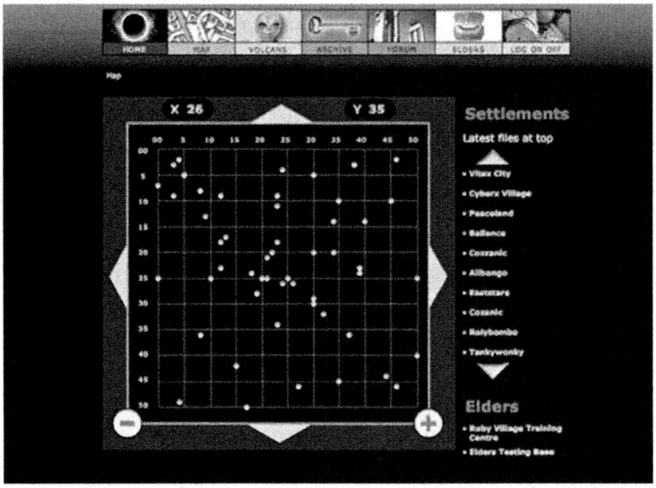

Figure 4.3 The *VOLCO* map page

had the opportunity to participate and, as a result, its data banks eventually incorporated the ideas of over a thousand children. Understanding of the paucity of school resources I had gained from the *Awakenings* project, together with the prospect of involving multiple participants, led me to make this project truly transferable. To enhance this I also developed a teaching pack and training that would enable teachers and youth leaders to run it for themselves. These enabled the project's widespread use and children eventually took part from London, North Carolina, Berlin, Chicago, and Shetland.

I had witnessed my own children playing computer games in which there was a choice of character, although only within the limits of imagery created by others. Similarly in virtual worlds such as *Second Life*[8], I had seen how "residents" could create their character, clothing, homes and environment. In the early days of these online environments increasingly sophisticated, images and graphics in this and similar resources were made available *for* their users, but not created by them. In contrast, I felt it important for participants in *VOLCO* to have the facility to produce the visual materials themselves, and remain in charge of representing their own identities and ideas. This was achieved through scanning, photography and downloading from the Internet as well through more traditional art processes. I again worked closely with designer Henry Iles and several programmers to make the web site attractive and accessible to primary age children and to enable them to do their own uploading to its database. Even though their entries were not "live" until moderated by their teachers, participants received immediate visual feedback to review what they had done, and it was through this process of adding their characters, dialogue and ideas to the Volcan archives that the planet grew and evolved.

The purpose of *VOLCO* was ultimately to involve children in considering new and co-operative ways of creating a better life for their own planet. As with all the projects, *VOLCO* could not guarantee change, and if this were to happen it was most likely to encountered through individual experience and at unspecified times in the future[9], although I still meet young people, teachers and parents who recall its impact. The project in fact drew on lessons learned through the campaigning of the Docklands Community Poster Project—the creation of alternatives as the most effective means of creating change. This time however the site for development was located in the imagination and its realisation in the future adult minds of the young participants.

Cascade, 2002–07

I taught on the BA in Public Art at Chelsea College of Art in the late nineties when small commissions were often offered to students by external organisations via the college. Although beneficial in providing production experience in the real world, this work also put students in competition with each other in ways that could sometimes be counter-productive and of limited educational value. It occurred to me that I was already running projects with young people in the public domain that could offer professional development together with workshop experience, and the art students would be well placed to offer back valuable role modelling for the young project participants. Hearing that *Widening Participation* funding was becoming available through the Higher Educational Council for England to address discrepancies

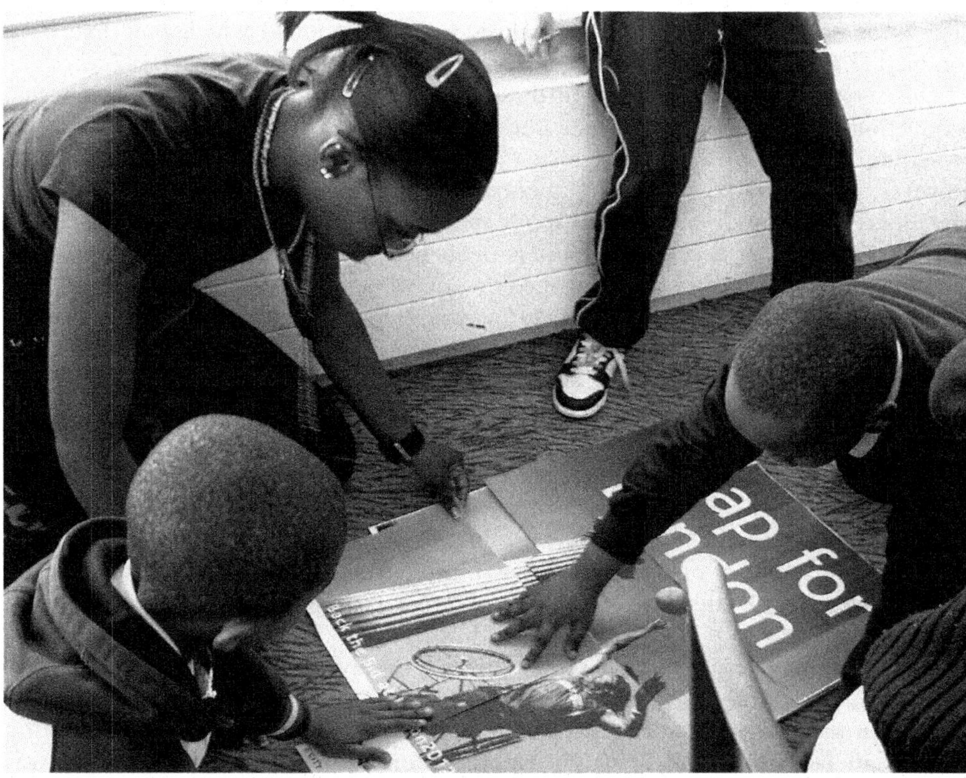

Figure 4.4 Cascade: College student working with primary school children
Photo © Loraine Leeson, 2003.

in the take-up of higher education, I approached the London Institute, the parent body for Chelsea College, to partner a project that would take the approach I had identified. As a result, undergraduates were involved in projects over a two-year period, and The Art of Change hosted a placement for a postgraduate student, through which she realised an MA in Design for the Environment.

When I moved my practice to the University of East London I took this process with me and formalised it into a mentoring scheme that would link students across three institutional levels—higher, further and statutory education. The work that cSPACE had already begun around issues of regeneration provided themes for the projects while the mentoring was able to take place through a process of shared production. *Cascade* enabled skills and experience to be passed from the arts organisation and university into the wider community—then back the other way, with each layer of participants learning from and supporting the other. While I directed the project, Anne-Marie Pereiro de Mello, the Chelsea graduate who had originally undertaken The Art of Change placement, co-ordinated a small team of freelance artists who collaborated closely with staff from participating institutions to deliver the projects. Every year or so we took a different regeneration-related theme, starting with the opportunity afforded by *The Catch*. Later topics included the bid for the London Olympics, the potential impact of this event on the environment, and then the *Young Person's Guides* described below. Each project culminated in an exhibition, production or event whereby participants used their expertise to present their ideas and interact with public figures from the field in which they had been conducting the creative work.

This series of projects was the furthest step I had taken away from direct visual production at a time when this was not widely accepted in this art world. In terms of setting a framework within which the creativity of others could be expressed, however, it was related closely in intention and outcomes to previous works. In this case, apart from some photographic input and documentation, my creativity was used solely in processes of development and management, leading me to question whether this was a new form of socially engaged art, or whether I had turned into a project manager. As with other recent projects, *Cascade* raised questions as to where the art, and indeed the aesthetics, ultimately lay.

The Young Person's Guide to the Royal Docks, 2005–07

Cascade provided a process that could be utilised for the collective involvement of large numbers of young people in creative work, while establishing additional learning opportunities for all concerned. Since production in the early projects was limited to exhibitions or books of participants' work, I began to feel that something was missing in the wider social effects of the *Cascade* projects beyond the direct benefits to participants.

An opportunity to address this arose through an approach made by the Museum of London Docklands to the London East Research Institute at University of East London in the early years of the millennium. The most easterly part of the London Docks had been overlooked by the eighties' development, and the museum was concerned about the lack of materials available that related to the cultural heritage of that area. The London East Research Institute, of which I was part, embarked on a series of visitors' trails. However I felt that using processes that cSPACE already had in place for collective work with young people, we could extend this concept through the production of a guide to the area by teenagers in the locality[10]. This would help to develop the sense of ownership that the young people felt towards their neighbourhoods while also situating them as local experts in the making of a professional product for public use. Further to this, mentoring by university and college students through *Cascade* would model for them how their skills and interests in this field might be developed through further and higher education. And so the concept for *The Young Person's Guide to the Royal Docks* came into being.

A great deal of fundraising resulted in a grant from the Heritage Lottery Fund matched by an assortment of finance from trusts, foundations, sponsorship, educational and public sources. This allowed for the contracting of freelance artists, photographers and designers[11], and for the project to run for the next two years with a local secondary school, excluded pupils, students from two colleges of further education, and university undergraduates. The young people learned basic photographic skills and, accompanied by students and a photographer, made site visits to document their chosen locations, researched factual information and wrote reviews, while college students made sound collages for each site.

The Docklands Light Railway supported the project by financing the production of extracts from the guide as visual panels[12] for their trains, and three hundred car cards depicting ten different locations were displayed to coincide with the project's launch. The web site containing all the materials produced was launched at the

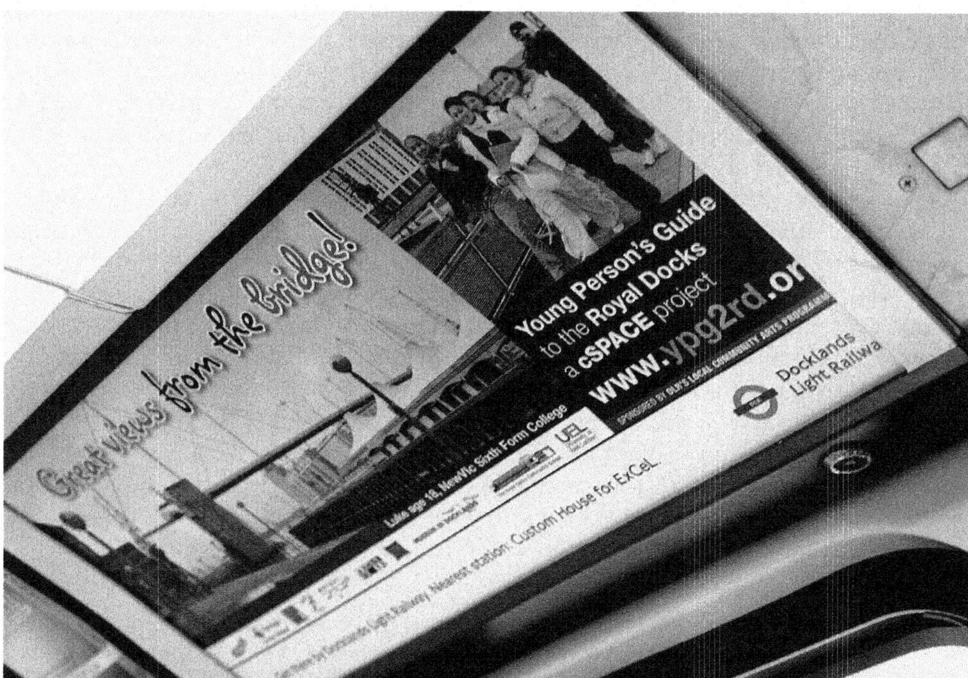

Figures 4.5 The Young Person's Guide to the Royal Docks: DLR car card
Photo © Loraine Leeson, 2007.

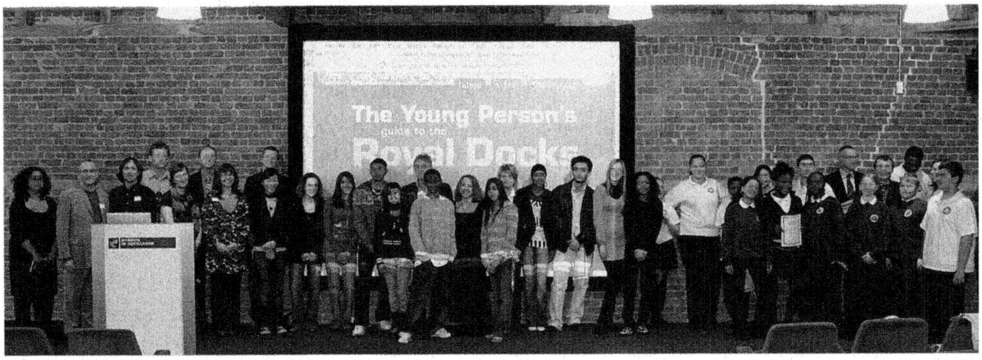

Figure 4.6 The Young Person's Guide to the Royal Docks: Launch event at the Museum in Docklands

Museum of London Docklands in March 2007, where participants presented the guide and its making to an audience of more than a hundred people. The director of the Royal Docks Partnership for business organisations in the area addressed the gathering and identified plans for the proposed regeneration of that locality. Although a rather "corporate" presentation, it was of particular interest to these young people, who knew the area very well but had not been aware of some of the proposed developments. At a "question time" event with roving microphones, participants began to realise that the answers they were receiving about the area's future were less than adequate, and with growing confidence their hands began to go up and prepared questions were discarded. Young people who normally found it hard to speak in public led a lively debate, raising issues of climate change, homelessness, accessibility and inclusion—they had indeed found their voice.

An evaluation of this project conducted by artist John Cockram helped to inform our next initiative. Participants suggested that the guide should now have wider application to offer opportunity for more involvement of young people in that age group, and also because they saw its potential to convey a different idea of East London to counter the media depiction of "hooligans and things like that". With the approaching Olympics in mind, and knowing that this global event might otherwise offer little real engagement for local youth, I began to develop the concept of a *Young Person's Guide to East London*, this time working with young people through schools and youth groups across the whole East London region. This would require significantly more funding for a searchable web site, a more streamlined production process that would draw on the experience of *VOLCO*, further design and programming input, and some careful orchestration.

The Young Person's Guide to East London, 2008–12

This project continued the evolution of a process developed through *VOLCO* and *The Young Person's Guide to the Royal Docks*. Web technology was again the means for generating a shared entity through the collective input of many participants—this time a teenagers' view of East London created entirely out of their own material.

As in *Cascade*, the project focused on a theme of local regeneration, this time in relation to the London 2012 Olympics, as a "hook" to encourage local youth to think about the potential impact of this development on their futures. The project brought into visibility the views of a marginalised age group within a hitherto neglected area that would soon become a focus of global attention, and ensured that they too would receive some benefit. The teenagers' first hand knowledge of the area was able to generate an unfamiliar sideways look at East End life and insight that would be hard to achieve by more conventional methods. Although there had been other projects in which young people documented their neighbourhoods, what made this work well for those who took part was its professional and usable public output that valued not only their new skills in photography, but also their previous knowledge and experience.

Over four hundred teenagers from the Olympic host boroughs participated in the making of the guide through youth, sports and disability groups, schools, college, after school clubs, referral units and a youth offending team. Initially I employed freelance photographers to lead the workshops, but funding restraints caused me to eventually lead the remaining workshops myself, supported by student volunteers. Although this at first seemed a compromise, I discovered that returning to a more hands-on approach was beneficial in the specific support I was able to offer the young people in looking differently at their world and I could also better adapt the workshop processes to different circumstances.

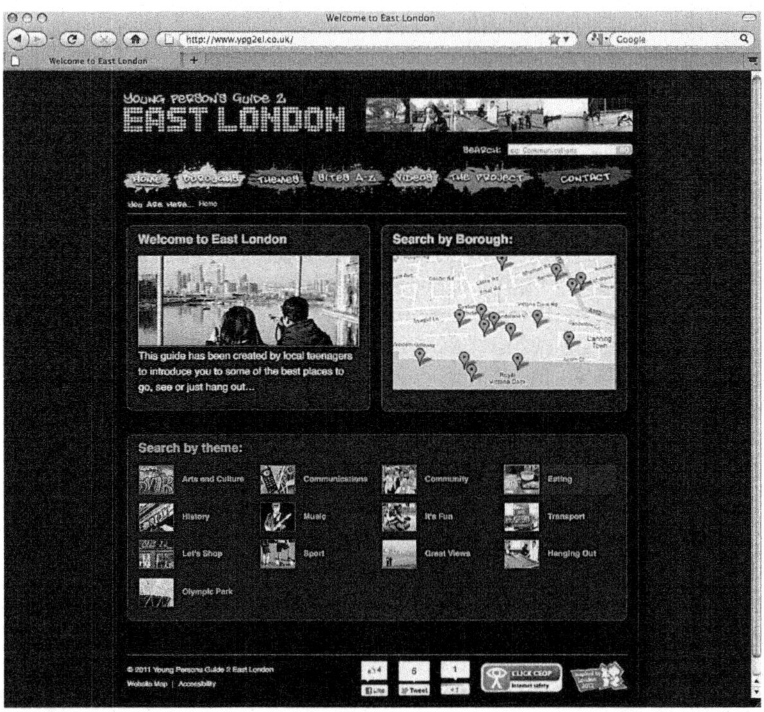

Figure 4.7 Home Page for *The Young Person's Guide to East London*

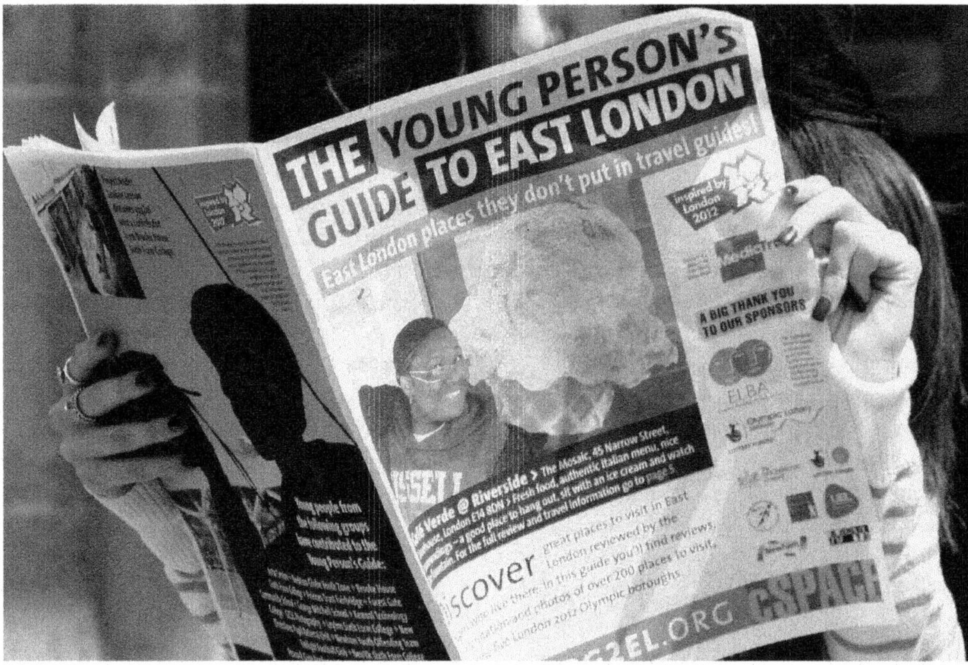

Figure 4.8 The Young Person's Guide to East London free newspaper
Photo © Loraine Leeson, 2009.

The project process involved participants identifying locations known to them that they thought would be of interest to others in their age group, then photographing, researching and writing commentary about these. I generally ran sessions over two days, starting with a small group workshop that took the young people through a process of using a camera to "see" with. Then we would go out with them to photograph their chosen sites, accompanied by student assistants, and sometimes centre staff. The project was adapted to include participants with different abilities. Those with particular difficulties or behavioural issues were supported by specialist staff from their centre, and we would, if necessary, "scribe" for them or hold the camera for those unable to do so. On the second day participants selected and edited their photos to create a set to represent each location. They also researched and wrote up factual information as well as their recommendations, which they organised into a web-ready format. Five thousand free newspapers containing all the participants' work were distributed by the young people during the summer of the Games. The web site received 38,495 hits over the life of the project, and is still in regular use.

Like *VOLCO*, *The Young Person's Guide to East London* involved hundreds of contributors and a great quantity of material, the organisation of which was facilitated by the use of Internet technologies, careful project structuring and above all the continued collaboration with Henry Iles. It was the expertise of this designer that made possible the development of an accessible and engaging web site with a young-person friendly interface and production values that enabled their work to be presented in its best light.

Many of the constituent elements of this project were comparable to those in previous work in the way that they embraced multi-layered collaboration and a number of external interests, needs and opportunities, although the aesthetics depended progressively less on visuals produced by myself. The project also brought with it additional challenges of fundraising. It took four years and was finally achieved with finance from trusts, foundations, local government, a sixth form college and a grant from the National Lottery, the only fund designated to support creative work by local people around the Olympic site. Although there was a heavily publicised Cultural Olympiad, most of its dedicated resources were for its own commissioned projects and artworks. Despite its youth focus the London Games failed to take into account the wealth of long-established arts activity in East London, particularly with the young people of the area. The rapidly shrinking economy also meant that funding as a whole was increasingly scarce and I was forced to make twenty-eight different grant applications, many for very small funds, to achieve the ten that finally supported the project. Although the rate of return was still high, the effort involved in financing projects was now beginning to overtake that involved in their delivery, heralding a shift in how I would continue to resource my work, as well as a turning point in the funding culture of the UK.

Lambeth Floating Marsh 2013–15

In September 2015 large-scale images of river organisms projected along the Thames embankment in London were used to draw attention to the importance of biodiversity in urban rivers. This was one of the outcomes of a collaboration with biophysical chemist Nithin Rai that included new reed bed habitats for microorganisms and invertebrates, realised through a fund that recycles landfill tax for environmental purposes. The project addressed the need for invertebrate and microorganism habitats along the shored-up the banks of urban rivers, since despite the return of fish to the River Thames, their survival is not sustainable without the remainder of the food chain. The central London reach of the tidal Thames is particularly challenging for smaller life forms due to its hard, vertical walls, turbulent tides, wash from river traffic, and changing composition of fresh and salt water. The project explored how a "floating marsh" secured to a barge might encourage growth of these organisms and the larger creatures that feed off them. Long basket structures along the hull of the *Tamesis Dock*, a floating pub close to the Houses of Parliament, were planted with various species of reeds, which rose and sank with the changing tide while drawing nutrients from the river. The plan was to create habitats where there had previously been none and enable the barge to host new resident river life around its perimeter. To bring the issues of biodiversity to the attention of the public, we took water samples to identify those organisms that are to be found in that reach of the Thames using microscopy at University of Westminster. Moving sequences of these were then projected onto the embankment pavement to be encountered by passers by. Visitors were also able to access the project web site[13] via their phones to further investigate the issues.

Unlike many of my projects, *Lambeth Floating Marsh* did not have a participatory element beyond the interaction of visitors and passers by, although the collaboration itself included three scientists and a visual effects specialist. I have a concern about

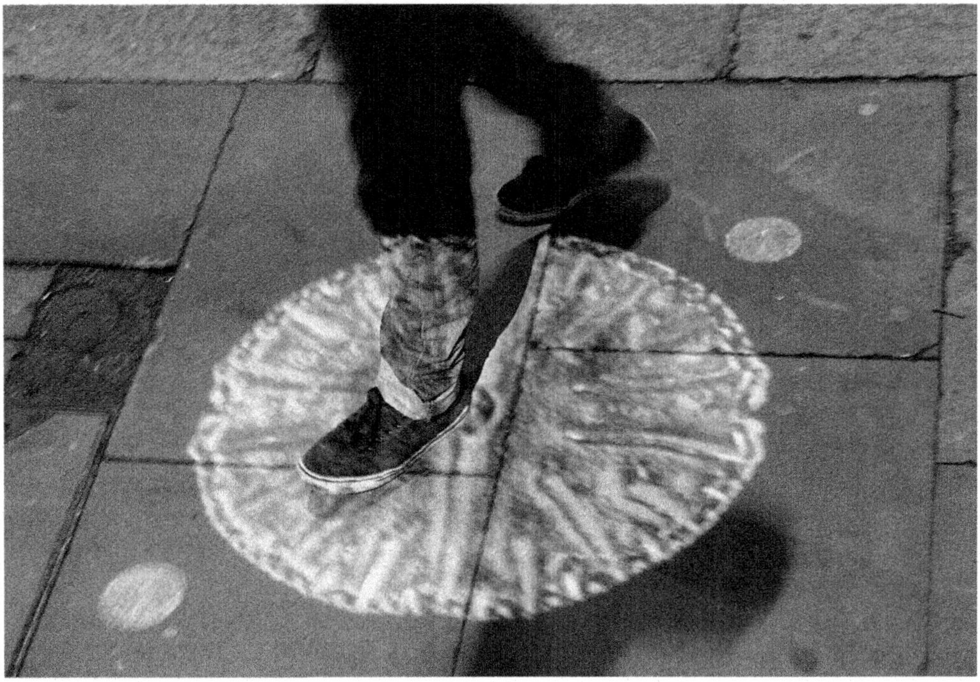

Figure 4.9 Lambeth Floating Marsh: pavement projections
Photo © Loraine Leeson, 2015.

the notion of the "general public" as the main constituency for a project. If the work is going to have any ongoing effect, it has to be to some extent targeted, and it would have been preferable if its outreach legacy had been further integrated into the overall concept. Our original proposal included the involvement of a local secondary school where young people would have monitored the river organisms in their science lessons and provided much needed data for research. They were also to produce images of the organisms in their art lessons to create an exhibition that we would have used to publicise the issues. However the funders did not consider this sufficiently "public" and preferred the idea of projections. They failed to realise, as had the commissioners of *The Catch*, that the involvement of the young people would have drawn in a much wider community and had greater possibility of long-term impact. Nevertheless we were too committed to the project to withdraw at that stage. Instead we aimed to achieve some influence through the project launch, which included involvement of an environmental agency with a remit to improve rivers and canals for people and wildlife, and has led to further collaboration. Although *Lambeth Floating Marsh* itself had the potential to expand and some possibilities for further development arose, they did not progress in this instance, and so the scope for any real change became limited. Many of the projects have started in this way, with an opportunity taken up, and then grow from there, but this is an unpredictable process. The marsh nevertheless continues, maintained by the scientist who instigated it, who plans to use it as a model for turning floating mooring pontoons into similar habitat.

Active Energy 2008, ongoing

In contrast *Active Energy* is still going strong after eight years. It began with a six-week commission by SPACE[14] to respond as one of three artist groups to research on the democratisation of technology[15] underway by researchers at Queen Mary University of London, with an exhibition to be held at the end of that period. The research team had been examining how the experience of older people was not only being excluded from the development of new technologies, but often left this age group victim to the technological design and control of others.

I started by meeting a group self-named The Geezers who ran a club at an Age UK centre in Bow, East London, to mitigate the effects of isolation and loneliness on older men. In reply to my question "What technology would you invent that could improve life for yourself or your community?" one member commented on how tidal power had not progressed since its early development, while wind power had predominated in UK alternative energy provision. Another recalled how in previous centuries a water wheel had been attached to London Bridge. By the end of the first session the whole group were keen to focus on nothing less than harnessing the tidal power of the River Thames. While I had no experience or particular knowledge of these issues, I pledged that I would help take them as far along this route as it was possible to go.

The group was made up of retired working class men including an engineer who had worked with steam turbines, others with mechanical interest and experience, and

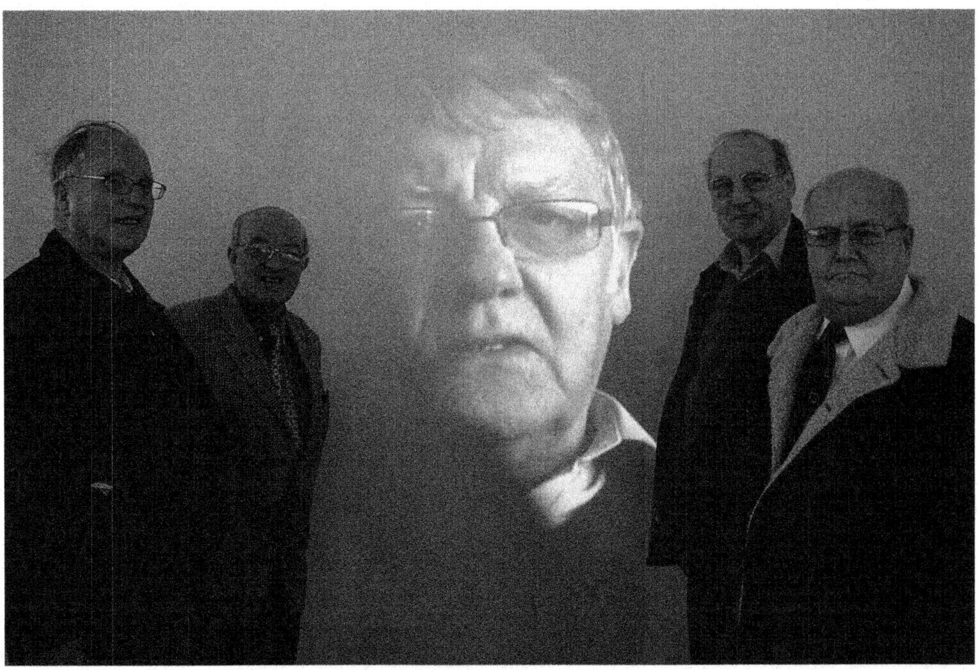

Figure 4.10 Active Energy: Projection at SPACE gallery

Photo © Loraine Leeson, 2008.

also ex-lorry drivers who were able to take the group on trips in a community minibus. We started by visiting a local tidal mill and, after taking advice, sought out wind turbines with designs that could be adapted for underwater use. Understanding that a barrage was required, we also explored the Thames Barrier as a possible site where such devices could be effectively located.

The Geezers were enormously engaged in the potential of their idea, which tapped into their existing skills and interests. Unprompted, they drafted new turbine designs and debated how these would work. *The Not Quite Yet* exhibition at SPACE provided an opportunity to draw this material together through a large-scale visualisation and video projections featuring members of the group making their case for the local resourcing of renewable energy. These interviews were particularly engaging due to the way that The Geezers were able to lay out the issues in very straightforward terms, which enabled them to relate to and inform segments of the community that professionals would struggle to reach. Although few had experience of public speaking, the group presented their idea to great acclaim at the research project's final symposium *On the Margins of Technology*, attracting particular interest from local media. Interestingly, this attention was much to do with the very nature of group members' senior status, which caught people's imaginations, turning on its head their initially marginalised position.

The creative energy generated by the project gained its own momentum, and at the end of the commission we all felt that it was not possible to halt the work there. I found a small amount of funding for equipment and training, which got The Geezers computerised so that they could pursue their research. Then SPACE, seeing that the project was still going strong, set out to do more fundraising and re-joined us for a further stage of the project. This allowed the group to continue developing

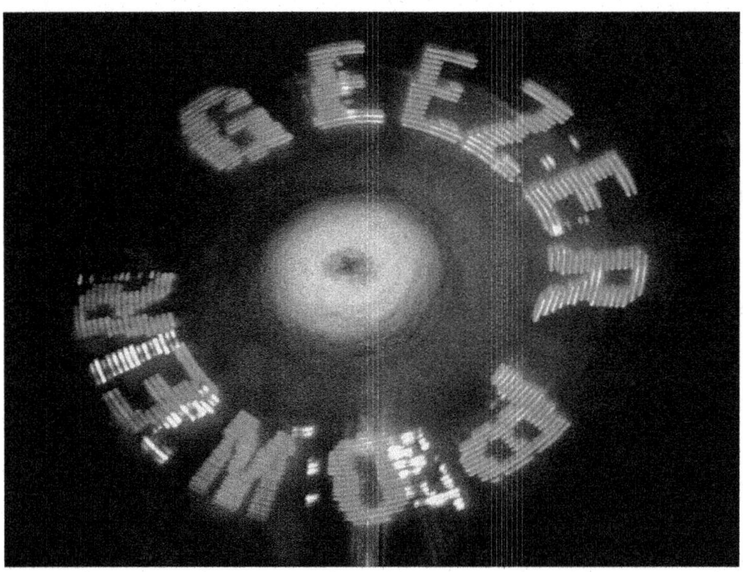

Figure 4.11 Active Energy: wind turbine on Age UK centre, Bow
Photo © Loraine Leeson, 2010.

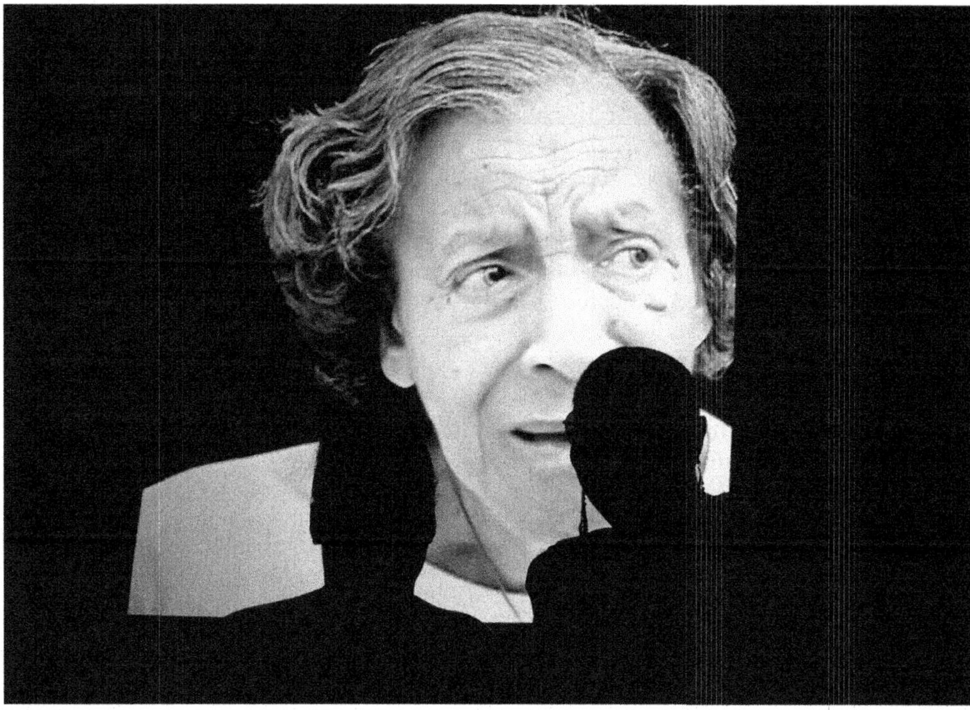

Figure 4.12 Active Energy: Pittsburgh
Photo © Loraine Leeson, 2012.

their ideas for tidal turbines and also to undertake an intergenerational project at a local boys' secondary school. Two engineers, Toby Borland and Stephen Dodds[16] from the University of East London, had been drawn into the project's growing vortex and were now assisting without charge. They provided essential input to the school project, particularly Toby Borland who ran a prototyping laboratory at the university. Collaborating closely with Fiona Fieber, Head of Learning and Participation at SPACE, who managed this stage of the project, I facilitated Toby Borland to lead the school workshops, assisted by Stephen Dodds, while previously isolated older men from The Geezers Club now found themselves mentoring underachieving boys. At the school's request the work focused on wind power, and so the young people learned about aerodynamics and tested their designs in a makeshift wind tunnel. The best design was then used for a wind-driven lightwork for the roof of the Geezers' AgeUK centre, which rotated to spell out "geezerpower".

In the meantime Professor Ann Light, who had been involved in the initial *Democratising Technology* research, returned with an opportunity for the Geezers to contribute to the *Participants United* research initiative at University of Central Lancashire, which was exploring effective community engagement. Following this the combined team has now presented the project on several occasions as an interdisciplinary panel with artist, engineer, social scientist and participating Geezers. In 2012, an art commission[17] I was offered in the US opened up an opportunity for me to connect the group with seniors in Pittsburgh. Their online exchange was an exciting experience for us all, and the first time that any of the participants on either side of the Atlantic had used Skype. Through this dialogue the US group developed their own research project, choosing to explore the dissemination of information on dementia, which we pursued with the support of University of Pittsburgh's Alzheimer's Disease Research Centre. Researchers there welcomed the contributions of participants' personal experience to their ongoing investigations, and introduced the group to further expertise[18]. Members of Northside Seniors recorded their concerns and experience through video interviews similar to those I had conducted with the Geezers. These were combined with researched information and material from the UK project to create a six-projector installation for the *Feminist and ...* exhibition at the Mattress Factory museum, highlighting the significance of the contributions that these groups could make. Alongside the exhibit were displayed materials by local producers of renewable energy and a video booth for visitors to record experiences of dementia to contribute to the work of the research centre. It is no coincidence that, given the opportunity, these two groups of working class elders set out to tackle some of the key issues of their respective nations. The strength of the desire of each to leave a legacy for the next generation ably contradicts those who write off the value of older people's potential contribution to society.

The UK project continued with the ongoing involvement of engineer Toby Borland and in 2013 the Geezers finally tested in the Thames a tidal turbine constructed from low-cost and recycled materials. All the design work has been open source and made available through the project web site[19] for others to access.

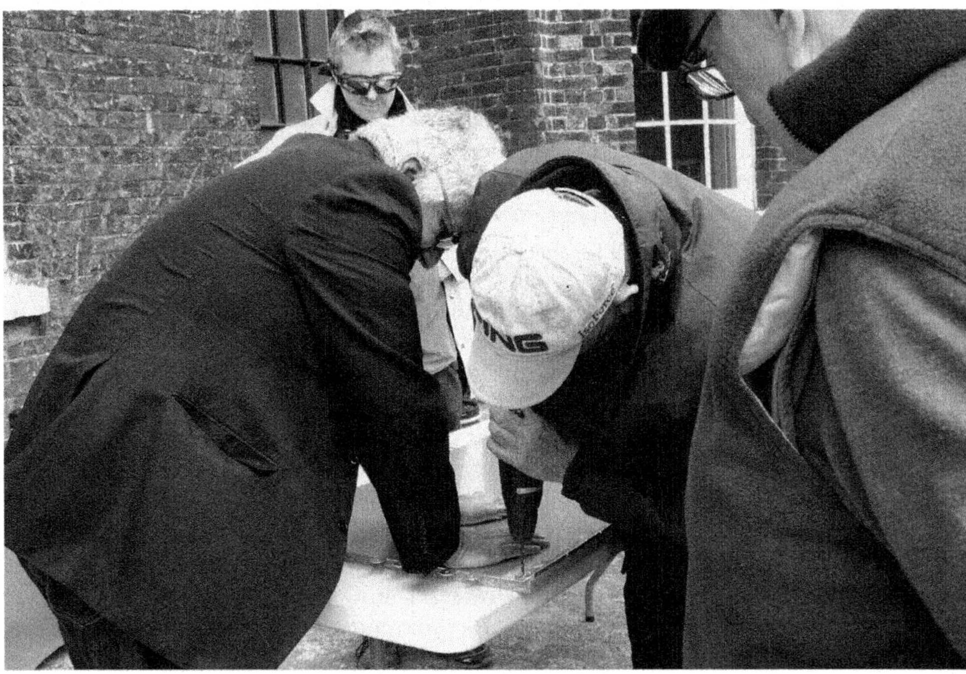

Figure 4.13 Active Energy: constructing stream wheel at Three Mills
Photo © Loraine Leeson, 2016.

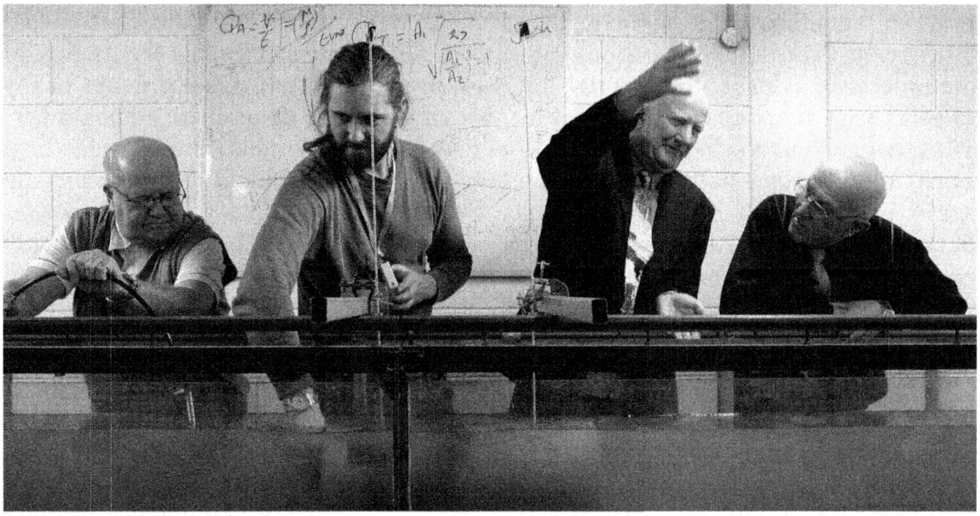

Figure 4.14 Active Energy: testing tidal turbine efficiency

Photo © Loraine Leeson, 2010.

The next stage in *Active Energy*'s ongoing trajectory is being managed between cSPACE and the *Hydrocitizenship*[20] research project at Middlesex University. Under certain weather conditions, when London's sewers become flooded they overflow into the Lower Lea, a tributary of the Thames, and the pollution makes it impossible for fish to breathe. We are therefore creating a working prototype of a stream wheel that will drive an aerator to oxygenate the water. Although some of this work has developed tangentially to the original aim of encouraging tidal energy for the capital, the opportunities that have arisen along the way have enabled the project to expand its scope and address related issues. Further work is planned for the tidal turbine, which has already been identified as particularly suitable for use in slow-moving tidal rivers in developing countries. We are hoping to do more renewable energy workshops for schools and develop these into a teaching pack for wider use, and we will also be engaging further with the providers of sheltered housing in the Geezers' locality with the aim of ensuring that renewable sources of energy are incorporated into their new build schemes. Meanwhile the stream wheel is being designed for replication in a low cost "flat pack" form.

It has been intriguing to all concerned to observe how this project has continued to develop with such energy when the positions and intentions of each participating party have been so diverse. At one point members of the team took the opportunity to comment on what it meant to each of us. From this it emerged that the Geezers' purpose has been to improve the lives of the older population, particularly in their impoverished area of East London. The social scientist was primarily interested in "citizen-led innovation" and the project's "co-design" process. The engineer has been particularly focused on the challenge of constructing, with the active input of communities, working prototypes of "socially accessible micropower generators" that have readily accessible parts and "open hardware". All parties were nevertheless agreed that the project would not exist without being facilitated through an arts process.

From my standpoint this is due to the fact that, unlike other disciplines, art has no other remit than the construction of meaning, a purpose that guides the totality of the process to achieve its potential. As with any kind of art, the experience of my role has been to bring together the elements that presented themselves, adding others as necessary, and to "hold" the work with this unwieldy alliance until something began to take shape, not knowing what would emerge. That could be said of making a painting, and is nothing more than the creative process applied to a different set of factors. Since my artistic role in this, as in successive projects, has been increasingly one of overview and facilitation, it is a reminder of how on a previous occasion, when asked whether I was not the "god" of *VOLCO* I replied how, far from that, I was simply the turtle on whose back that virtual world was situated.

Notes

1. All members of the cSPACE board had been involved in some way with previous work. Over the years they have included: Jean Lowe, previously Joint Docklands Action Group; Graham Downes (who remains as Chair) and Debra Reay from Cultural Partnerships; Belinda Kidd, the first administrator for DCPP, who is our current treasurer; Clare Connor from Stratford Circus, the original commissioner of *VOLCO*; Prof. Phil Cohen of UEL, collaborator on several Art of Change projects; current director Penny Machin, who for many years ran the Art Practice and the Community modules at Middlesex University before I took on that task; and accountant Margaret Trotter, who both advised and worked at The Art of Change, is now a board member of cSPACE, and has enabled both organisations to survive financially during hard times.
2. Extract from the Dutch lullaby Wynken, Blynken, and Nod by Eugene Field (1850–1895).
3. In 2016 the original fish were replaced with a new design made from hinged stainless steel.
4. London 2012 landmarks, which included Tower Bridge and Big Ben, were each commemorated by a pin badge issued during the Games. www.londoncouncils.gov.uk/node/24501
5. Sherry Turkle, *Life on the Screen*, New York: Phoenix, 1995, p.268.
6. Robinson, op. cit. p.6.
7. Newham Education Business Partnership funded primary school teachers to identify suitable subjects and produce a *VOLCO* lesson plan.
8. http://secondlife.com
9. To avoid quantitative evaluation of outcomes, I mainly sought funding for workshop delivery rather than for the project as a whole.
10. The suggestion of a "Young Person's Guide" was made by Warren Lakin, a friend and associate who worked at that time for the London East Research Institute.
11. These included John Cockram, Henry Iles, John Nassari and Anne-Marie Pereira de Mello.
12. The "car cards" for the Docklands Light Railway were designed by Henry Iles from the materials generated through the project.
13. http://lambethfloatingmarsh.org.uk
14. Not to be confused with cSPACE, SPACE is visual arts organisation based in Hackney, East London that provides creative workspace, residencies, bursaries and training opportunities for artists. It has an established reputation for community engagement and its gallery hosted my retrospective *Art for Change* when it toured to London in 2006.
15. *Democratising Technology* (DemTech—www.demtech.qmul.ac.uk) was a UK research project that involved a number of community groups to ask whether together a generative, open-ended form of engagement with digital technology could be produced and brought to bear on the design of our society and its tools. It worked with participants' values and aspirations for the future, using arts development methods as a transformational tool.
16. Toby Borland, who ran the prototyping laboratory at University of East London, had a remit to offer services to the local community, and has been key to all further developments

of the project. Professor Stephen Dodds, renowned for his development of the control systems for the European Space Commission, gave the project much time and valuable expertise.

17. Curated by Hilary Robinson, the residency and exhibition *Feminist and . . .* (2012) was designed to demonstrate how the concerns of feminism have wider influence than in work more traditionally seen as "feminist art".
18. Professor Kenneth Langa from University of Michigan, a world-leading scholar in this field, had recently delivered the keynote at the Alzheimer's Disease Research Summit in Bethesda, May 2012 and provided materials for our installation and information to inform the group's research.
19. www.active-energy-london.org
20. www.hydrocitizenship.com

References

Ken Robinson, *All Our Futures—Creativity and Culture in Education* (Suffolk: Department for Education and Science, 1999).

Sherry Turkle, *Life on the Screen* (New York: Phoenix, 1995).

5 In Hindsight

Taking a long view of the practice has demonstrated the extent to which shifts in the wider social, economic and political environment have affected the work, particularly in terms of the general turn away from collective action at the end of the eighties towards a more personal politics for the next couple of decades. At a time when activism was no longer prevalent, I began working with young people to help spark in them a sense that they could indeed be the future engineers of a new world. This happened literally in *VOLCO* and implicitly in other projects through a process that encouraged individual expression within a collective whole that was ultimately aimed at a wider public. More recently the growing urgency of climate change has led to collaboration over ecological issues, with scientists in *Lambeth Floating Marsh* and with engineers in *Active Energy*. The latter also typified those long-term projects that have managed to develop over an evolving trajectory through the patching together of funding and opportunity while retaining overall purpose.

A process of "joining up" seems to typify much of the practice, which has come from the need to address social issues with expertise and input from people, groups or institutions with divergent disciplines and experience. These collaborations have had to be managed in a way that allows each party to contribute their particular skill or knowledge, while gaining what they themselves needed from the engagement. This "joining" process has not just been about accumulating competencies however. All the projects described, including commissions, have woven together elements of need, opportunity, research, skills, context and funding. Creative development of this nature, whatever the discipline, has a way of taking on its own momentum, with each opportunity opening new doors, and serendipity frequently taking the lead. A process of "holding" is then required. The development of a project can be thought of as adding ingredients to a pot. When sufficient elements have been included and before they overflow, a lid must be put on, effectively at that point determining the recipe. The pot then heaves and strains as these different factors come together and begin to form together the substance of the project. I have felt my role to be one of keeping the lid in place while this process is underway, preventing the vessel from exploding and fragmenting while the transformative procedure takes place. The project, although made up of those ingredients that went into it, gradually takes on its own form and emerges as a new entity. This process is nevertheless generally more the concern of the artist than others involved, and one of the *Active Energy* project partners, while excited by the burgeoning possibilities, did express some anxiety about where it would all lead, and what in the end would constitute the project. I realised that I was, in contrast, on familiar ground and had just been waiting for the appropriate moment to remove the lid. While this procedure is simply the creative process, as experienced in other forms of art as well as in different disciplines, in the case of socially situated work the "ingredients" involve people, their skills and knowledge in addition to other ideas and materials. The medium through which the different elements come together is that of dialogue, while the alchemical process that takes place is one of negotiation and interaction. The process is not necessarily concluded once this has taken place however, since the combined energy of those taking part can also provide the momentum for a project to continue along its evolutionary trajectory and has led to the longevity of much of the work described here.

In an interview for *What We Made*, artist Mierle Laderman Ukeles observed how the outcomes of a piece of work increase according to the ability to recognise the contribution of each person alongside the whole[1]. Similarly, while collective expression might be a regular outcome within my own practice, its initial articulation is often one of individual experience. Staying true to the input of each participant has been of primary importance, since it is through the accumulated fragments of these experiences that a deeper reality can eventually be glimpsed. The process could be seen as analogous to a psychotherapist's understanding that any starting point taken by a patient will lead to their underlying issues. In this sense, however arbitrary a choice of place, object or reference might seem, it will function well so long as it remains the participant's own. In projects such as *The Young Person's Guide to East London* or *VOLCO*, the effect of this becomes evident where the outcome is a collective amalgamation of this material. A similar virtual planet constructed by teachers, or a guide created by adults imagining what teenagers would like would result in a very different outcome when viewed as a totality. The participant's sense of ownership of the project is also deeply embedded in this process.

One of the methods for gathering these experiences I have described as construction of organisational and material "frameworks", which will be further explored in Part 2. The large-scale images of the nineties and the web sites of more recent work served as structures for bringing together these nuggets of human experience. *VOLCO*, for example, drew on very simple technologies of representation, using a template to allow children to construct a character online by compiling a set of objects, images and text rather than reverting to avatars or simulation. The history and nature of this virtual planet could similarly be "read" through a seemingly arbitrary collection of information systematically stored in its archives, but which the children had no difficulty understanding. Asked what Planet *VOLCO* was like, participants would generally describe a coherent environment and society. This is not very different to how people perceive the world. An array of fragmented information comes together to form a mental picture of life on earth and, while there may be some disagreement between social groups, most share a broad concept of the planet in a way that overrides the disparity of individual experience. The medium that amalgamates these fragments is one of imagination, indicating why the arts can prove so fruitful a means for mediating understanding across difference.

Fundamental to the work throughout has also been ensuring that the "drivers" of the content and/or social purpose come from those with direct experience of the issues. This was explicitly the case in the early work on health as well as the Docklands Community Poster Project and has re-emerged in *Active Energy*, although this time combined with a participatory approach[2]. It is nevertheless implicit in other projects where participants have not started out with a clear message or intention. The young people's experience of their own neighbourhoods as expressed in *West Meets East, Celebrating the Difference* or the *Young Person's Guides* was as important to those projects as had been the input of local or professional knowledge elsewhere; it simply required a different project structure to facilitate it.

Another feature of the practice has been the way that it has constantly functioned "on the edge"—of institutions, finance, disciplines and personal capability. While there are many times that I would have benefitted from greater financial stability and institutional support, it has also been important that the developmental processes have been able to remain fluid. Since the projects were largely developed independent of institutional concerns, they were able to evolve and change until the time came to apply the "lid" and determine the shape of the project. Achieving this has nevertheless also required staying "on the run". Like many artists, particularly women, I have had to juggle domestic and work commitments, run a household single-handed, manage an organisation and in better times hold down two jobs, while also making the art. It may not have been easy, but this process of its realisation could be seen to have also informed the work in unintentional ways.

Notes

1. Mierle Laderman Ukeles, "Spirituality and Cooperation" in *What We Made: Conversations on Art and Social Co-operation*, Durham and London: Duke University Press, 2013, p.294.
2. I was inspired to return to this way of working through witnessing the energetic and active involvement of members of the Rialto Youth Project, who arrived from Dublin with artist Ailbhe Murphy for the symposium that accompanied my retrospective exhibition in London in 2006. Through ongoing experience of culture embedded in daily life, Rialto has employed its own resident artist Fiona Whelan and the organisation has become a model of the productive role of art in regeneration, instigated from the bottom up within in a working class community.

References

Mierle Laderman Ukeles, "Spirituality and Cooperation" in *What We Made: Conversations on Art and Social Co-operation* (Durham and London: Duke University Press, 2013).

Part 2
Reflections

Having laid out the practice in some detail in Part 1, Part 2 considers the methodologies that have been involved in this work. These include the ways that projects and their outputs have been initiated, conducted and evaluated, as well as difficulties addressed. I will look at issues that arise from the act of social engagement, indicate the value of collaborating across difference, and suggest why it can be so important to work across disciplines. Different strategies for engagement will be discussed, together with the role of organisational support and ways in which funding or commissioning approaches can impact, for good or ill, on both the work and the wider community. Much has already been said about the role of aesthetics in socially engaged art. While acknowledging existing debates I will make an argument for the importance of "resonance" in work of this nature, and where this can interface with practical function. In conclusion I reflect on what is required to encourage art practice that sets out to make a difference, and how this might be imagined in our rapidly changing world.

6 Process and Product

In this chapter I aim to reveal some of the wider ramifications of those practical procedures, concerns and issues that have underpinned the practice, and which are often not discussed except among those directly involved in the work. First, process—from the way that projects come into being and are developed through negotiation between different parties, how collective input is managed, together with those structures and devices that have helped to facilitate engagement. After that, the role of "product" in both its material and virtual sense, indicating some of the challenges of collaborative working in the public domain. Consideration of aesthetic function is, however, left till Chapter 8 in order to situate this within wider debate on this issue. For the moment I will focus more on the means through which an artwork is conceived and constructed, either intentionally or developmentally, the significance of its initiation upon the way it interacts with the world, who it serves and belongs to, and, finally, ways it can be disseminated and gain an "afterlife". I will touch on methods of both formal and informal evaluation, and include reflections on those instances when not everything goes to plan. Finally, I will look at the complexity of concrete as well as less tangible outcomes to which both process and product can give rise.

An Invitation

In David Harding's insightful description of the community arts movement in the small Scottish town of Craigmillar in the seventies, he reminds us of Theatre of the Oppressed founder Augusto Boal's injunction to artists to "never go into a community until it has articulated its need for you[1]."

The projects described in Chapter 1 were initiated, developed and also evolved in many different ways. Addressing need has nevertheless been key to the instigation of each. It enables the artistic activity to become part of a movement towards change rather than standing outside of it, or worse, attempting to generate change solely through the intervention of art. This is the difference between *The Present Day Creates History,* instigated solely by Peter and myself around issues of personal interest, albeit of social relevance, and the work we produced in support of the campaign to save Bethnal Green Hospital together with all subsequent projects. The role and intention in the later projects was by comparison much clearer, both to ourselves and others.

Need might sometimes be expressed through a direct "invitation", as in the initial request from the East London Trades Councils in 1981 to produce the poster about imminent changes in the London Docklands. However, it may also be filtered through a number of different agencies including practitioners themselves. Artist Ailbhe Murphy (2004, p.188) has described the way an invitation may be directed from a community or curator to the artist, or to both the artist and community, or vice versa. She points out that, whichever way this happens, the quality of this invitation makes an enormous influence on the integrity of the work as well as on those involved in the process.

Expression of need and the resulting artistic responses can be complex, and also a developmental process. *The Infinity Story,* for example, was developed in recognition of a series of opportunities and dissatisfactions. The former included new developments in Internet technologies and the instigation of the National Grid for Learning, which introduced networking and computer hardware into schools. Some unmet needs at that time came to my attention through observation from my position as a parent and a school governor. Limited creative use of these technologies in schools was already apparent, as was my own children's growing disenfranchisement with a curriculum through which they seemed to find diminishing opportunities for self-expression. The introduction of SATs[2] testing and commencement of rigorous OFSTED[3] inspections in schools reflected an increasingly target-driven economy, which left little or no space for the arts. This eventually led to recognition at policy level that creativity was disappearing from the curriculum, and the beginning of "in principle" support for initiatives involving cross-curricula and project-based learning. A further signal for the project came with the recognition of the poor standard of learning materials available to schools at that time, and the coincidental observation of a colleague's[4] inventive use of interactivity on the web. All this was then underpinned by my own interest in experimenting with the Internet as a site for collective creativity.

The *VOLCO* project later built on these factors, adding to them the growing sophistication of web technology that was becoming available at the end of the nineties. As part of a national goal to encourage the embedding of computer technologies into the curriculum, it became a requirement for teachers to use them in nearly every subject taught. It was clear that there were few resources to support this aim, and so I developed *VOLCO* as a cross-curricular virtual learning environment for use in both primary and secondary schools, and simultaneously a collaborative artwork that could evolve through collective input.

The multiple factors informing these two projects highlight the interrelatedness and complexity that the process of "invitation" can take. These also indicate why top-down forms of arts patronage, which attempt to control and limit outcomes, can fail to encourage the innovation they seek unless applied with a great deal of flexibility. That is not to say that commissioning as a means of project instigation is unable to achieve this and, indeed, it has taken a very positive role in a number of the projects I have described. It nevertheless becomes problematic where commissioning is the main means through which social engagement is initiated, or where it follows agendas that do not necessarily include creative growth. *VOLCO* in fact was brought into being through a commission. The sum of £1,000 was offered by an imaginative and open-minded arts officer[5] to develop some pre-programming workshops for a new art centre. When I indicated that there was little worthwhile I could do for such a small amount of money, proposing to use it instead for research and development and raise the remaining funding myself, she agreed. The value of that original commission could not be underestimated since it enabled the project to start. When it concluded its ten-year span it had attracted £200,000 of support, and involved over a thousand children.

The Art of Negotiation

> The idea of participation, of negotiation, be that political or cultural ... is consistent with the idea of civilization ... It can, it must, be made central again, rather than marginal.
>
> Declan McGonagle[6]

Sometimes an invitation and a question are the same thing, as at the commencement of the Docklands Community Poster Project or *Active Energy*. Whether this is the case or not, the necessity of finding the right questions to put to others involved remains central to the building of any collaborative project, despite the fact that there may well be a different set of questions for each of the stakeholders. One lesson from the training I undertook in conflict resolution during the early nineties that has always stayed with me is that, when a situation seems "stuck", this is more frequently due to the "presenting problems" being at odds, rather than underlying needs. The conciliation process stresses the importance of getting underneath seemingly insurmountable differences to discover what each party *really* wants. When this is identified it is extraordinary how much more readily conflicts can be resolved, and recognition of the relevance of this for collaborative working has become integrated into the ways that I have approached projects since that time. During the development phase I often employ a process of questioning to uncover what each party most wants or needs from the proposed work. While answers will almost certainly differ, projects are generally capable of delivering multiple outcomes, most of which can co-exist without contradiction. Thus *VOLCO* provided a much-needed resource for schools, training for teachers, enjoyment and learning for the children and a list of social and educational outcomes for its funders. To the children, the project offered not only fun, but a glimpse into their own potential to create a better world. For myself it was all these together with the opportunity to work with hundreds of children, who would each bring the power of their imagination to bear on an immense collective and purposeful artwork. I always feel that the practice works at its best when it offers something real and tangible, though not necessarily measurable, to all involved.

It is this conscious sharing and meeting of needs that forms the backbone of the negotiating process, together with respect for the different positions of others. In *Conversations before the End of Time* Suzi Gablik described this process as a willingness to sit with the emerging difficulties as the differing sides connect and communicate[7]. Flexibility is necessary, but it is important that outcomes are not simply a compromise. As I understood when learning about the conciliation process, compromise is a solution where nobody gets what they want. The other way is that everybody does, since projects can also be built around disparate needs. Strangely, it seems to work. Perhaps this is because it functions in a similar way to Freire's "problem posing theory and practice"[8], which takes as a starting point people's histories and background experience. I have similarly found it essential to start where people are and treat the project development as a vast problem-solving exercise. This does not of course mean giving up or watering down the original intention of the project, which is one of the key factors to be taken into account. In *Conversation Pieces* (2004, p.65) Kester described how, in the development of their environmental projects, artists Helen and Newton Harrison used to "knit together" connections across disciplines to enable them to ask larger questions[9]. A further effect is that, when a person is getting what they need from a process, they give of their best. Where people are involved in larger numbers, then the energy that drives a project becomes multiplied many times over.

During my conflict resolution training an experienced mediator[10] explained that once all the standard processes have been employed and still do not work, there is only one thing left—creativity. Well, I thought, I'm on home territory here! I have always seen the creative process as the *terrible* (in the biblical sense) coming together of ideas/energy and matter. This is equally true whether the outcome is to be a sculpture, a cake, a new planet or the satisfactory involvement of different participants working towards a shared creative outcome, since all elements need to pass through a transformative process. The enormity of this passage arises through the states of disembodied idea or energy and material substance being of different orders, which simply do not fit together in any way that an "additive" process can solve. Rather, an external agency is required—heat, motion or intention, to impact on the elements. The process can be swift, is more often slow, but is always complex and at the time can often seem impossible. What one can bring to this process of transformation as a creative practitioner is the desire and intention to bring about a resolution of these forces. The outcome is never certain. In my experience no successful project has failed to have a "sticky moment" when, for an interminable short space of time, one comes up against the impossibility of the task at hand. Yet there are processes that can help bring creativity to bear on a "stuck" situation, and simply staying with it, as Suzi Gablik advised, is one of them. This is no different to how any creative endeavour might proceed, although the constituent elements here are people, organisations and perhaps some social issues. With relief I have discovered that the understanding that comes with experience, while not reducing the enormity of the transition from one state to another, removes some fear of the unknown. Feeling more enabled to draw on these processes has encouraged me to extend the scope of collaborations, and while the social and creative rewards have become proportionately greater, I nevertheless remain in awe of the unexpected challenges that can emerge.

I have indicated the importance of initial consultation with potential collaborators and participants, whether verbally or otherwise, which enables the hopes and desires of each to become embedded in the project. It is, however, not simply the nature of the questions that count here, but the quality of the listening and responsiveness. Gablik has shown how becoming a "compassionate listener" can help one to move beyond the dualisms and decisiveness and free up a developmental process of "cultural unfolding"[11]. Grant Kester has phrased it as "vulnerable receptivity" or "empathetic identification", and sees interaction with others as a useful means of moving away from any sense of fixed identity[12]. In this way the artist's intention is not abandoned, but rather develops through the dialogue. Although others might see some suppression of self-interest in the process of developing connectedness with others, I do not find that any altruism is necessary. One's own interest becomes so completely bound up with the interests of others that it is only through the collective needs being properly fulfilled that it is possible to realise one's own. This process of "conversation" actually enables one's own ideas to be formed—an experience akin to Mikhail Bakhtin's proposition that dialogue taking place between two parties allows both to move and arrive at new positions[13].

If creativity is to be employed as a problem-solving device, then there is also an art to creating the frameworks within which the questions are asked. Sometimes this dialogue is best conducted through non-verbal means. In *West Meets East*, my first experience of working with young people, I found the students did not respond well to the kind of brainstorming process I had previously employed with community groups, and it was through the intervention of the teacher that we together worked out an almost entirely visual approach to the development of ideas. While these approaches are all the familiar stuff of arts workshops, it was only through the experience of this project that I realised they could also be used to work through the tricky business of negotiating collective ideas for a shared artwork. Projects such as *VOLCO* and the *Young Person's Guides* then built on this to ensure that a sense of individual ownership could be retained, even by multiple participants.

Managing Collective Input

In describing the means by which Peter and I engaged with communities, Grant Kester wrote:

> Their artistic identity is based in part on their ability to listen, openly and actively, and to organise scenarios that maximise the collective creative potential of a given constituency or site[14].

Kester was referring to the way in which the process of listening turns into the structuring that will enable the production of the artwork. The "scenarios" he describes are the frameworks, both organisational and visual, that for me are now pivotal to the process of turning the general into the specific, and the ideas of many into a cultural entity that can then transmit their knowledge in the wider social sphere.

West Meets East was where I began, at least consciously, to use such a structuring process. It may have been that this was already present in the Docklands work, with the regular meetings of community activists—a pooling of ideas from which Peter and I would create images for discussion. However the school project presented a different starting point and a puzzle to be solved: how to create a coherent and professional public artwork with the combined ideas of twenty teenagers in such a way that they would also retain a sense of ownership in the result. I drew on a number of approaches to facilitate this process, as described in Part 1, moving from loose collages to a highly structured set of montages designed to draw out content in a format that was in keeping with the final output. This structuring also helped to ensure that whatever each participant contributed would come across in a resonant and coherent way. While this project developed through several more stages, the principle of providing a framework for ideas was sustained. Reflecting on this, I recognise that it was a different process to that which might be employed in a workshop with a sole remit to support creative self-expression. The process I used required facilitating the emergence of ideas while ensuring that the visual means used for this was compatible with the final public output. From the outset a central intention of this work had been its implicit offer to bring participants' issues and concerns into the public domain. It was their ideas that were important, albeit conveyed through visual means. The importance of representing their first hand experience relates back to Freire's notion expressed in *Pedagogy of Hope*, where he demonstrated how respect for the cultural content provided by participants was due to the window onto the world opened up by their knowledge, since it is their experience that "in the last analysis, is the primary and inescapable face of the world itself[15]."

An example of how this translates into later work can be found in *VOLCO*. Although dissimilar in outcome and appearance to *West Meets East*, the projects are very much alike in the structuring processes employed. A key element that *VOLCO* nevertheless took and developed further was the importance of not wasting participants' ideas, a principle that has re-affirmed itself many times over as significant both in terms of respect and efficiency. If a child, or any participant, has been encouraged to develop an idea that is subsequently rejected, the lack of value signalled to that person can be very negative. I am not referring here to teaching the editing process, which can, on the contrary, be affirming, but rather the generating of material by participants through a process that has been insufficiently thought through. Each image that has been developed in the course of such a project constitutes an expression of their experience, and it is on this that the quality of the project rests. Efficiency also applies where valuable time and resources may have been taken to support each young person in the production of their set of ideas.

In *VOLCO* the formal interventions of *West Meets East* were enhanced by the use of technology significantly more advanced than the photocopier of the earlier project. One of the tasks of *VOLCO* was for children to represent who they wished to be through development of a virtual "Volcan" identity, and an online template served as the receptacle into which they could upload their own materials. This was designed to hold a specific range of imagery and text, and teachers trained to run the project were advised of various devices—the close framing of objects, for example—that would ensure images were at their most effective. In the project's early days participants had to crop and resize their imagery to fit the templates and, if they failed to do this adequately, the results could suffer. Later, though still encouraged to manipulate images to their satisfaction, the programming was improved to provide a "fail safe" device for those who had not done so, "grabbing" and re-sizing the uploaded images and inserting them into the correct place on their template, a process now commonplace, but one that had to be thought through at that time. This also had to be instantly visible if it was to provide immediate feedback to the children. The design of the *VOLCO* web site incorporated a number of similar features that ensured the children's work appeared at its best, while at the same time remaining true to what they had created. The attempt to achieve this was initiated as a response to feedback from teachers, parents and the children themselves, coupled with recognition of the importance of those things they wished to communicate within this context. In this situation the children were the experts in regard to the imaginative expression of their ideas. *VOLCO*'s function was to harness the power of their imaginations and put it to creative and social use, which included the children's own sense of being able to change or shape a new world.

In *VOLCO* the programming, design, opportunities for digital imaging and formal limits combined to ensure visual resonance for all the children's contributions. The provision of frameworks, devised with designer Henry Iles, enabled their contributions to look at their best, while respecting and foregrounding the particular expertise they

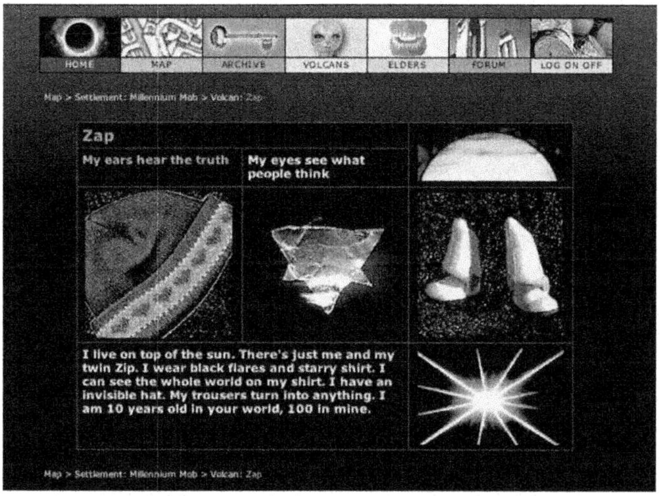

Figure 6.1 Character created with a template for *VOLCO*
© Loraine Leeson, 2002.

were contributing and avoiding reliance on dexterity of hand, which is not highly developed at such a young age. A similar approach was later taken in *The Young Person's Guide to East London* with a process of information gathering that paralleled in many ways that used in *VOLCO* and *West Meets East*. In this project the young people were shown how to create a range of different digital photographs to make a sequence about their chosen site. They were encouraged to initially edit their photographs in camera to ensure that they ended up with a manageable quantity, then edited and manipulated the rest on computer. In this way they remained in control both of production and selection, although within given boundaries. The remainder of the information they entered into a template in a format suitable for uploading to the web site.

In all these projects the "frameworks", whether templates or visual devices, enabled questions, needs and issues to emerge without the need for translation into words. They constituted a process of visual negotiation and development through time, holding and respecting difference while facilitating communication. In *VOLCO*'s pilot project, children in North Carolina and East London had no difficulty in "reading" each others' characters, even though much of the content was unfamiliar; in fact, the familiarity of the structure made the differences exciting rather than strange. A further function of such a framework is to create a context within which new ideas may be born. Just as Planet *VOLCO* evolved through the accumulated knowledge held in its archives, so did the ideas that emerged from it. The structure that contains this information needs to be strong and appropriate enough to act as a "holding mechanism" so that new information may begin to emerge in coherent ways. Gablik has described how allowing the truth of the subject to emerge not from any one point of view, but from many, makes an entrenched position open to question[16]. The idea of employing this process not only with small groups but with participants in much larger numbers initially became consolidated for me through reading Sherry Turkle's *Life on the Screen* (1995). I was drawn to her description of "artificial evolution" in which simple boundaries imposed on random dots on a screen would eventually lead to recognisable animal behaviours, then go beyond this to develop self-replicating, open-ended, and evolving artificial life. In a similar way I wanted to see what would emerge through *VOLCO* if hundreds of children could together create the elements of a new society. Although the *Young Person's Guide to East London* lacked *VOLCO*'s veil of fantasy, a new perspective on East London was similarly produced through the input of hundreds of local teenagers.

From Communication to Community

> . . . the process of communication is in fact the process of community.
>
> Raymond Williams[17]

Nearly two decades before the commencement of my practice Raymond Williams identified how community is constructed through networks of relationships and the ways in which communication systems, including the arts, form an intrinsic part of social organisation. He also demonstrated how the interaction arising from the selection, interpretation and sharing of ideas and attitudes creates its building blocks. This interpretation of "community" has been central to my practice in terms of both the networking through which projects are realised, and the shared goals, interests or experiences that it seeks to express. The premise has been that the process of making visible or uncovering shared needs, desires or intentions can encourage or move society to realise changes that are required.

My early work with health workers and Docklands campaigning involved engagement with ready-formed groups brought together by the common experience of geographic location when shared ways of life were under threat. However group activity rarely starts out with cohesion, but rather through disparate individuals with diverse experiences, who then perhaps discover that a common thread runs through these. The activities of the tenants and action groups in the London Docklands came out of a history of local experience where residents and workers recognised the necessity of self-organisation for survival itself. The concept and name of the Docklands was imposed on the area as a development strategy by government, and only eventually adopted by local groups through counter-strategy. What held these different organisations together was not just the experience of shared oppression and threat, but the information that was regularly circulated among them through meetings, newssheets and word of mouth. The Docklands Community Poster Project became one of the vehicles of communication in the wider campaign, and art a tool of consolidation and celebration. In this way the project was able to contribute to the strengthening of bonds within the campaign while helping to facilitate its outward expression.

The Art of Change in the nineties held a different relationship with its groups. It was no longer working to support campaigning activity, although what remained in common with both previous and later work was the process of making public the views of those whose voices are rarely heard in mainstream society. Freire described this process when he wrote about the right of an individual to "name their own world", seeing the uncovering of this worldview as a key part of the revolutionary process[18]. The participants we worked with during the nineties belonged to preexisting groups such as a school classes, but what they brought to the project was individual experience. They did not "represent" communities in the way that tenants and action groups during the Docklands campaigning had identified people to speak on their behalf. On the contrary, the aim of these later projects were first to enable individual expression and then, through the structure of the project, to allow commonality to manifest itself. In her article *Community Engagement* Catherine Wilson recognised the nature of dialogue set up in these kinds of projects, describing how a community or social group, far from an independent universe, constitutes a shifting site of invention and negotiation and an interface between individual subjectivities and realms of meaning. She also noted the importance of communications that start from the specific and so avoid modernism's homogenised and universal sense of "public"[19]. Suzi Gablik has similarly identified the importance of this kind of discursive interaction, which enables shared understanding to develop without coming to any conclusion or judgement[20], while Freire reminds us that "authentic thinking [takes place] only in *communication*"[21].

To what extent then, and under what conditions, is art able to build community? My experience is that it is unlikely to achieve this on its own, and that it is also dependent on the extent of an artist's intention and desire to engage in social process. Miwon Kwon in fact prefers to call this process "collective artistic praxis" as opposed to "community-based art", since she sees in the latter that "the community" can end up functioning as a self-referential social entity[22]. This insight, however, is clearly not taken on board in much of the recent practice of commissioning artists to meet social and political targets within regeneration schemes or to fulfil the agendas of political or institutional targets—an issue to which I will return later.

Objects, Fragments and Narratives

> One can know what every individual object will do, but still have no idea what the system as a whole will do . . .
>
> Sherry Turkle[23]

In earlier sections I have mentioned the use of visual devices to both generate and structure content. One of these has been objects selected or brought into workshops by participants to represent themselves or their ideas. In the seventies I came across D.W. Winnicott's *Playing and Reality* and was drawn to the concept of the "transitional object" with its associative meanings[24]. Over a decade later, when embarking on my first schools project *West Meets East*, and searching for a means to facilitate the exploration and communication of identity without verbal brainstorming, the use of objects came to mind as a potential vehicle for this. They proved a far richer device than I had first envisaged. With the criteria for this exercise that participants should choose an object to represent who they felt themselves to be, each one provided a seemingly endless repository of meaning. The position of the object as a separate entity to the person helped to facilitate discussion of individual ideas and feelings, while simultaneously offering further layers of association and memory. Perhaps most important in the light of my proposition regarding the role of creativity in the negotiating process described earlier in this chapter, objects provide the "matter" of the creative equation. As opposed to concepts of one's inner reality, they constitute an element of the "stuff" or material that can be worked on. I discovered that, having chosen a set of objects, participants were already well advanced on the journey towards realising their ideas through making. *Making Stuff*, an online article by Francoise Dupré, has addressed this role of materiality in what she has referred to as "ethical collaborative-participatory practice". She discovered how, in her own art practice, this material engagement facilitated connection with participants' identities by tapping into their experience and history, and enabled them to become active social subjects in the work[25].

My own use of objects developed though a number of projects in the nineties before taking a step into the virtual domain through *VOLCO*. Despite taking place almost entirely online, this project used many of the same processes as *West Meets East*, although this time with participants creating new identities for themselves through their choice and manipulation of imagery. *VOLCO* participants were much younger than in the former project, starting at around eight years old. They brought objects and images from home or selected them from an assortment brought to workshops. These were scanned or photographed, while other visuals for the character layouts were created through painting, collage or downloaded and digitally manipulated. It almost did not matter what imagery was selected; it was the choice that counted. Once selected, that object became imbued with all that needed to be expressed. Feedback from the children confirmed that they found it much easier to write about their character after creating a set of images in this way, a process diametrically opposed to the task of illustrating stories that is the more usual way for schools to encourage children to work with word and image.

While developing *VOLCO*, I had been reading Sherry Turkle's account of the *Game of Life*, created in the late sixties by John Conway at MIT[26]. Through the repeated generation of random black and white squares following a small number of limiting rules, increasingly complex patterns and shapes would begin to evolve. These were referred to as "emergent objects", an early form of artificial life. Turkle went on to describe the development of the StarLogo game for children by Michel Resnick, which took the process to another level, producing entities that resembled the movement and behaviour of flocks of birds, a colony of ants or cars in a traffic jam[27]. As a result of *The Infinity Story* I had become interested in how the combination of the disparate elements contributed to the story by the children had created such a coherent whole. It seemed that the structure of the project had provided an equivalent to the simple rules that enabled the emergence of Conway's artificial life and Resnick's flocks of birds. *VOLCO* was designed to take this a step further regarding content, enabling a whole new world to emerge from the fragments contributed by hundreds of children through a similar framework. The children's online Volcan identities were similarly created through the images and text that made up each character layout. Turkle saw this kind of play with multiple identities and fragments of identity as paralleled in the deconstruction of the unitary self of contemporary psychology. She referred to Levi-Strauss' notion of "evocative objects-to-think-with" to identify a new practice of creating identity through multiplicity in online life, and saw the virtual personae created in this way as another version of these "objects-to-think-with"[28].

The processes of socially situated art, which aim to engage with, consolidate and celebrate shared meanings, are not new. I have for a long time, for example, felt that the complex matrix of frescoes by Giotto that adorn the walls of the Basilica of San

Francesco d'Assisi in Umbria provide the visitor with a narrative experience paralleling multi-media. The chapel provides an immersive environment that has communicated non-verbally to its visitors since the fourteenth century. Moments from the life of St. Francis are depicted in horizontal sequence around the walls, while ranging vertically upwards from these are stories of the Old and New Testaments. Their meanings are linked to the St. Francis story and each other through the repetition of fragments of colour, shape and gesture—as interactive as any set of HTML pages. Before I had heard of multi-media, the memory of this environment, first seen at a young age, provided inspiration for the montaged photo-murals. A further encounter with the Giotto frescoes in 1997 certainly resonated with the way I thought about the *Infinity Story* and subsequently *VOLCO*. A form of narrative runs through most of the work discussed here, either explicitly as in the photo-mural sequences of the eighties, *Between Family Lines* and *Infinity Story*, or implicitly as in *West Meets East*, *Awakenings* and *The Catch*. It offers an accessible route to the uncovering of meaning without undermining the complexity of issues at stake. The slow unfolding of the photo-murals and ongoing use of montage techniques also draw directly on my early experience of working in film as an undergraduate. The concept of "new narrative", which informed debates around photography and new media in the eighties and nineties, usefully identified an approach based upon non-linearity and customisation. This concept referred to a matrix of information related to an over-arching concept or theme, which then becomes the vessel for specific inputs from other participants. Those who interact with this matrix, whether through directly producing or consuming, become actively engaged in customising their "journey", in making their own sense of the narrative, which they create or navigate for themselves. This is true of most of the work, but particularly addresses the way in which narrative functions through both *VOLCO* and the *Young Person's Guide to East London*.

Narrative has, however, not only acted as a formal consideration in the work, it has also provided a means of pinpointing the perspective represented by its content. In 1991 Peter and I were commissioned by the Agnes Etherington Gallery, Ontario, to produce a work with Canadian artists Carole Condé and Karl Beveridge[29] for the exhibition and conference *Fragmented Power: Art voices for 2000*. The outcome of this was *Digital Highways, Local Narratives*, which took the global narrative of the digital highways and corporate lines of communication crisscrossing the globe, and contrasted this with the "local narratives" of their impact on specific communities and work places in Canada and the UK. In a chapter for *Mapping the Futures* we highlighted the importance of these in relation to the viral-like spread of corporate culture globally along its "digital highways". Local narratives' are not only about geography but the specificity of what it is like to be working class, female, black, gay, or differently abled. In other words, the voice of those defined as "other"[30].

When It Goes Wrong

> . . . all must be examined in their particular unique context.
>
> Martha Fleming[31]

The concept of "wrong" is a nebulous one in a socially situated practice. When work is developed with others it builds on a range of needs and expectations and so evolves—shifts in the way a project is delivered are merely part of its development. This process is nevertheless rarely easy or straightforward and can certainly stretch one's patience and social skills. However, without this constant dynamic of give and take, adjustment and re-adjustment, there would be no collaboration, no project and nothing new would emerge. It can take time to satisfactorily negotiate these interactions and, on occasion, when things have not turned out as expected, it may be necessary to allow some extra time and space for a process of reworking. It is hard to say therefore whether the work "always" goes wrong, or rarely does, since in one sense the whole process of its realisation is akin to Freire's "problem-posing theory and practice" with every stage of each project becoming part of an ongoing informal evaluation, transforming the process as it progresses. While this can apply to most creative work, the involvement of collaborators and/or participants means that these projects often contain complex matrices of relationships to be managed, and therefore also enormous scope for discontent. In Part 1 I referred to my experience as a volunteer neighbourhood conciliator and mediator, which gave me the confidence to develop projects around collaborations involving a number of different institutions, groups and individuals. Recognising the value of the outcomes that could be created in this way I felt able to draw on these tools to manage the inevitable difficulties as they emerged. The *Cascade* series of projects were the best example of this, each involving a school, a college of further education, a university and cSPACE itself. It was not only necessary to maintain good working relations with staff in each institution, the positive experience of hundreds of children or young people was also dependent upon the quality of these relationships.

The *Cascade* projects were realised by a team of freelance artists[32] employed by cSPACE, each possessing a high level of inter-personal and communication skills. They passed these skills on to the undergraduates who would work alongside them as project volunteers, and in turn mentored young people from further education who assisted them in facilitating the school workshops. The "cascade effect" was therefore not just limited to skills being passed down, but also functioned in the other direction through the layers of support built into the process. After each set of workshops volunteer undergraduates would be de-briefed by the mentoring co-ordinator, while the cSPACE team met periodically to share experience. The whole process was regarded in a sense as a vast trouble-shooting exercise. After a particularly harrowing workshop I might check with the mentoring co-ordinator on how the different parties were feeling—children, teachers and student volunteers. Quite often we established that each was in fact comfortable with their own part in the project, and that this had been due to her expert management of a difficult situation. The emotional toll of this could then become discharged through myself as director of the project, or within the supportive larger group.

cSPACE's position as a small and flexible organisation enabled it to interact with the larger institutions involved in the *Cascade* projects, which may have had difficulty maintaining a similarly complex web of relationships. On occasion however the vagaries and internal politics of these institutions would throw up problems that we were unable to deal with. These included issues with college staff who had been unwillingly assigned to the project by their line managers, and resentments or jealousies about the other institutions involved. Most difficulties were handled through keeping communications open and, where necessary, calling on the institutional hierarchies. Difficulties can sometimes get out of hand, however, and one incident between students from a sixth form college and a member of staff from a secondary school caused the internal politics of each to collide, leading to an insoluble issue. A secondary school teacher behaved badly towards some of the college students assisting with workshops resulting in blame being passed both ways, with cSPACE caught in the middle. It was only through significant time and effort put into meetings and communications, plus the swift introduction of another school partner, that we were able to conclude the project without detriment to participants. The college, which had been financially supporting the project, took nearly a year to release its contribution, causing cSPACE considerable financial difficulty. As a result of this I removed a tier of the "cascade" process, so that undergraduates subsequently worked directly with the young people and no longer mentored college students. I also shifted the work to youth groups rather than schools, where we would be more likely to be liaising directly with those responsible. While this in itself was a positive development, it was regrettable to no longer work with a local school and college with which we had otherwise built longstanding and positive relationships. It also highlighted the issue of the financial vulnerability of cSPACE with its dependence on project funding and lack of long-term institutional support.

Issues can also arise in collaborative projects where there is dependence on a collaborative partner for their skills and knowledge. This can be particularly the case when working across disciplines, with tensions exacerbated by deadlines and the different approaches each party brings to seeing a project through to conclusion. At times when this has caused stress I have been grateful to something I learned through conflict resolution—that difficulties in a work situation are rarely caused by personalities, even when they seem to be so, but rather by lack of clarity in roles and responsibilities. It has proved useful therefore to ensure that contracts that outline responsibilities and timeframes are issued early on in the process, so that they can act as a point of reference when needed. Sometimes this is not enough, however, and it can be useful to remind oneself, with an eye on the bigger picture, that along with the different skills that are valued in others come different approaches. Occasionally, as director of a project with the ultimate responsibility and perhaps the largest creative stake, it can become necessary to take on extra tasks. It is very important at these times to keep communication open and positive, and remember that good lessons are being learned for the future.

There are few projects that I would consider to be actual failures, although in seeking one I have remembered a schools commission that I undertook with Peter in the early nineties. Interestingly, the commission itself was not unsuccessful in its own terms—an installation in a secondary school resulted, of which I believe the participants were proud, while the process of working with the students had been positive and informative. Its "failure" was more in terms of our broader intentions and became manifest through the lack of desire by either Peter or myself to include it in our promotional list of Art of Change projects, or make use of its documentation, so that it has now been lost to history. Looking back, I believe that this lack of interest may have been due to the project being realised through what I now think of as an "additive" process and with no public outcome. Although a reasonable set of workshops and personal outcomes for participants did take place, the project did not go through that transformative creative process that I described earlier in the chapter, while its lack of presence in the public domain meant that, for us, its function as a tool for social transformation was only partially realised.

Another example of a project not proceeding as desired took place during the development of *VOLCO*, when it was being piloted in a primary school in the London Borough of Tower Hamlets. At that time the web processes that were later added to help structure the creation and uploading of digital materials by participants had not yet been implemented. Apart from some student support I was running the project single-handed on a newly developed web site with many glitches, with pupils using a suite of school computers that were both inadequate for the task and unfamiliar to myself. I was attempting to work across a whole year group rather than just one class, as had previously been the case, and the school had allocated a group of young children who needed significant support. On this occasion the difficulties spiralled out of control to the extent that teachers were becoming unhappy with the way things were proceeding, which in turn threatened to have a knock-on effect on the pupils' enjoyment of the project. I made an unprecedented decision and stopped it there. On reflection, while none of the problems that arose were unfamiliar, there may have been just too many difficulties with insufficient resources, exacerbated by some personal issues, which prevented me from throwing myself into a sufficiently rigorous, problem-solving mode of behaviour. I proposed splitting the project into two parts, with the second to be concluded the following term. On returning to complete the work under better circumstances, things went a lot more smoothly and *VOLCO* continued over several more years with ongoing success.

The greatest external destructive impact on a project that I can recall was the unannounced demolition of the Docklands Community Poster Project's first photo-

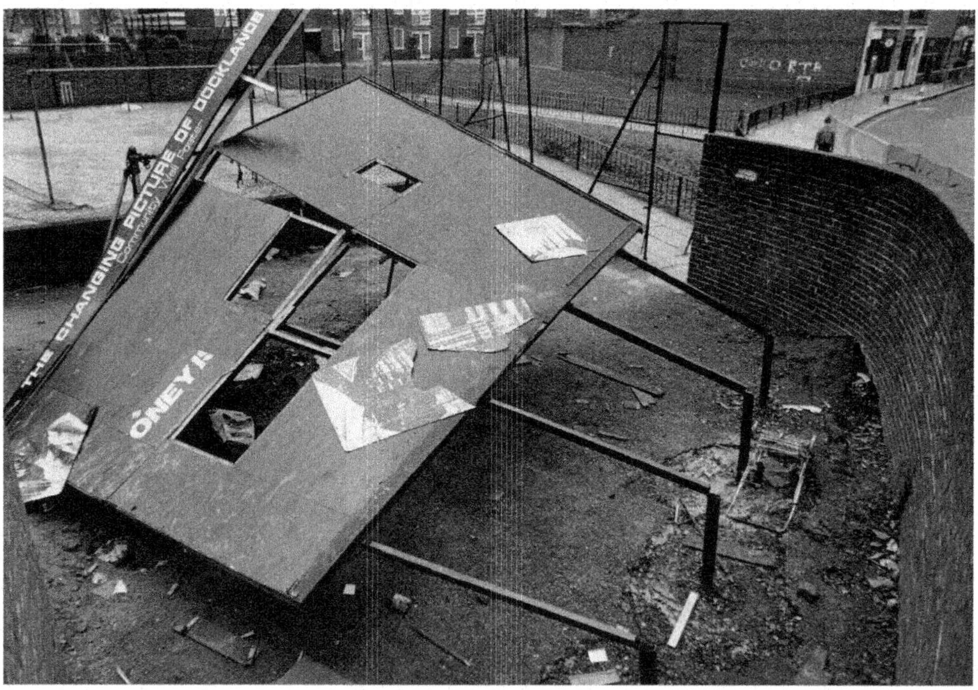

Figure 6.2 Demolished Photo-mural, Wapping Lane

Photo © Peter Dunn and Loraine Leeson, 1983

mural in Wapping in the early eighties. The London Docklands Development Corporation had become the planning authority for the newly designated Docklands and responsible for planning permission for our billboards. Understandably this organisation was not keen on our critical stance against their development, but had only restricted grounds on which to refuse permission. Our first photo-mural structure in Wapping Lane had in fact been erected prior to the LDDC gaining its new powers, and they could do nothing to remove it. One morning, however, we found it demolished. The photo-murals were large eighteen by twelve foot wooden boards supported by steel girders. There had been no warning and no indication of who had done this, although it clearly had not been spontaneous vandalism, since the steel girders had been completely cut through. This could have been a disaster for the project since at that time it was our first and only standing photo-mural, and its removal was both a blow to our continuing work and a political statement. Two factors nevertheless worked in our favour. The first was our steering committee of local people, who were outraged at this assault on the public airing of their views. They regarded the photo-mural as one of the few means of communicating their side of the issues, and took action with the full force of that campaigning community. Letters appeared in the local papers decrying this act of "municipal vandalism". In addition, we had the support of the Greater London Council, which had funded the building of the structure, and saw this as an affront to their own position. They provided swift financial recompense to enable re-building, and before long the photo-mural was continuing its ongoing narrative as though nothing had happened. We nevertheless had to fight for every planning permission. Peter even had to attend a tribunal where the LDDC claimed that the photo-murals were "advertising political ideas". He argued that they were art and, calling on historic examples including Picasso's *Guernica*, demonstrated how art has often done this. As a result we were given leave to erect the photo-murals, providing they were for "art and community use" only. Members of the tribunal commented that the debate made it one of the most interesting cases they had judged.

Outcomes and Products

> . . . the field of collaborative art practice must set out to destabilise, challenge and finally dissolve the very terms within which it has been constructed and contained: the community, the artist, the artwork and the audience.
>
> Ailbhe Murphy[33]

In his first book *Conversation Pieces* Grant Kester made the case for socially engaged work to be considered in dialogic terms, and outlined a new theoretical paradigm for the work of art as process. This shift in the way art can be perceived has been immensely liberating. In some projects the activity is the totality of the work; however, where there is "product", this can also be seen as part of a continuum, as it has in many of my own projects. In my experience the resonance of whatever is produced, whether tangible or experiential, remains of immense importance, and I shall say more on this when I touch on the issue of aesthetics in the last chapter. For now I will offer an image of how I perceive that output to function with an analogy based on my understanding of artists as providers of frameworks through which the world can be seen and re-considered. In this respect artists act as a lens that brings meanings into focus. It can be turned towards any chosen source—a landscape, a set of concepts, or the ideas of others—the light reflected from these sources then forms an image that appears on the far side of the lens. This image is of a different order to the source material, however, holding the original information but in a compressed form—the artwork or art project. The "compression" of meanings in its new form makes it analogous to a dream that transforms the material to create a new, self-contained entity through which new insights can occur. Where this culminates in a public setting it is able to connect with others, who bring their own ideas and pre-conceptions, and as the two sets of information mingle, potential is created for a shift in perception. In a situation where the light entering the lens embodies the experiences of those whose views rarely reach the public domain, then these offer a new set of ideas with which society can engage, creating opportunities for change. If artists indeed serve in this way as mediators of meanings, then my own practice is to frame and focus the ideas of those who have insights to offer, ensuring that any outputs are as resonant as possible so that a wider engagement with the ideas can ensue.

This analogy confirmed for me an understanding that the point of wider engagement of a project, that is, the means through which others are able to engage with the embodied idea once it has become accessible in the public domain, is a key element of its function in terms of social change. From experience, the nature and quality of outputs within this process are always of great consequence, whether produced by the "hand" of the artist, or otherwise. This issue is perhaps most clearly visible in fine art education where a student might take a highly sophisticated approach to studio work, yet feel it is sufficient to realise a module in community practice through a series of workshops in which they apply a much reduced level of aesthetic scrutiny. Both process and any artefacts produced along the way require a similarly rigorous approach if they are to fulfil their respective functions.

Although there can be one or more concrete outputs to a project, there are likely to be multiple outcomes. I described earlier in the chapter how initial questioning of collaborative partners in the early stages can identify the different needs around which a project may then be constructed in order to offer each party or group involved their desired result. For young people it may be that they have fun while engaged in creative activity, a school might gain a learning resource, while others might place the greatest value on participation in a launch event. This has subsequent bearing on the sense of ownership each partner feels in the resulting work. Those without first hand experience of this kind of practice sometimes express concern regarding ownership of any artwork produced, missing the fact that it is more important that each of those involved receives what they need from a project, which should ideally have been identified early on in the process. In a practice where outputs are not for sale, concern with the product would be better focused on ensuring that creative outputs are used for their purpose and thereafter cared for, displayed or archived appropriately.

Each project that I have described has resulted in one or more physical outputs that are central to its function, but cannot "stand in" for the work, which has a greater totality. This is why, if elements from it are exhibited after the event, they most certainly require contextualisation. The *Art for Whom?* exhibition at the Serpentine Gallery in 1978, where we showed work from the campaign to save Bethnal

Green Hospital, was a case in point. Exhibiting the contextualised products of process-based work can clearly provide a positive means of both disseminating methodologies and extending the reach of the practice. The retrospective *Art for Change* in 2005, which documented thirty years of my work, attempted to do just this, and a team of artists and academics from Berlin[34] spent significant time gathering background material to convey the processes through which each project was realised. Galleries still form the main nodes of communication and dissemination for visual art, and play an important role in showcasing different kinds of work, whether designed for the gallery or documenting external practice. These were issues keenly debated in the seventies and eighties, a time when our proposal to exhibit documentation from the Docklands work in a major gallery met with derision[35]. Exhibiting this kind of work is in many ways less problematic in the present time; however, finding ways to effectively communicate social process in settings primarily designed for object-oriented experience is an issue that needs to be continually addressed by artists and curators.

If social change is the purpose of the work, then it is not just the initial project that matters, but what happens to it afterwards. In 1995, *Awakenings* offered an early lesson in transferability after our discovery that other classes in the school were simultaneously doing similar projects based on the same materials—the school's Head of Art, on his meagre budget, being very adept at making the most of resources. In addition to its direct purpose, the project was inadvertently serving as a non-prescriptive model for further creative work. It was difficult to obtain adequate funding for school projects due to the argument that a relatively large amount of money would benefit only a few pupils and, while it was desirable that larger numbers should be involved, this was not always practical in a classroom setting. It seemed that it would be better therefore to design projects in such a way that would allow greater numbers of participants to benefit at a later date. This lesson of "transferability" experienced through *Awakenings* led to *VOLCO* being created as an ongoing learning tool, *The Young Person's Guide to East London* to function as a resource for and beyond the London Olympics, and the *Active Energy* turbines to be designed for open source dissemination.

Feedback and Evaluation

> ... my tendency was to review and review promptly, and thus, adopting a consistency with the practice I had, to perceive that practice as steeped in the dialectical movement back and forth between consciousness and the world.
>
> Paolo Freire[36]

I have experienced three types of evaluation in relation to my practice. The first is that ongoing dialectic described by Freire, a re-evaluation of working process and outcomes, which supports the development and realisation of community-based projects and also feeds into the identification and management of arising difficulties, as discussed above. Working with people, particularly where many different interests are involved, can be a complex process and calls for great adaptability and, even where the core theme and output of a project does not change, the means of achieving these have to be flexible. One might first plan on involving schools, but youth groups turn out to be a better solution. Workshops might be designed to run over full days, as in *The Young Person's Guide to East London,* but if a group that wants to be involved generally meets after school, then it may be best delivered in two-hour slots. While I had assumed that this particular project required a computer suite, I was not going to turn down the opportunity to work with a youth offending team, even though this meant running the project from a laptop on the side of an Astroturf pitch during their football sessions. Each of these changes to original assumptions needs careful consideration and assessment as to what is most important to a project and cannot change, or whether any such shifts will destroy its *raison d'être*. One has to be clear about a project's ultimate objectives and, as in the example above, whether fitting workshops around football practice will be a compromise or an opportunity. How each participant, partner, teacher or participating artist feels about their involvement also matters, since, if a group or person is dissatisfied, it will be detrimental to the project if this is not addressed. Running such a project therefore requires an organic and flexible process of checking and re-checking, since, although the goal may already be decided, the shape of the project itself can never be entirely predicted. While this is not different to other creative work—in making a painting most of the decisions will be intuitive, and the dialogue internal—when working with people the process is equally intuitive but the dialogue is held with others. These changes may be documented in a project report, but most of the time it is the outputs and outcomes that are of most interest to others, rather than the process through which they are delivered.

The second type of evaluation involves a more in-depth look at the project experience by an independent or semi-independent evaluator commissioned either externally or internally where funds allow. I have only been in a position to experience this on a few occasions, and mostly in the last fifteen years. Each time this process has resulted in a useful documented record of the kind of information that could otherwise only be gathered informally. In his 2001 article on evaluation *Did it make a difference?* François Matarasso described a process of "internal evaluation" as necessarily subjective and advocated its purpose to be learning from experience, while warning against setting "unrealistic standards of truth"[37]. The systematic process of information gathering involved in this type of study often allows a wider range of views to be taken into account than would otherwise be the case, while the more structured questioning can elicit a more considered response from participants. The evaluation for *The Young Person's Guide to the Royal Docks* undertaken by John Cockram[38], who also worked on other aspects of the project, was additionally useful for developing future work. In this case his wider involvement in the project and deep understanding of the issues resulting from this, led to a helpful review that was able to enhance my own sense of participant experience gleaned from direct involvement. The more reflective responses elicited through focus groups, suggestions made for future work, the views of staff from participating institutions and feedback from undergraduate volunteers all contributed to a more rounded view of the project that could be fed back into the practice. The fact that they were documented in written form also made useful material for future funding applications.

The third type of evaluation is an analysis of process, outputs and outcomes as regularly required by commissioning and funding bodies, particularly where public monies are concerned. The purpose is to justify the spend and to meet the social and economic criteria of the original source of finance. The extensive monitoring that is often required together with "proof" that certain changes have come about can be a debilitating experience, with criteria tending towards the quantitative and evidence-based. Unrealistic evidence may also be requested, such as participant attainment of employment or improved academic achievement following a very short-term intervention. Generally these requirements are a simple reflection of the bureaucratic processes attached to the social policies governing the funding source in question. Given a particular mindset, they may seem quite reasonable to those who draw up and administer the targets.

A downside of the wider perception of art's social role is that it becomes subjected to the same kind of scrutiny that is applied to other publicly funded activities. While those giving out public money need to be accountable, it does not make these methods any more appropriate for activities that have never been quantifiable in this way. Although the production of material for such feedback can have the advantage of encouraging regular documentation and record keeping in arts groups, its function is ultimately for outside agencies. This can drain resources from small organisations, taking time that is rarely covered by budgeted management and overhead costs, which are often capped by funders to ensure value for money. Where unrealistic outcomes are expected, the addressing of these can have the additional effect of diverting valuable creativity and "drive" away from the project and one can find oneself "playing the game" of this type of evaluation procedure in order to ensure that further resources will be forthcoming. While it would be possible to explain the inappropriateness of some of these expectations to these agencies, this generally cannot be risked by practitioners already operating on a financial tightrope. Those involved in the distribution of public money indeed have the onerous task of obtaining necessary information without inadvertently supporting artists who have little concern for the social effects of what they do. Some administer this with sensitivity; however, the system suffers from an apparent lack of accepted qualitative methods and tools to assess truly socially situated work.

In an article for *Creative Transformations* Kerstin Mey called for a shift to a qualitative approach capable of assessing the impact of creative practices, whether on quality of life, community cohesion or urban regeneration. She has pointed out how critical this is if an argument for the value of creativity and the arts in society is to be maintained, since current methodologies as they stand are often highly counterproductive to the field of work that they purport to encourage[39].

While Matarasso's document on evaluating community-based arts projects was comprehensive and, without doubt, a useful handbook for funding providers, its section on "Guiding principles for community-based arts projects" contained a list from the Department for Culture, Media and Sport's 1999 Report on Social Exclusion, which identified principles of "good practice" in relation to social exclusion. Although clearly written with the best of intentions, nearly two decades later we are reaping the disempowering effects of the utilisation of these principles for the social control of artistic activity. One irony of this is that they embody the kind of approach to projects from the eighties and nineties described in Part 1. To give an example, a section entitled "Embedding Local Control" described processes of involving members of the community in a way not dissimilar to the Docklands Community Poster Project. However, when I was attempting to raise finance for *The Young Person's Guide to East London* and *VOLCO*, I found myself repeatedly asked how participants would be involved in managing the process—a perfectly legitimate idea, but not for those particular projects. It is not just that times change—*Active Energy* does happen to involve its participants in this way—it is simply that not all projects are the same, and "good practice" cannot be judged by a universal points system. One might ask if it were not possible to create a young people's management group for the *Young Person's Guides*. At a stretch I could have done this but, in the context of those particular projects, it would have been both irrelevant and at odds with the respect for the authentic contribution of the participants that lay at the heart of those initiatives.

There is a difference between understanding what has made a particular approach work and assuming that this constitutes a universal truth. The former can provide grounding for open-ended creative development, while the latter limits from the outset. Within UK institutions responsible for arts commissioning or funding there seems to be a notion of "good practice" from which principles can be extrapolated and re-applied to ensure value and sustain artistic quality. This turns the very purpose of research into this area on its head, converting it into bureaucratic thinking that bears little relation to the way creative practice actually develops. Art in its many forms has operated as an intrinsic part of social engagement since civilisation began, and there has never been one way of doing it. Its processes are fluid: they evolve and change according to circumstance. One artist can work creatively with others in many different ways, so multiple practices will result in a myriad of engagement strategies. While it may be tempting to use reflections on these practices as a directive, the notion that getting the rules and principles right will ensure a positive outcome is deeply flawed and it is better for institutions to support and learn rather than assume greater knowledge. Collected in this book are themes that have emerged from activities employed by one or more artists within a particular snapshot in time. If taken literally as "rules" and used by those holding the purse strings, the same observations could become a straightjacket to stifle innovation through denying other artists the freedom to address different circumstances in new ways. It is appreciated that institutions do need to use criteria against which to make judgements, particularly where public funds are concerned. However, in a situation where resources are tight and staff time is stretched, these can end up more arbiter than guide.

It could be argued that many of the studies carried out in the nineties with the purpose of advocating the social value of community-based arts practice succeeded in their goal, since during subsequent years government ministries became convinced of the power of the arts to deliver social outcomes. It may be that the case was made too successfully, however—a proposition to which I shall return in the next chapter.

Notes

1. Augusto Boal (as quoted in Harding 2004, p.31).
2. The UK's Standards and Testing Agency for schools.
3. Office for Standards in Education, Children's Services and Skills.
4. Camille Dorney was at that time running Arthouse, a virtual gallery on the Internet, which contained a story that visitors could access and add to.
5. Clare Connor was the first education officer, later Creative and Cultural Development Manager, for Stratford Circus in East London. Some years after this commission she served on the cSPACE board of trustees.

6. Declan McGonagle, "From Community Arts to Civil Culture and back again" in *An Outburst of Frankness: Community Arts in Ireland—A Reader*, Dublin: Tasc at New Island, 2004, p.56.
7. Suzi Gablik, *Conversations before the End of Time*, London: Thames and Hudson, 1997, p.23.
8. Paolo Freire, *Pedagogy of the Oppressed*, London: Penguin, 1970, p.65.
9. Grant Kester, *Conversation Pieces: Community and Communication in Modern Art*, Berkeley, Los Angeles and London: University of California Press, 2004, p.65.
10. Masana de Souza became manager of Newham Conflict and Change in the early 1990s. She later went on to become Executive Director of Mediation UK and a Sir Winston Churchill Fellow, delivering training, mediation and facilitation across three continents.
11. Gablik, op. cit. p.35.
12. Kester, op. cit. p.77.
13. Mikhail Bakhtin, *The Dialogic Imagination*, Austin: University of Texas Press, 2002.
14. Kester, op. cit. p.24.
15. Paolo Freire, *Pedagogy of Hope: Reliving Pedagogy of the Oppressed*, London: Continuum, 1992, p.85.
16. Gablik, op. cit. p.35–36.
17. Raymond Williams, *Culture and Society 1780–1950*, New York: Columbia University Press, 1958.
18. Freire, op. cit. 1970, p.5.
19. Catherine Wilson, "Community Engagement" in *Collections*, Newcastle upon Tyne: a-n The Artists Information Company, 2008, p.4.
20. Gablik, op. cit. p.25.
21. Freire, op. cit. 1970, p.58.
22. Miwon Kwon, *One Place after Another*, Cambridge MA: MIT Press, 2004, p.154.
23. Turkle, op. cit. p.167.
24. D. W. Winnicott, *Playing and Reality*, Harmondsworth: Pelican, 1974.
25. Francoise Dupré, "Making Stuff" in *Axis* online journal, 2008a.
26. Turkle, op. cit. pp.154–158.
27. Ibid p.166.
28. Ibid pp.259–260
29. We first met Carole Condé and Karl Beveridge in the early eighties and were greatly impressed by their work with Canada's Labour movement. Their complex photographic imagery was largely achieved, not through physical montage as our own, but by means of intricately constructed sets. Carole was present at the installation of our first Docklands photo-mural, and a fruitful reciprocal relationship has continued since that time. They have been the artists whose work is mostly closely akin to our own, both politically and stylistically.
30. Peter Dunn and Loraine Leeson, L, "The Art of Change in Docklands" in *Mapping the Futures*, London and New York: Routlege, 1993, p.143.
31. Martha Fleming, cited in Kwon 2004, p.148.
32. Anne-Marie Pereira de Mello organised the mentoring, John Cockram coordinated undergraduates and John Nassari provided specialist photographic input to workshops. Each worked on several of the *Cascade* projects.
33. Ailbhe Murphy, "The Fine Art of Floating Horses" in *An Outburst of Frankness*, Dublin: Tasc at New Island, 2004, p.191.
34. The Art for Change working group comprised Katja Jedermann, Carmen Mörsch, Birgit Kammerlohr, Thorsten Streichardt, Jole Wilcke, Nanna Lüth and Christian Mayrock. The exhibition opened at the Neue Gesellschaft für Bildende Kunst in Berlin, November 2005, then toured to London, Toronto and Dublin.
35. At the end of the 1980s the director of the Whitechapel Gallery turned down an exhibition of work from the Docklands Community Poster Project, saying that it belonged on the streets and would not be understood if viewed in a gallery.
36. Freire, op. cit. 1992, p.105.
37. François Matarasso, *Did it make a difference? Evaluating community-based arts and business partnerships*, London: Arts and Business, 2001.

38. John Cockram, *The Young Person's Guide to the Royal Docks: evaluation report*, London, 2007.
39. Kerstin Mey, "How do we Know it Works?" in *Creative Transformations*, Londonderry: University of Ulster, 2008, p.111.

References

Mikhail Bakhtin, *The Dialogic Imagination* (Austin: University of Texas Press, 2002).

John Cockram, *The Young Person's Guide to the Royal Docks: evaluation report* (London, 2007).

Peter Dunn and Loraine Leeson, "The Art of Change in Docklands" in *Mapping the Futures* (London and New York: Routledge, 1993).

Francoise Dupré, "Making Stuff" in *Axis* online journal (2008a).

Paolo Freire, *Pedagogy of the Oppressed* (London: Penguin, 1970).

Paolo Freire, *Pedagogy of Hope: Reliving Pedagogy of the Oppressed* (London: Continuum, 1992).

Suzi Gablik, *Conversations before the End of Time* (London: Thames and Hudson, 1997).

David Harding, "Cultural democracy, Craigmillar style" in *Arts: the Catalyst—Craigmillar* (Edinburgh: Craigmillar Communiversity Press, 2004).

Grant Kester, *Conversation Pieces: Community and Communication in Modern Art (*Berkeley, Los Angeles and London: University of California Press, 2004).

Miwon Kwon, *One Place after Another* (Cambridge, MA: MIT Press, 2004).

François Matarasso, *Did it make a difference? Evaluating community-based arts and business partnerships* (London: Arts and Business, 2001).

Declan McGonagle, "From Community Arts to Civil Culture and back again" in *An Outburst of Frankness: Community Arts in Ireland—a Reader* (Dublin: Tasc at New Island, 2004).

Kerstin Mey, "How do we Know it Works?" in *Creative Transformations* (Londonderry: University of Ulster, 2008).

Ailbhe Murphy, "The Fine Art of Floating Horses" in *An Outburst of Frankness* (Dublin: Tasc at New Island, 2004).

Sherry Turkle, *Life on the Screen* (New York: Phoenix, 1995).

Raymond Williams, *Culture and Society 1780–1950* (New York: Columbia University Press, 1958).

Catherine Wilson, "Community Engagement" in *Collections* (Newcastle upon Tyne: a-n The Artists Information Company, 2008).

Donald Woods Winnicott, *Playing and Reality* (Harmondsworth: Pelican, 1974).

7 Themes and Issues

Many skills and strategies are required by artists wishing to engage with the wider world beyond those of art production. Interpersonal skills and methods are needed to interface with the public, to share knowledge, experience and to find the tools that will enable this to happen effectively. The way one structures and finances one's practice also has a bearing on what is achieved, including consideration of how and where the work is situated. In this chapter I will be unpicking some of these processes to understand more about what enables art to function in a social context. First to look at are concepts of "collaboration" and "participation", terms that are sometimes used interchangeably. Drawing on examples from different projects, I will demonstrate how their distinct but sometimes overlapping approaches affect the nature of a project. Interdisciplinary working has underpinned much of my practice, whether through collaboration with activists, locals, children or professionals with differing expertise, and I will explore the importance of this, as well as how understanding one's own discipline can support the wider aim of working with others to make a difference.

What is the relationship of diversity and innovation? I will be excavating a number of past projects to address this question and to see how these concepts continue to inform current work. I shall also be reflecting on the intersection of these issues with those of ethnicity and migration and the changing social and intellectual climate within which projects engaging with these issues have been enacted. In relation to this I will then look at the shift from the activism of the seventies' and eighties' projects to a focus on identity, which underpinned most of my work of the nineties. This offered a new perspective from which to address change in the social environment, and was subsequently expanded through the linking of educational with cultural outcomes in the work with young people.

Technology has both facilitated and informed the practice through all its stages. Developments in digital imaging and the Internet have offered new means of combining collective input, while the far greater numbers of participants that it is now possible to involve has progressed and changed how the notion of "community" is understood. I will therefore consider the experience of individual participants in relation to the impact of technological innovation on the practice itself. Behind these shifts in the structure of the work changes in funding policies over several decades have influenced, supported or sometimes undermined my practice. A critical look is required at those ways in which current commission-dominated and target-driven funding aims to control artistic output, threatening to undermine both sustainability and new ways of working. I will make a case here for the support of initiatives that are not only "engaged" but "socially situated" and stem from an organic and developmental relationship with community.

New Labour's programme of regeneration for the UK under its 1997–2010 administration promoted a positive re-thinking of the property-focused urban development implemented by the Tories under Margaret Thatcher in the eighties. Along with the New Labour agenda of "social inclusion", concepts of education and culture were seen increasingly as key elements in the process of revitalising neighbourhoods. While acknowledging the commitment of some regeneration schemes to community involvement, I will take a critical look at this top-down support of culture[1], which has developed from that time and frequently led to artists becoming used as a cheap panacea for social ills within the imperative of government targets. At the same time I will outline some of the "small changes" where artists and others help to facilitate meaningful shifts in the social fabric at a local level alongside massive urban development programmes. Finally I will consider the issue of social change itself, what this has meant in practice over the years, and how the social effects of community based art practice, so challenging to quantify, might begin to be assessed.

Collaboration or Participation?

> I do not authentically think unless others think. I simply cannot think for others, or without others.
>
> Paulo Freire[2]

Collaboration has been for me both a personal preference and a means of social enactment. It is a process upon which Peter and I embarked, first in relation to each other, then with groups and individuals within the wider community. In *Conversations before the End of Time* Gablik discussed how one voice lacks dialectical resonance[3], and we certainly glimpsed the difference when, as artists, we could move our work from being a "drop in the ocean", our experience of *The Present Day Creates History*, to part of a groundswell through our subsequent involvement in the Bethnal Green Hospital Campaign. The video *Emergency* we produced for this campaign also offered up an early differentiation between participation and collaboration. I have described in Part 1 how the workshop approach to producing a video for use in the campaign threw up a number of contradictions. People involved in a learning experience, who may be handling media for the first time, cannot be expected to have expertise in skills that are new to them, whereas the context in which we found ourselves working required a swiftly produced and effective campaigning tool. Through this experience we discovered the benefits of a collaborative over a participatory approach, borne out through the subsequent production of an exhibition and posters developed in consultation with the campaign committee. This process became honed and refined through the East London Health Project and Docklands Community Poster Project, and it was not until the work with schools in the early nineties that I revisited participation as a potentially positive working process.

What, then, is the difference between collaboration and participation? Artist Françoise Dupré has acknowledged the complex set of overlapping relationships involved in each, while proposing collaboration as the equal involvement of individuals in a project's content, concept and ownership, who share the logistical conceptual and creative decisions. She sees participation as not requiring such a demand from those involved, leaving responsibility for the project with the lead artist[4].

Several different levels of collaboration run through my practice. One is the equality of involvement described by Dupré, experienced in work with other artists and professionals such as the projects with Peter Dunn, Karen Merkel in *Between Family Lines*, and Anne Thorne Architects in *The Catch*. Another form of collaborative working is reflected in the sharing of expertise that ran through the East London Health and Docklands Community Poster Projects. These differed from the later work in that responsibility for production lay with ourselves as artists, while the equality was to be found in the relationship between the groups and individuals of the wider campaigning community. *West Meets East,* although essentially a participatory project, was not entirely distinct from this. The pupils who took part were also collaborators in a similar way to the Docklands campaigners who had brought their expertise to the table in the previous project. In this situation, although I led the project, they led the content and there was a sense that we were in this project together, combining our ideas and abilities to make a statement to the world. In an interview for Tom Finkelpearl's *What We Made*, Mierle Laderman Ukeles has described how, even though the artist might identify the first move, the creative answers reside elsewhere. She goes on to describe how there are nevertheless authoring or directing moves or judgements that she does not hesitate to make because she understands those to be part of her job as the artist[5].

I have continued to find it both useful and inevitable that different stakeholders in a project take differing roles. Kester usefully coined the phrase "co-participants" to describe the way that artists might work with others towards transformation of both self and society[6]. This process goes further than making connections, but is rather one of building bridges that allow each party to contribute from where they are and with what they do best. Commencing with *West Meets East*, this approach to working with participants in a collaborative way through a workshop environment has remained key to my practice, even with the young children involved in *VOLCO*.

Gablik has described dialogical work as a process of first creating solidarity among those with similar experience, then communicating this to a wider audience[7]. I had been able to understand this approach in the practice of others, such as the work that Carole Condé and Karl Beveridge carried out with the Canada's labour movement, but had not previously thought of applying it to my own work beyond the Docklands Community Poster Project. However I since came to realise that the boundaries encompassing "similar experience" can also be constructed. Therefore in a similar way becoming a "Volcan" brought a participant into the planetary community of *VOLCO*, enabling them to discover what they have in common.

Why are these processes important? Gablik has seen them as an attempt by artists to balance the global parts of a social system, helping it to process its edges and incongruities. In her view relationship is "the key insight of ecology" and acknowledged collaboration a means of social change[8]. For me it has been a means of linking into the "groundswell" of local activism. While individuals may sometimes play key roles, social change is necessarily the act of many. The individualism that has emerged in visual art in western society over the last few centuries has simply failed to encompass the tools and processes required for effective social intervention, since its economic role has been to create capital. Artistic methodologies for supporting social change have occurred in such disparate historical circumstances as the Russian Revolution, May '68 and Greenham Common. Excavation of whatever precedents exist would be useful at this moment of world upheaval to re-inform and re-invigorate current practice.

Interdisciplinarity

> Sometimes art's storytelling is profoundly revolutionary in its evocation and enactment of *something else*.
>
> Alana Jelinek[9]

My experience of events connected to Joseph Beuys' Free International University in the seventies offered an early introduction to the value of dialogue and collaboration across disciplines. Beuys saw this integration of diverse forms of research as transdisciplinary[10], with art as the primary medium. In the catalogue accompanying the exhibition *Art Into Society, Society Into Art* at the Institute of Contemporary Arts in London he stated,

> Only on condition of a radical widening of definitions will it be possible for art and activities related to art [to] provide evidence that art is now the only evolutionary-revolutionary power. Only art is capable of dismantling the repressive effects of a senile social system that continues to totter along the death-line: to dismantle in order to build 'A SOCIAL ORGANISM AS A WORK OF ART'[11].

My projects have certainly been influenced by this approach, particularly in relation to the transdisciplinary aim of involving active collaboration with community-based stakeholders and professionals in different fields. Unlike Beuys, however, I do not regard art as the only possibility for evolution, or the primary means of changing the world. Rather I see it as having the power to draw attention to social issues as a cultural, not a social tool. My experience of the transition from the artist-driven *Present Day Creates History* in the seventies to the subsequent work with activists on health and Docklands issues, through to my current work with seniors, social scientist, engineers and environmentalists on the *Active Energy* project, has confirmed for me that my most effective role is to work through cultural means alongside those skilled in other disciplines and/or with people who have different lived experience. In doing this it has felt important to remain within my own discipline, albeit augmenting my capabilities with some wider skills. I have described in Part 1 the enlightening experience of the East London Health Project, in which each member of the steering group contributed their specialist knowledge. In situations such as these it would have been completely inappropriate to assume as an artist superior knowledge of the issues to the health professionals leading the campaign.

Alana Jelinek has written helpfully on the disciplinarity of art practice, particularly distinguishing between art and activism[12]. In recent years many emerging artists who have effectively been left behind by a top-down economy have become keen to work in an activist way. I know from my teaching[13] how confused students can be when they start to collaborate with an external organisation or group, and can easily become unsure of their role. Yet if art has the power that I believe it has, it is the more important to enter these situations as an artist and to put those skills together with a different range of experience without attempting to subsume one into the other.

Working across disciplines has its challenges, as touched on in the previous chapter. The process calls for openness and flexibility, while keeping a hold on one's own aims and values. It can also be disorientating to venture outside the familiarity of one's own area of expertise. There is little that can be taken for granted and it can even be undermining to discover that people from other walks of life have completely different ways of working and thinking, and not at all the same expectations. There is also a particular danger of losing one's footing in the bigger imperative of a scientific, technological or activist aim. Strategies learned throughout the course of the practice, and particularly in conflict resolution, have nevertheless offered awareness of how important it is to be clear from the outset about one's overall objectives. They have also demonstrated the importance of talking through early on in the process what each party wishes to gain from it, drawing out if possible any additional unstated aims, and then to build the project around these. Given this, it is probably no coincidence that I have found the projects with the leeway to develop organically to be the most successful, although if money is involved, it is also important to ensure letters of contract are in place before the project begins. There is therefore a creative balance to be drawn between openness and closure as the project develops.

The issues described above may make the process of working across disciplines seem overly problematic; however, the benefits cannot be understated since working with others in this way not only opens up possibilities but can also be enormously inspiring. I did not enjoy science at school, but was very excited to have the opportunity to don a lab coat and explore microscopic river organisms for *Lambeth Floating Marsh*. At the same time I have become familiar with an underlying feeling of ignorance that I encounter in many situations, one that might begin to undermine one's confidence until the realisation dawns that it is not your role to have that knowledge—that you have in fact created this situation precisely because you do not have all the answers. It is also a privilege to be able to step into the domain of others and see the world anew through their eyes. All artists are familiar with the crucial role of "not knowing" in the creative act. Working across disciplines can take that to an extreme, but with equally far-reaching possibilities.

The Dynamics of Difference and Issues of Multiculturalism

> ... we are beginning to see constructions of just such a new conception of ethnicity: a new cultural politics which engages rather than suppresses difference.
>
> Stuart Hall[14]

Most of my work has been carried out among the diverse communities of East London where the ethnic mix is such that in some areas there is no majority ethnicity or culture. Issues of diversity have underpinned the work not only through the different experience contributed by collaborative partners and participants, but also through the perspectives that this has in turn brought to individual projects. My desire to work in this location has involved me in engagement with people from ethnicities, classes and cultures that are not my own, which has on occasion brought up the issue of the appropriateness of working as a white, middle class artist with people who have a different life experience. Touchstones I have used in negotiating if and where my work will be of value have been very much those of the processes and methodologies described in Chapter 6. In these projects an "invitation", whether direct or developmental, has triggered each intervention. Following this, the first stage of each project has been an act of "listening". This may have taken the form, as in *West Meets East*, of discussing with each participant their previous cultural production. In *Between Family Lines*, preliminary work had already been undertaken by Women Against Fundamentalism, and the next stage of our task was literally to hear each woman's story. Other projects not specifically addressing issues particular to minority cultures have equally presumed that each participant will have a very different tale to tell. This might be through the choices each made regarding their representation, as in *Awakenings* and *I.D*, the identities created by children for *VOLCO,* or personal depictions of what is to be valued in their neighbourhood, as in *The Young Person's Guides*.

In his article "Against Multiculturalism" for *New Humanist* in 2002, Kenan Malik described how diversity enables the expansion of horizons together with the comparisons and contrasts between values, beliefs and lifestyles, which lead to new perceptions and ideas[15]. This resonated profoundly with my creative experience during the nineties, and was further confirmed through the understandings I was developing through my voluntary work as a neighbourhood conciliator and mediator. Key issues relating to conflict resolution in this context included the way that conflict often arises from fear of difference—of "the other", that it generally occurs where personal or group identity feels vulnerable or threatened, and that characteristic of people in conflict is a difference between their stories of the same situation. It is when their stories converge that a transformation of the conflict itself can begin.

While creative collaboration between different parties with diverse skills and experiences certainly produces fertile ground for new ideas, that potentially positive scenario can be turned on its head where the differences play on vulnerable identities—particularly where power and status are involved. Fear of "the other" can then turn into prejudice or worse. If people are to work across difference, they therefore need to feel that their own identities, whether individual or group, are valued and free to be defined by themselves. I could see a role for a new cultural activism, articulated by Stuart Hall as the need to engage difference and involve the cultural construction of new ethnic identities[16]. Such activity would require the development of suitable contexts where diverse ideas could be brought together.

In *The End of Tolerance: Racism in 21st Century Britain* Arun Kundnani echoed Kenan Malik's concerns in identifying problems that came out of the shift in the political solidarities of race and class of the sixties and seventies towards the issues of cultural diversity that came to the fore in the Thatcher era[17]. Racial tension reached a height in the nineties when the British National Party tried to gain seats in council elections, with a recent resurgence following the 2016 Brexit referendum in the UK and Trump's victory in the US, both focusing on migration. In the intervening years, however, the fight against racism was transformed into battles over cultural issues, with the new "multiculturalism" not simply entrenching the divisions created by racism, but making cross-cultural interaction more difficult by encouraging people to assert their cultural differences. Kundnani's warning against attempts to institutionalise stereotyped utopias of cultural identity[18] had to some extent been embedded as an approach in *West Meets East,* which was built around participants' exploration of their own emerging identities. *Celebrating the Difference,* taking its name from a political campaign of that time, approached these issues in a similar way. While it resulted from a teacher's request for an anti-racist project, it seemed that this might only serve to retrench existing divisions in his culturally mixed classroom. In this situation it seemed more constructive for pupils to take a step towards valuing each other's differences. It remained important, however, as in *West Meets East,* that the representation of identities was not prescribed and only culturally based if that was the participant's choice. Pupils constructed collages using fragments of image and text, building up content pertaining to their lives and interests. These in turn became part of a larger picture, incorporating visual information from the wider group, so that the final image was able to reveal something of the complexity of the community it represented.

The Infinity Story some years later picked up on aspects of this approach, both expanding and turning it around, so that the children's different contributions became part of the overarching narrative, mirroring the position of each child in their wider community. The "multicultural" family that embodied *The Infinity Story*'s main characters described in Chapter 3 were not so much a representation of a "pluralistic nation" than the organic result of three hundred children from the same community telling their different stories from their own personal perspectives. This paralleled to some degree Stuart Hall's recognition that "we all speak from a particular place, out of a particular history, out of a particular experience, a particular culture, without being constrained by that position"[19].

The way that new and unexpected outcomes continually arose from the combined fragments of diverse experience in these projects led me to consider the "dynamic" created out of this approach, and to research opportunities for new contexts that would facilitate it. *VOLCO* was one of these with a framework that used the Internet to combine collective endeavour. While the first stage of activity involved a similar construction of identity as in the earlier projects, in the second stage the task of participants was to invent an aspect of life on the planet. Initial ideas had nevertheless to be first debated through the discussion forum with "Volcans" from other settlements and the children's archive entries only uploaded once they had been subjected to such dialogue, during which process their ideas were able to expand and develop. In *Art and Otherness* Thomas McEvilley stated that "by learning to appreciate the value stance of groups other than the one we were born into, we in effect expand our selfhood"[20]. In this way the children interacting with others from different backgrounds through *VOLCO* were able to move forward and expand their ideas. The Volcan "settlements" represented classes or groups of children, which could be located anywhere in the world. Links were made through the project and the children found themselves discussing their ideas with others who they knew only through their online personas. The template format through which their characters were created provided accessibility in the reading of each other's identities, and their differences became interesting characteristics within this. In constructing the project in this way, I took a calculated risk that children would have more in common in their imaginative lives than through their direct life experiences, which was indeed borne out in practice. In Chapter 4 I described the effects of participants "meeting" through video conferencing following participation in the project, having already exchanged communications with their online partners. Their excitement and interest in each other's different attributes and circumstances was generated through getting to know the real personalities behind the online identities with which the children already felt familiar.

In a review of *Between Family Lines* Clara Connolly noted how that project was able to go beyond the "cultural conflict" popularly portrayed in relation to minority ethnic families and was also interested in its foregrounding of "new political identities" in its critique of aspects of minority cultures and religions[21]. In their article on "Transversal Politics and Translating Practices" for *Soundings* in 1999 Cynthia Cockburn and Lynette Hunter voiced concerns regarding the process of denying difference in order to demonstrate community cohesion[22]. Their notion of "transversal politics", developed with Nira Yuval-Davis, was an attempt at conceptualising the democratic process of "talking across difference" and in a separate article for the same journal Yuval-Davis described this as both an alternative to the assimilationist "universal" politics of the Left, and to identity politics. Like Kundnani and Malik, she warned at that time against reifying boundaries between groups and homogenising and collapsing individual into collective identities. Yuval-Davis was herself involved in *Between Family Lines* as a member of Women Against Fundamentalism, a collaborating partner organisation. In this project, although the women portrayed were from different religious backgrounds, their experiences were represented from their own perspectives through words and images chosen by themselves. Yuval-Davis concluded her introduction of transversal politics with a call for more "thinking and doing", indicating a place where further cultural activity could indeed lead the way[23].

Activism into Identity

> the key political question of our day: how can we develop a coherent programmatic perspective . . . that integrates redistribution and recognition?
>
> Nancy Fraser and Axel Honneth[24]

Yuval-Davis warned against the divisiveness of "identity politics", emphasising that community activists should not see themselves as representative unless democratically elected or accountable. This effectively described the shift in the role of representative activists on the Docklands Community Poster Project steering group to the roles of participants in the later projects where issues of identity were addressed within a broader context of urban renewal. The politics of the eighties work was framed by "redistribution", the struggle for economic equality, echoing the values of the Labour movement allegiances held by the Docklands activists. It gave the campaigning its organisational base and the representational structure that enabled it to function so efficiently. The Docklands Community Poster Project would not have been able to come into existence without the ability to approach and question representative groups, and neither would it have had the support of a committee that spoke on behalf of the population of an extensive geographical area. There would have been nobody to "speak for" if committee members had only represented themselves. However, the concept of identity also underpinned the culture of many of these working class communities. Those who had not been born and bred within a very small geographic area were considered by many to be "outsiders". Although there was an openness to co-operation across class and culture, there could also be a narrowness of vision within them—consternation, for example, at the fact that an incoming Chair to the Association of Wapping organisations had not been born in Wapping, even though he had lived there most of his life.

The nature of the campaigning gradually changed, however, and alongside this the way that residents regarded themselves. In Chapter 2 I referred to a quotation that was included in the final image of the first sequence of photo-murals, which stated that Docklands is not about land, but people. It went on to claim that the "ownership" of the land goes beyond monetary value to constitute a birthright and heritage for its communities. This statement accompanied two shifts in the activism of that community. First was a recognition of community identity beyond the hitherto traditional neighbourhood boundaries and, second, a move away from oppositional campaigning to a more pro-active set of strategies. This latter approach, described at greater length later in this chapter, built its strength on the creation of alternatives, as in the case of the *People's Plan for the Royal Docks,* which, abandoning oppositional tactics, re-framed the issue from a position of greater experience and in-depth research into the needs of the area. This positing of alternative meanings opened up the potential for the cultural strategies that came to be further developed through The Art of Change and cSPACE. From *West Meets East* to the *Young Person's Guides,* project outcomes emerged increasingly from totalities of collective experience built up from fragments of knowledge that could only be accessed individually, and in so doing the notion of representing communities became replaced by the authenticity of personal experience. In *West Meets East,* for example, as in subsequent projects, it was important that the girls whose families came from Bangladesh did not see themselves as representatives of the culture of that region. In this way the work managed to sidestep the cultural stereotyping of identity politics and engage in a process described by Clara Connolly whereby culture becomes a dynamic practice that "women can help to re-define and re-create"[25]. By translating individual and anecdotal evidence into collective expression in the public domain the young people gained historical validation for their experience.

The concept of identity continued to be a central element of the practice into the new millennium. The Art of Change in fact described its aim as that of addressing the "transformation of the urban environment and its impact upon quality of life and cultural identity"[26]. Meanwhile more recent projects have re-worked the photo-mural statement of the relationship of people to their land. Rather than deriving identity from a sense of place, *VOLCO* created its own, while *The Young Person's Guides* re-framed localities from the perspective of individual and group experience.

Where Education Meets Production

> . . . the revolutionary process is eminently educational in character.
>
> Paulo Freire[27]

There is much in common between the processes involved in initiating projects such as those described in Part 1 and the pedagogical work by Freire, which he recognised as in keeping with the revolutionary process. His educational practice was likened by Tom Finkelpearl to what he described as "problem posing art", since it involved researching the area, setting up meetings, asking "permission" of participants to run the project and eliciting their views on its content[28]. In her article for the *Art for Change* catalogue (2005), however, Carmen Mörsch lamented the way that the work of artist educators in Germany was socially devalued[29]. She acknowledged that this state of affairs was not unknown in the UK, but perhaps underestimated the attempts by Bernard Levin[30], Peter Suchin[31] and others to denigrate artists working in the social sphere as glorified teachers. From the seventies onwards it had certainly felt important to keep one foot firmly in the public arena of the art world in order to enable work without a gallery showcase to remain within public thinking and to stave off the ever present threat of marginalisation[32]. The precariousness of this position has since been partially alleviated by the work of Gablik and Kester, who have striven to situate dialogic and socially engaged practice within their own traditions and history, a critique that has provided much needed nourishment for this field of work. However self-contained and successful in its own terms socially situated practice might be today, critical textual frameworks are nevertheless required if it is to be positioned within a body of thought that is new to the wider domain of visual art. For, indeed, the work described here is art and even though, unlike most products of recent history, it is both interdisciplinary and collaborative, it has its roots in the same cultural soil as the most esoteric products celebrated by our major art institutions. The difference is that, through its processes of engagement, it is able to operate in a range of different contexts, while in common with any cultural activity and perhaps more so, it has a great deal to offer educationally. Furthermore, artists involved in this type of practice often engage actively with the educational potential of their work, rather than keeping separate the activities of education and production.

While the disciplines of art and education have different core values and intentions, their realisation can indeed overlap. I conduct my practice as an artist and not a teacher, but the educational process nevertheless remains relevant in terms of the Latin root of "educate", which means "to draw out", and precisely describes the process of enabling participants to express their ideas, identities, imaginative constructs and aspirations. Learning experiences are also created through collaboration with project partners and participants who contribute their expertise and abilities to a common purpose. This transfer of knowledge features in projects such as *VOLCO* with its training for teachers, instruction in digital photography in the *Young Person's Guides,* and the upskilling of the Geezers in computer technologies and engineering design for *Active Energy,* although equally travels in the other direction. However, important though these aspects may be, they are not the main purpose of the projects. Perhaps it is this certainty that the core of the work is cultural rather than educational that has enabled me to engage wholeheartedly with educational institutions and structures and deliver these projects without experiencing a compromise. In this respect an interface between *VOLCO* and the UK National Curriculum did not put the project in danger of becoming "education" rather than "art", but rather allowed it to reach children in large numbers. The fact that teachers, participants and institutional partners gained specific benefits for their own situation, meant that they lent their energy to it, which greatly enhanced its outcomes. The teacher training element of *VOLCO* enabled the project to be run without my direct involvement, allowing for many more participants than I could possibly have reached on my own. I delighted in the enjoyment experienced by the children taking part and the extraordinary ideas they came up with, while taking satisfaction from the fact that, through its connection to the curriculum, the project was able to replace other lessons that may have been somewhat less exciting[33]. Most of all, however, I gained creative fulfilment from watching *VOLCO* grow as an entity in surprising ways. Akin to one of Conway's "emergent objects" that I had read about in Sherry Turkle's *Life on the Screen*, *VOLCO* evolved as a largely self-governing community, members of which I had increasingly never met.

The one exception to this approach was *Cascade*, which began as an attempt to bridge my artistic and teaching work while bringing effective professional practice and community involvement into higher education. Witnessing the extent to which participants from different levels of education were able to enhance learning experiences for each other, I took the step of expanding the institutional collaborations involved. These were centred around a series of projects relating to different aspects of East London regeneration, with students and young people involved in a mentoring programme developed as part of the *Cascade* process. Some years it was possible to achieve one-to-one mentoring between students in higher and further education, who would then jointly facilitate classroom workshops, overseen, trained and briefed by freelance artists. At other times graduates and undergraduates would work with small groups of students in further education as informal tutors and demonstrate through their own practices how they had come to develop their skills and interests through educational progression. Descriptions of the often unconventional route each had taken on their individual journey towards higher education, together with campus tours of the university, frequently proved inspirational for the younger participants. All this interaction worked very well, and it was only the facilitation of so many institutional collaborations at one time that caused *Cascade* to eventually become overly draining on cSPACE's small resources.

I have already indicated how, in the earlier *Cascade* projects, I was aware that something was missing. On re-reading extracts from my interview with Carmen Mörsch[34], I note how my comments of that time indicated how well the participation processes had developed, with the satisfaction of seeing the participants of different ages creating with and learning from each other. However, I also noted that all this could be further enhanced with a more satisfactory final output. A few years on, this intention came to fruition with *The Young Person's Guide to the Royal Docks* web site and the later version for East London, which helped to create much-needed focus. *Cascade* was also a way of developing legacy for my own practice, which allowed me to pass on the learning I had gained, aspects of which I have since incorporated into my university teaching.

Technology as Facilitator and Transformer of Social Engagement

> Because culture is mediated and enacted through communication, cultures themselves—that is, our historically produced systems of beliefs and codes—become fundamentally transformed, and will be more so over time, by the new technological system . . . its global reach, its integration of all communication media, and its potential interactivity is changing and will change forever our culture.
>
> Manuel Castells[35]

The *Interrupt* series of symposia[36] organised by the Arts Council of England in 2003 included the topic "Artist as Engineer". This took as its starting point the concept expounded by Walter Benjamin in his 1934 article "The Author as Producer" for *New Left Review* of the transformation that can ensue when creative practitioners not only use available technology, but adapt it to the aims of social change[37]. While the symposium itself focused on developments in digital technologies, the more general link it made between socially engaged practice and innovative use of technology was entirely appropriate. Benjamin's interest had indeed been in how such "apparatus of production" could be adapted to meet the aims of revolution.

Seeking tools to use in campaigning materials in the seventies, Peter and I turned to several historical precedents including the cultural outputs of various revolutionary movements. While the work of John Heartfield offered a particular use of photographic montage, it was rooted in a journalistic/literary tradition that was not our own. The imagery of Constructivism and Suprematism, reflecting an era of social, political and technological change, felt more akin to the visual dynamics we were seeking.

Montage has frequently been used for revolutionary ends. In describing Brecht's "epic theatre", Benjamin referred to the disruptive function of montage: "the element which is superimposed breaks into the situation on which it is imposed"[38]. The technique of photographic montage provided us with many opportunities for disruption as well as the construction of new narratives that drew on our documentation of campaigns and related events. It also suited our low-budget darkrooms of the seventies and early eighties, established in the converted cellars of short-life houses. In the East London Health Project video, tape/slide and fly-posters were all considered before a form of poster was agreed upon that comprised a combination of montaged image and text for display in doctors' surgeries and waiting areas.

The photo-murals of the eighties were produced prior to the widespread availability of the personal computer. At that time full colour imagery could only be achieved on a large scale through a three-colour lithographic printing process, as used in the production of advertising billboard posters, and would have necessitated large print runs rather than the one-off imagery required. We came up with our own solution in the form of hand-montaged A1 artwork created with black and white photographs, which we sent to a lab for re-photographing into eighteen large-format negatives. The final 18' × 12' (5.5m × 3.6m) images were reproduced in 3' × 4' (0.9m × 1.2m) sections that were in turn pasted onto panels of marine plywood, their dimensions in part determined by the size and weight of backing boards that could be carried up ladders on site. The black and white enlargements were hand coloured, and coated with yacht varnish before being individually screwed to the photo-mural backing boards. Each of these processes went through many stages of trial and error before problems of warping, colour fading and varnish discolouration were solved.

While photographic imagery was able to address audiences on the street in a way that could not be done in film at that time, my undergraduate experience of filmmaking nevertheless fed into the narratives that played out in the photo-murals like slow-motion animated sequences. Peter meanwhile was largely responsible for developing the photo-mural production process, realising their construction, and hand colouring the large-scale images once pasted onto the panels for installation.

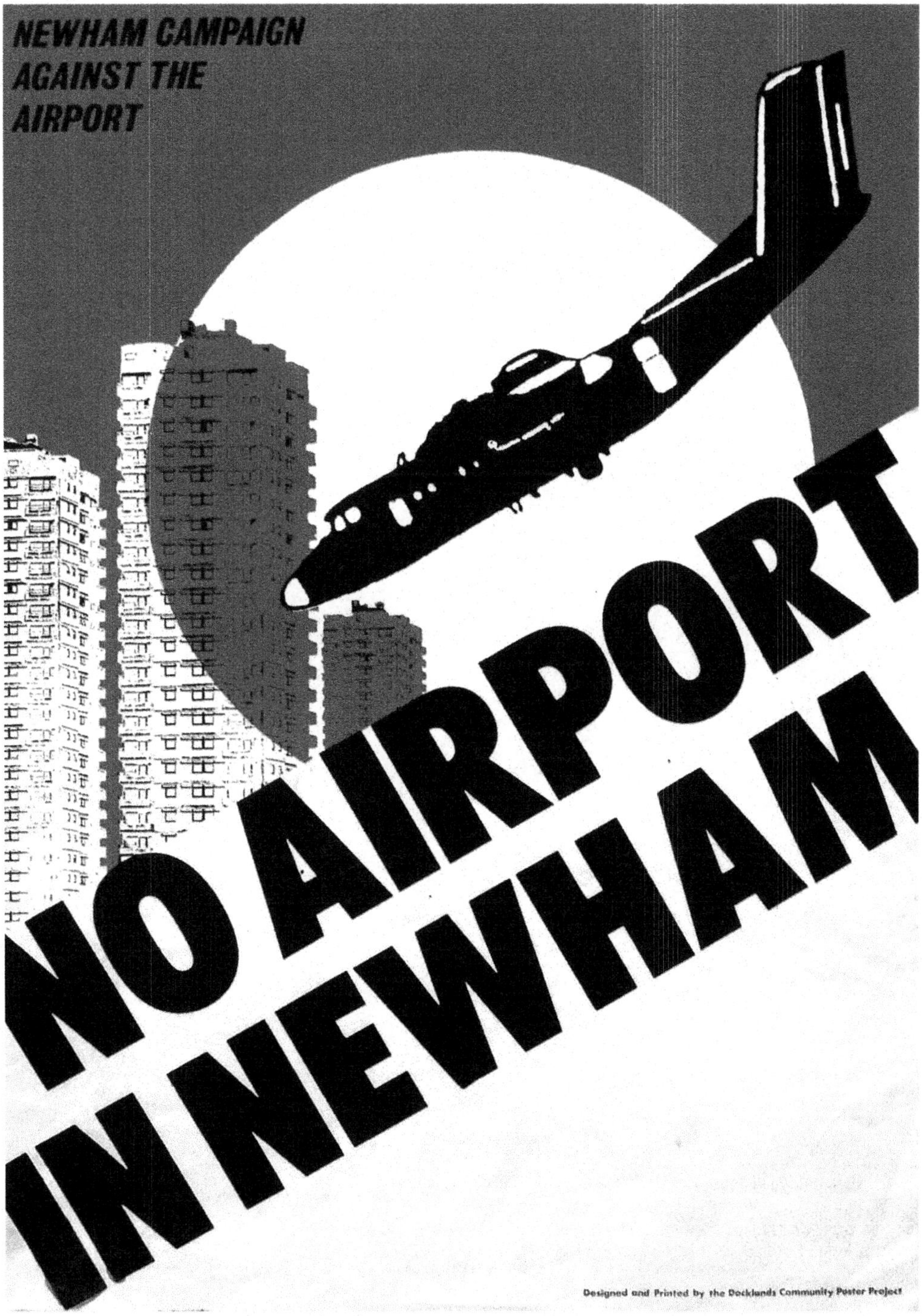

Figure 7.1 No Airport in Newham

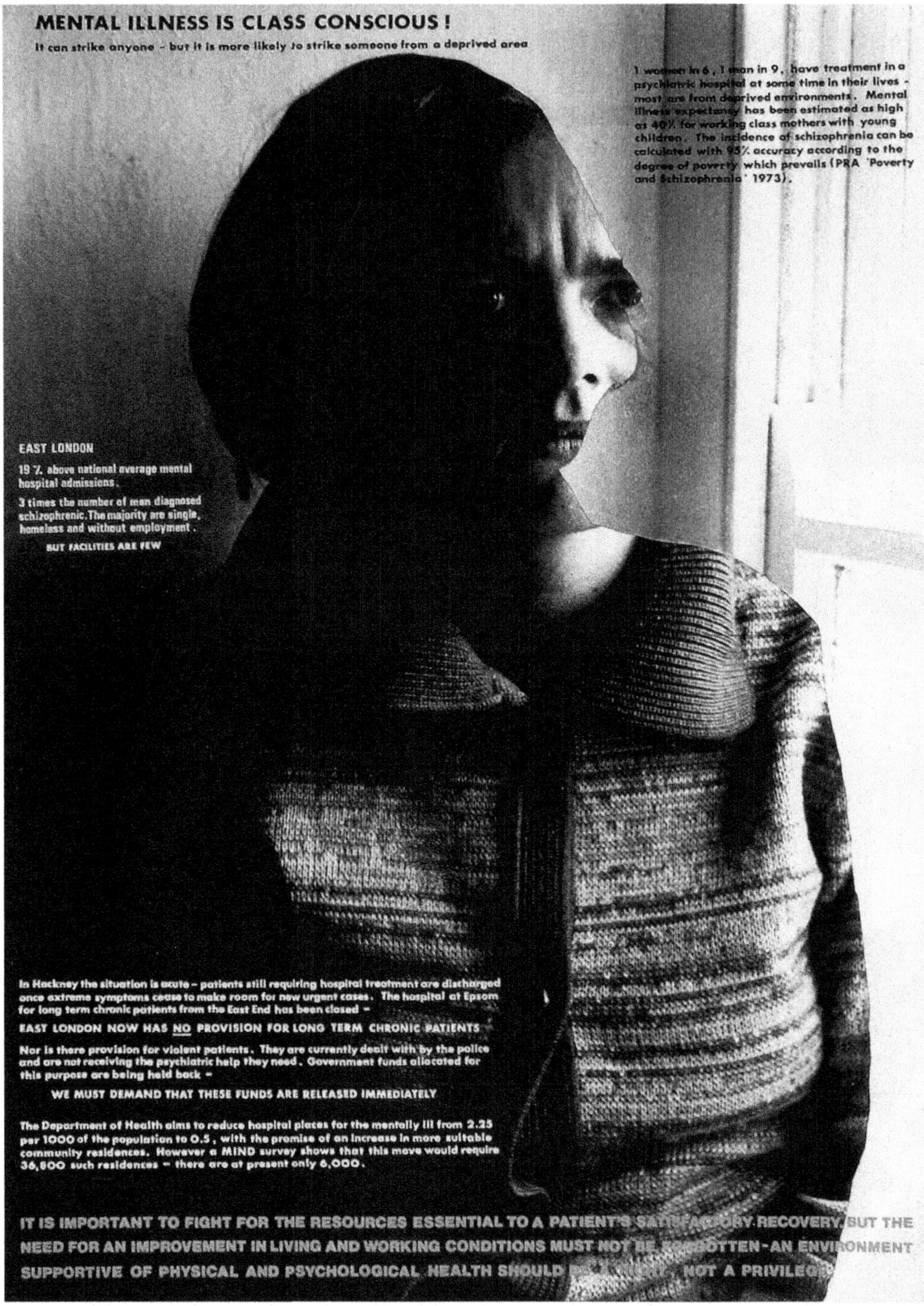

Figure 7.2 Mental Illness is Class Conscious

Each photo-mural was produced as a set of eighteen panels to facilitate assembly on site, and this gave rise to the opportunity for changing each image gradually over time. Initially this was done relatively systematically. In the first sequence of photo-murals for example, replacement of some of the *What's Going on Behind Our Backs* panels, with others from *Big Money is Moving In* gave the impression that some of the corrugated iron had been taken down to reveal what lay behind it. We soon grew more adventurous and *Shattering the Developers' Illusions* was actually montaged on site. First a new caption was screwed over that of the previous photo-mural, then its four central panels replaced with others suggestive of the next image breaking through. At artwork stage I had photographed parts of the removed segments behind pieces of broken glass. Enlargements of these were then sandwiched between clear acrylic sheets to give a glass-like effect and situated in shallow relief over parts of the previous photo-mural to represent its shattered fragments (see Figure 7.3). In the Housing Sequence the earlier images combined photographic montage and drawing to bring together documented and undocumented historical activity into one picture. Diagonal segments were then used as devices through which layers of meaning could be revealed.

Our montage techniques gradually became more sophisticated into the nineties and drew on technological innovations. *Digital Highways, Local Narratives* used *Digital Darkroom,* one of the earliest digital imaging tools, while the many-layered *Awakenings* in the mid-nineties stretched the first version of *Photoshop* to its limits. This latter project identified for us an increasing role that new technologies might begin to play in all aspects of the production process itself, allowing for the creation of visual elements at a scale and with materials suitable to their context of origin. In *Awakenings,* for example, this meant that small clay models could be constructed in the classroom, and then combined with photography and fabric printing through digital imaging. This considerably expanded the scope of both process and product in a way that would thereafter influence all our work of this nature.

In subsequent years, the Internet increasingly became the site for the public output itself. *I.D*, completed in 1999 and *Momentos* later that same year, were initiated as commissions for website projects by institutions looking for outcomes akin to our previous work. However the briefs were limited in scope and I was keen to experiment with the Internet's potential for collective creativity and discover if it could successfully support the involvement of much larger numbers of participants. This led to development of *The Infinity Story* with artist Camille Dorney. Unlike the more straightforward web commissions, we could barely obtain funding for this, and yet it opened up more innovative possibilities than all the previous web based work and laid the foundations for the more extensive creative interactions of *VOLCO*.

In 1995 Sherry Turkle had discussed the opportunities of digital technologies for creating simulations in which she described the computer as still a tool but less like a hammer and more like a harpsichord[39]. This echoed Jean Baudrillard's concept of "simulacra" published in his 'Simulacra and Simulations' of 1983, but which I did not read until after the initial development of *VOLCO*, at which point I realised that this project was indeed "proving the real by the imaginary"[40]. Inspiration for *VOLCO* as a simulated environment had in fact mainly come from the chat rooms and multi user domains of the late nineties where young people were using virtual spaces for exploration of identity and online interaction. I was struck by Turkle's descriptions of people who conducted most of their social life in these virtual realms and felt it

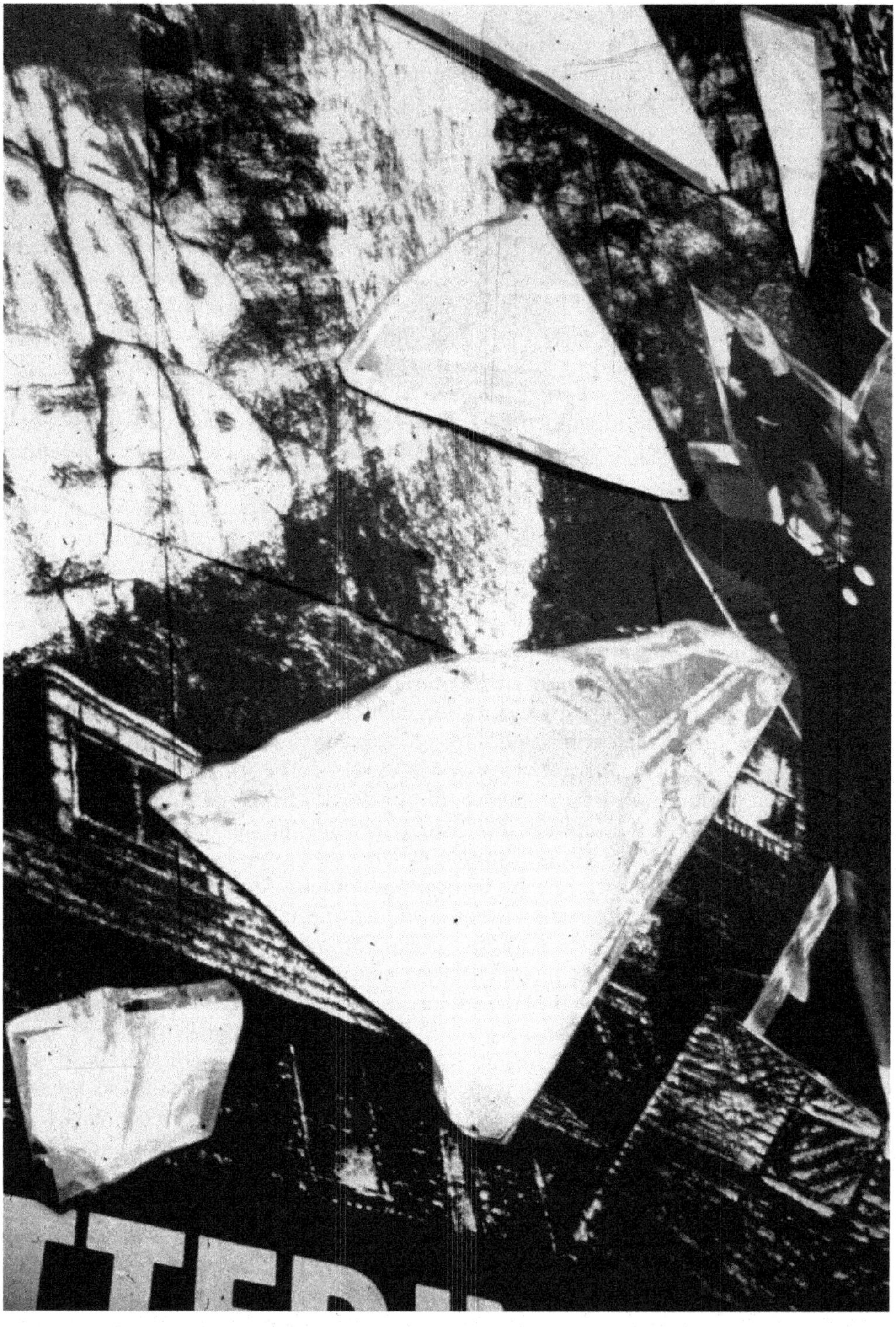

Figure 7.3 Detail from Shattering the Developers' Illusions

© Peter Dunn and Loraine Leeson, Docklands Community Poster Project, 1982–85.

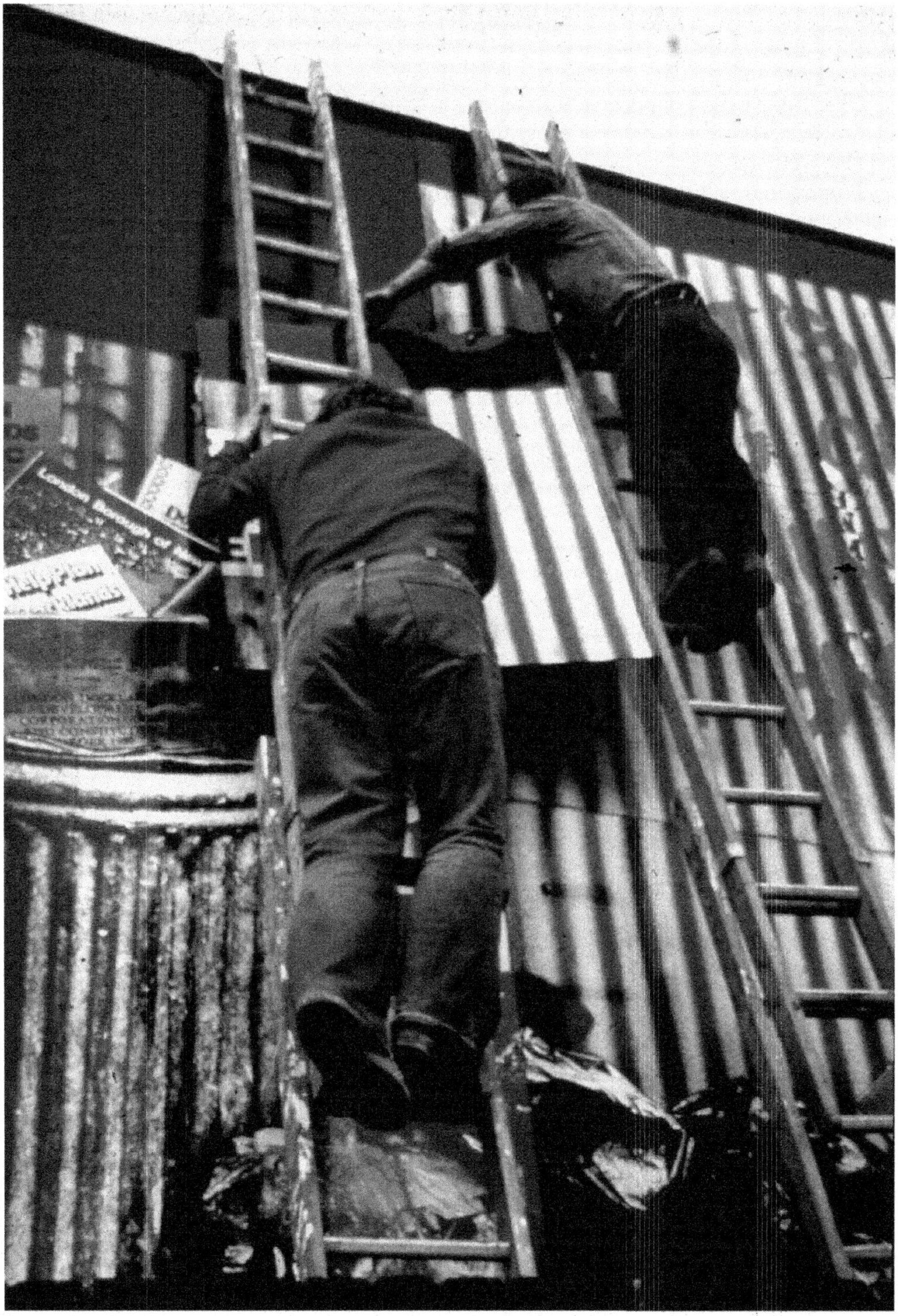

Figure 7.4 Photo-mural under construction

Photo © Peter Dunn and Loraine Leeson, Docklands Community Poster Project, 1981.

important to find a way of using *VOLCO* to facilitate social engagement in the real world. I had wanted particularly to address Turkle's proposition of a situation where the real and the virtual could be made permeable and enrich and expand the other[41].

Over a thousand children contributed their ideas to *VOLCO*, for which designer Henry Iles and three different programmers provided background support, working on the web site over ten years to develop an interface that was both child friendly and functional. While participants learned how to format their own images, a failsafe device framed and sized them to the correct dimensions in a way that was still not commonplace, so that justice could always done to the children's ideas, even where insufficient image processing has been undertaken. We also discovered how important it was for the young participants to gain immediate visual feedback once images were uploaded, even though they were not accessible online until they had been moderated. Programming had to be developed to do this and also ensure that the web site was secure with a tiered system of moderation that would allow teachers to check the work of their own classes without access to others. While the project ran it remained under constant development, with new indications of how it could be improved coming to light each time it was implemented with another group of children. All this knowledge not only improved its functionality, but also fed into new projects such as *The Young Person's Guide to East London.*

I had been interested to know if the far greater numbers of participants facilitated by the technology would affect the nature and depth of participants' engagement as cautioned by Dupré[42], and what difference this might make to the project's social outcome. While there was no doubt that the actual activities of each child or class contributing to *VOLCO* were important, the way the children talked about the project indicated that something more had been achieved. Its success or failure in their eyes appeared to be not only connected to individual experience, but also with the perception of the whole that each gained through their engagement. The more that participants experienced the project's outcome as feeding through into the wider world, the greater it seemed was the recognition of their own importance within that process.

From Co-op to Charity: Working from an Organisational Base

> A "laissez faire" group is about as realistic as a "laissez faire" society; the idea becomes a smokescreen for the strong or the lucky to establish unquestioned hegemony over others.
>
> Jo Freeman[43]

Visual artists still work for the most part as individuals, and this is the way that most Fine Art students are taught in higher education. Despite many attempts over recent decades to re-think this nineteenth-century model of training for genius in our art academies, student practices are still often defined by the medium in which they work and adherence to autonomous production as the norm continues to dominate the art institutions. Yet this method of working has not always been, and is not everywhere, the case. The production of cultural artefacts and use of art to represent and communicate social and spiritual meaning has accompanied the development of the human race since pre-history. The notion of visual art as a product created by an individual has followed the development of capitalism and growth of market economies and cannot be seen as only reflecting the requirements of the creative process. In performing arts, music, film and other cultural fields, teamwork is the norm, however, and although financially successful visual artists employ assistants, these are normally not acknowledged. Renaissance artists worked through studios where teams of artists and apprentices would collaboratively produce large murals or sculptural work, developing their skills and gaining increasing autonomy. The *Cascade* approach is certainly not new.

When the Tower Hamlets Trades Council set up a steering group for the East London Health Project, they were following a process of organisation familiar to them through the trades union movement and voluntary sector. It was an arrangement that respected expertise, ensured accountability, and offered a forum for the brainstorming of ideas. In founding The Docklands Community Poster Project in the early eighties, Peter and I sought a similar structure. This initially functioned well; however, as the organisation expanded, it required a formal constitution to enable it to fundraise, employ staff, apply for planning permissions for the photo-murals, and put in place policies and safeguards to cover its work. The newly appointed administrator[44] researched organisational structures that would reflect the way that the steering group functioned, and the group constituted itself as a Community Co-op. Its decision-making committee was made up of both community representatives and staff, with community members always in the majority. This ensured a sense of ownership on behalf of the community, and for us as artists, freedom of expression underpinned by accessible information and accountability. Roles were demarcated so that each member of the group represented an area of expertise, whether geographical or skills based, while our constitution enabled the organisation to raise the funding required to support large-scale work. The formal involvement of representatives from the Docklands communities also served to support the organisation in relation to setbacks such as the demolition of the Wapping photo-mural, as previously described. Co-op members responded to the attack on "their" mouthpiece with outrage and were instrumental in getting it re-instated.

If there was a problem with the co-operative model, it lay in the "flat" staff structure, where all had an equal vote in the decision-making process, irrespective of experience, responsibility or length of commitment to the organisation. During this time I undertook the training in conflict resolution to which I have already referred, and worked in my spare time as a volunteer neighbourhood conciliator and later as a mediator. Driven by both interest and need I progressed to participating in training for organisations experiencing conflict. The opportunity to work alongside experienced professionals offered many lessons. Co-operative and collective structures, so common in the seventies and eighties when people were experimenting with forms of organisation to support equality, were particularly at risk. Leaderless and structureless groups were popular in the early women's liberation movement as a reaction to the over-structured patriarchal social order of the time. However, these loose groups brought their own lessons, incisively described in Jo Freeman's article *The Tyranny of Structurelessness*[45]. Serving on the board of other organisations with collective staff frameworks, I had witnessed some of the destructiveness that could ensue from the exercising of personal power when insufficient boundaries were in place. It was a useful lesson that authority need not be conflated with power and that clear structures and designation of responsibility could avoid the inappropriate wielding of personal agendas.

When the Docklands Community Poster Project transformed itself into The Art of Change in the early nineties, a decision was taken not to change its structure. With a new programme of work that would include disparate projects and commissions underpinned by income generation, the community representatives now found themselves under pressure to act more like a management committee than a steering group. This was an entirely different task to that of contributing information from their local areas to a campaigning programme of action and, while broad goals were shared, the co-operative no longer had the specificity of the Docklands redevelopment on which to focus. The new programme of work was not of itself problematic, but did not fit the old structure and there was confusion among some community representatives as to their new role. Although all remained staunchly supportive, the skills needed on the new committee were more those of arts professionals than community activists. As a result, those with an arts background or professional experience bore the greater burden of management, which they carried out with great skill and commitment. However, there always seemed to be some confusion at its centre.

On establishing cSPACE I therefore strove for a simple structure appropriate to its small size and dependence on project-generated income. It was established as a "not-for-profit company limited by guarantee" and registered as a charity to maximise income generation opportunities. Its trustees have all been colleagues who have given of their time and expertise out of personal commitment to the practice, ensuring that the organisation has conducted itself correctly, while I have developed and delivered the programme with as many freelancers as could be afforded. Demarcation of responsibilities has always been clear—the board were in charge of the organisation and I was responsible for everything else, apart from company finances, which were managed by a skilled accountant, who has helped us considerably in steering through difficult times. I brief and de-brief freelance artists and administrative staff, who have received contracts, job descriptions and supervision or appraisal as appropriate. cSPACE is a hierarchical structure and could not be further from the collectives of the seventies, yet the remit of its work remains in line with that of earlier decades. For me it has evolved as the most efficient means of creating a platform from which that work can be delivered.

It may be asked, since the organisation is so small, what has been the point of all the paperwork, policies, audit and the rest? Why not simply function as an individual artist? It is because, although finances may be trim, the ideas are still expansive. Operating through an organisation makes it possible to work far more strategically and at much greater scale than could be achieved on my own. cSPACE has been able to apply for sizeable grants, collaborate with institutions and invite other artists and professionals to input to projects. Although at times the administration has felt onerous, the organisational approach still seems to offer greater opportunities for navigating a path towards changing the world–a desire that has not altered since those earlier decades, despite modifications to the platform of delivery.

I no longer only work through cSPACE, however. While the charity provides the most effective and efficient means for fundraising and managing smaller projects, my main base for several years has been in higher education[46]. The university environment offers opportunities for legacy through teaching and course development, as well as greater personal security and access to research funding, which renders the cSPACE financial goal less onerous. It also provides networking initiatives such as the virtual symposia on Art and Social Practice[47], opportunities for larger projects and pathways to interdisciplinary resources and collaboration. It has been advantageous for the organisational progression to be this way round. Although working through independent companies has been financially precarious, they have offered the flexibility needed to develop the practice while keeping the main focus on project work, which may have been lost with an earlier career in academia. It would have been difficult, however, to continue working only through cSPACE in the current financial climate, as I shall indicate in the next chapter.

Funding

> Consistency, it will be shown, is the "hobgoblin" of simple minds rather than a measure of professional competency. There are few sacred prototypes to follow, no best practices for export, no brand names that guarantee quality.
>
> Nabeel Hamdi[48]

While acknowledging the somewhat enviable position that the UK is seen to hold in terms of both its public funding and plethora of grant giving trusts and foundations, there have been significant shifts in UK funding and policy over the last four decades that have impacted on the way that practice in this field has been conducted.

Since the eighties my work has largely functioned through the support of public finance, whether designated for the arts or to facilitate other social outputs. This has not necessarily meant the luxury of regular revenue income, which was only substantially forthcoming during the earlier years, but rather resources raised through a patchwork of funding applications, bids and the occasional commission, with personal finances augmented by hourly paid university teaching. "Sustainability" in the arts has long been the goal of many who would seek to reduce, or perhaps accept as inevitable, reductions in public subsidy. Others have perceived it as an ideal, achievable through business training for artists. Having run an organisation without core funding since the withdrawal of regional arts board support at the end of the nineties, I am aware of the unlikelihood of being able to achieve this on project funding alone without an additional form of income. With process-based work there are no commodities to sell. Commissions, even where desirable, offer insufficient remuneration to those who are not stars of the gallery system, and art, particularly when involving long term relationships with communities, takes time. Its (initially free) university base and use of freelancers for additional expertise basis enabled cSPACE to function on project income alone for a number of years until the economic recession of 2007–08 took effect. Thereafter survival became increasingly challenging as larger organisations began to compete for even the very small grants that could previously have been relied upon. For myself, becoming an academic in my later years eventually solved the issue of personal finances, with funding then only required for the project expenditure. This is not a particularly useful model for upcoming generations, however, with university employment harder to come by and increasingly demanding in terms of workload.

UK public funding for visual artists is based on an assumption that most artists are individuals who survive through a mixture of selling work, commissions, some teaching or workshop activity, and supporting themselves through other means. Visual arts groups can apply to the Arts Council of England for project funds, but not revenue, and a diminishing number of organisations receive regular revenue funds as public finance becomes squeezed. There are other ways to manage the distribution of funds, however, and my own practice has indeed benefited from different modes of financial support. I should emphasise here that I am speaking from a practitioner's perspective, which is heard much less than the voices of ministers and policy makers. In so doing I am therefore not taking on board the struggles of those who do their best as arts administrators and managers to offer support to artists from a shrinking budget with governing structures and policies that are not their own.

In the seventies and eighties the Arts Council of Great Britain and regional arts associations were the first stop for much community-based work, and at that time both involved artists on their assessment panels. In the early eighties the Docklands Community Poster Project received its first funding from the Greater London Arts Association in the form of a six-month part-time artist residency that Peter and I shared. This was not a commission, but rather resulted from a meeting with an officer to propose our plans—an approach that could not happen now. However, without that flexibility we would have been unable to start the project. Later a more bureaucratic process of application was introduced, which became increasingly didactic, although the regional arts boards of the eighties and nineties varied considerably in their approaches.

Local borough councils also funded the arts. Some took this very seriously, as in the case of Tower Hamlets Arts Committee[49], which contributed to a thriving hub of arts activity in that borough and granted funds to cover the materials needed for the first phase of the Docklands project. Neither of these sources, however, compared with the impact on the arts made by the Greater London Council (GLC) in the eighties. In 1981, two years after the Thatcher government came into power, the political control of London turned Labour with the left wing of that party winning through, resulting in the implementation of socialist policies aimed at making the capital work for its people. The arts were not left out of this, although regulations meant that only organisations and not individuals could be funded. The GLC Community Arts Sub Committee, with an annually increasing budget that started at £1m, involved a panel of volunteer representatives[50] from across the art forms, who visited applicants and vigorously debated the shortlist. During this time there was a burgeoning of collective activity as the capital came alive with festivals, events and other forms of community-based production. The Docklands Community Poster Project achieved ninety per cent of its funding for the next five years from this source, with the rest provided by local councils. This enabled the organisation to develop a long-term programme and to build sustainable relationships with the communities it was serving. Following the disbanding of the GLC in the mid-eighties a transitional fund maintained our work until the end of the decade; then, from the turn of the nineties and the transition of the Docklands project into The Art of Change, partial support was maintained through GLC legacy funds administered by the London Arts Board, with the rest fundraised from different sources. At the end of the nineties, however, the London Arts Board cut "public art" production, having re-categorised our work in this way, in favour of support for agencies. This total loss of revenue funding required significant change.

During the nineties and up until that point we had been able to make some use of the "public art" label, since a proportion of the profits from the newly implemented National Lottery were directed into the arts. This was mainly channelled through public art commissions. However, after objections were raised about artworks commissioned through this scheme that were disliked by local people, priority was given to works that involved community engagement, a move that suited us very well for a time.

This source of National Lottery funding, particularly through its other priorities that have included community, heritage and creative work related to the London Olympics, has continued as the mainstay of the practice to this day. Nevertheless only rarely in the last twenty years have I applied for money to do art, asking rather for funds to support communities through project work—the term "art" has often been irrelevant and even an impediment to those proposals. This is also the case when applying to trusts and foundations, which have regularly provided much needed additional resources—another good reason for being constituted as a charity is that these forms of funding are generally not applicable for individuals. Regeneration of the inner cities also offered funding opportunities during this period, when government schemes called on the arts to help in the process of "building community", a rather dubious aim that I shall explore in the next section.

* * *

Since the nineties public support for the arts, in keeping with the public sector as a whole, became increasingly more directive, making it harder for individual artists as well as arts organisations to find financial support for proposals developed organically through dialogue or long-term collaboration with communities. Much public funding and commissioning of the arts has used the kind of "good practice" approach espoused by the 2001 Matarasso report to which I referred in Chapter 6, and this distilling and re-application of artistic and social value, denigrated by Nabeel Hamdi as simplistic and inappropriate, may be seen at work in a number of public agencies. An initiative that exemplified this was Creative Partnerships, "the Government's flagship creative learning programme" [51], which for several years subsumed the Arts Council of England's arts and education funding. It enabled schools to take the lead and choose the artist or arts organisation with which they wished to work. While this model functioned well in some regions, in the capital the temptation for schools to choose the "centres of excellence" to work with was too great and many smaller organisations lost access to funding for educational projects. Other limitations imposed included a division of labour between designated "creative agents" and "creative producers", with no overlap permitted. The role of "creative producers" was to simply deliver the work that had been negotiated between the "creative agent" and the school. Much resource was also diverted into promotion and frequent project evaluation. It would be wrong to imply that good work was not achieved under this initiative and I myself became "creative agent" for a while to a primary school doing excellent work with filmmaking[52]. The problem with it was more that in effect it "sucked up" all the public funding for this area into one imposed model of practice. Ironically I had to use income from my work as a "creative agent" to separately support different work as an artist working with young people, which did not address Creative Partnership criteria.

The replacement of funding with commissioning as a wider strategy of control unfortunately remains on the increase, and is used as a means of fulfilling governmental and institutional interests. Project development—arguably the most creative part of the process—is therefore largely carried out by those who have no recent (if any) experience of the work they are setting out to commission, so that the commissioning processes themselves are often ill thought through. Artists are regularly selected on the basis of ideas elicited before the main commission is awarded, without sufficient time or resources allocated for meaningful consultation or engagement[53]. *The Catch* was developed for Barking and Dagenham's planning department under such adverse circumstances, and it was only with persistence that I was able to involve a school and the *Cascade* mentoring process in the final stages.

The process of commissioning as experienced under New Labour at the turn of the millennium was a well-meaning but blinkered top-down exercise masquerading as bottom-up support, which proved particularly detrimental to the arts. Eleanore Belfiore and Oliver Bennett have outlined how evidence-based policy-making was vigorously pursued as part of New Labour's implementation of "third way" politics[54]. Highlighting the difficulties this caused in terms of enabling the arts to retain any degree of transformative power, they reported how this failing was even acknowledged by government ministers[55], who spoke on the shortcomings of the evidence-based approach. Its quotas and targets for ethnicity, disability and the like also contributed to the "mainstream multiculturalism" derided by Nancy Fraser[56].

If New Labour's aim was socially orientated but misguided, the ongoing development of the top-down approach under the Conservatives has been a more straightforward process of control, conducted not only through public funding, but also through institutions. This mirrors developments in the US, about which Grant Kester has voiced concern through a 2016 editorial in FIELD journal, giving as example *Guggenheim Social Practice,* a new commission by the Guggenheim Museum, New York, for two projects that "engage community participants . . . and foster new forms of public engagement". He cites Hammer Museum's *Public Engagement* programme in Los Angeles and MOMA's *Artist's Experiment* program in New York as further examples of major art museums "jumping on the social practice bandwagon", and points out that what differentiates contemporary socially engaged art from this is the way it enacts critique in specific sites of resistance. What does it mean when these sites of resistance are determined by government agencies and major institutions? It certainly all mitigates against any meaningful creative engagement on behalf of the artist.

Although commissioning may, in present times, be virtually the only kind of financial support encountered by younger artists working in this field, I would like to remind the next generation that this is not, and has not been, the only way of initiating socially engaged practice, although it will certainly take political will to turn this around. I am nevertheless keenly aware of the struggle to survive experienced by most young artists leaving education with an exploitative jobs market and overpriced accommodation—I recently heard that in the next five years thirty-five per cent of artists' studios in London will be lost to rising property prices in the capital[57]. In choosing social practice they will also be largely cutting themselves off from the art market as a source of income. New technologies offer some opportunities for support, but it will be a task for this generation to discover new means to carry out this work.

As a last word on the subject of commissioning, I would not like to denigrate this as a means of financial support, since if it is conducted sensitively and flexibly it can lead to meaningful community engagement. It only becomes a problem where this becomes the primary means of funding social practice in the arts. Where it is implemented, however, all concerned should be clear as to whose interests are at stake. Examples of my own projects where the initiating organisations offered positive support to work capable of development in the longer term include *Awakenings*, commissioned by Colin Grigg[58] from the Tate; *VOLCO*, which would not have been able to get off the ground without a small pre-programming commission from Stratford Circus[59]; the first stage of *Active Energy*, initiated by SPACE[60]; and *Active Energy: Pittsburgh*, a residency and installation for a group exhibition sensitively curated by Hilary Robinson in collaboration with the Mattress Factory Pittsburgh. These examples have in fact all been commissions by arts organisations rather than statutory bodies. The difference may well be that the people running these commissions had experience and understanding of the process. This only strengthens the argument for funders to be more open-minded in how public money is used, with some better balance between accountability and the creativity that can be unleashed with greater freedom. A re-instatement of practitioner advisory panels for peer assessment and grants for artists' own research and development would both be a positive step in that direction.

Regeneration

> It is here in this complicated and organic swamp of the everyday, with its adaptive and largely self-organising systems of people and collectives who think locally and act locally, where the intelligence of cities lies.
>
> Nabeel Hamdi[61]

From *The Present Day Creates History* to my work today, the field of urban renewal has provided a fruitful platform for addressing issues of social change. My location in East London has also offered opportunity for immersion in its mesh of overlapping social and cultural networks and history of self-organisation. Although initial engagement with issues of re-development was through invitation from local communities rather than personal choice, my regular return to these concerns has been no coincidence. Since the eighties the East End of London, traditionally the city's industrial quarter, has become an arena for successive governments to enact their vision for change. Space, both physical and conceptual, has been opened up in this otherwise overcrowded city through the replacement of manufacturing by service industry, the containerisation that emptied many of the up-river docks, and shifting patterns of employment caused by globalisation. Both commerce and government grasped the resulting opportunities. The site of the 2012 Olympics at Stratford, which lies within the Thames Gateway area, had already been scheduled for development before being proposed for the Games. Thames Gateway is one of the largest regeneration zones in Europe, and effectively extends the development of the London Docklands for a further forty miles from Tower Bridge to the Thames Estuary, using a similar legislative framework. Key to this plan has been the construction of a massive quantity of new private sector housing, intended to both reduce house price inflation and solve the housing needs of South East England. These plans had obvious contradictions including an initial collapse of the housing market in the 1990s and massive building development on the river's flood plains in the face of rising sea levels, planned prior to acknowledgement of climate change. The Thames Gateway regeneration scheme has nevertheless dominated plans for this area for nearly three decades and is destined to present enormous challenges for its future citizens.

Over the years the notion of redevelopment in the UK has been gradually replaced with one of regeneration. In its ideal form the latter not only refers to the urban fabric, but also embraces concepts of culture, community, participation and sustainability. In England, for example, thirty-nine New Deal for Communities (NDC) partnerships were created by New Labour in the late nineties to deliver these aims. These included Ocean NDC in the London Borough of Tower Hamlets, which contributed funding from its Education budget to *VOLCO*[62]. However positive these principles, the ideals of this bottom-up regeneration for the new millennium suffered from its top-down instigation. Officials on the Ocean Estate wondered why so few residents attended the "decision making" meetings, urging them to take "ownership" for something they had never requested. In her article "Participation and Local Urban Regeneration: The Case of the New Deal for Communities in the UK", Lorna Dargan reflected on the overly simplistic policy discourses of "community" and "participation" underpinning area-based regeneration programmes, and demonstrated their problematic use in regeneration policy[63].

Equally problematic has been the way that artists were wholeheartedly embraced within these schemes to deliver a range of desired regeneration outcomes at comparatively little cost, a process that still continues. In an article co-authored with John Cockram for *Engage* in 2005, I warned of how the arts were being seen as a necessary component to the agendas of most regeneration agencies and that, despite their best intentions, many artists were finding themselves pawns in a game being played at a much higher level and with large contracts at stake[64]. I was concerned how, under such circumstances, and particularly for the less experienced, this gave rise to some artists having difficulty in ascertaining to which agenda they were working, and indeed whether these were ones they would choose to support.

Eleanore Belfiore and Oliver Bennett reported how in 1999 the Policy Action Team 10 (PAT10)[65] argued that participation in the arts and sport should effectively contribute to neighbourhood renewal by improving communities' performance in four key areas of health, crime, employment and education[66]. A proliferation of "impact studies" were apparently designed to justify the "usefulness of the arts" in relation to government priorities. Similarly the Cultural Policy Collective in the introduction of their paper "Towards Cultural Democracy" (2003) described how UK governments had identified cultural industries as sources of urban regeneration and cultural activity as instruments of social change, appearing to be democratic but fundamentally market led and tokenistic. They described various forms of co-option as being the order of the day.

While the widespread involvement of artists in regeneration can be positive, this process is often undermined both through the way it is done and the resources it offers, or as the Cultural Policy Collective put it, "combating serious structurally-induced social problems with miniscule resources and no external support"[67]. *VOLCO*'s achievement of a £90,000 budget[68] from Ocean NDC was achieved through describing it as "education", which enabled the project to run for many years and reach hundreds of children. When funding specifically for the arts was introduced later in the scheme, applications were capped at £3,000 each.

So why continue to engage as an artist with regeneration? My own interest comes through recognition of the power of "local intelligence" of the kind referred to by Hamdi—a concept that the "local" not only matters but can create repercussions of a far greater magnitude. The arts are also well placed to draw out and assist the communication of direct experience to ensure that planning and design meet real need. Regeneration remains a fundamental force of change in the lives of East London communities, and requires addressing rather than ignoring—there are nevertheless many ways of doing this other than through agency-led commissions. *The Peoples Plan for the Royal Docks,* for example, initiated by local people and supported by the Greater London Council, is today heralded as a model for community planning. It remains, however, completely at odds with the way most community consultation is conducted.

For several decades following the eighties there was little broad based community campaigning with which to collaborate and my focus turned for a while to encouraging young people to think about their future lives and environment, as in *Cascade, VOLCO, The Catch* and the *Young Person's Guides*. Proposals for change to the urban and social environment has nevertheless provided material for encouraging participants to consider what kind of future they want for themselves and their communities, and then to find a voice through which to express this. Each *Cascade* project focused on a different regeneration-related theme and culminated in an exhibition, event or web site that brought the views of young people into the public domain, while reminding them of their own important role in their community's future.

Social Change

> good development practice facilitates emergence; it builds on what we've got and with it goes to scale.
>
> Nabeel Hamdi[69]

The Docklands Community Poster Project is probably the clearest example within the practice of the way that art can support communities and act as a political force to provoke reform. Local people from three London boroughs in effect took on central government[70] to oppose, and then provide workable alternatives to turning a site where generations of working class people had lived and worked into real estate to be sold off to the highest bidders. The art did not lead the campaign, but it became an increasingly important part of it, disseminating information among local people and also to a wider public. It was not a simple message. The campaign adopted more sophisticated strategies than being straightforwardly oppositional, rather proposing ways of developing the area to include local needs and infrastructure. It was also aware of how this massive development would engage with the wider global economy of the capital. The imagery therefore needed to reflect this complexity as well as the unfolding of different approaches within the campaign. In order to achieve this, the practice had to be embedded in ongoing dialogue with the activists, community members and professionals involved. It was also necessary to communicate the issues in diverse ways for various audiences, leading to a programme of photo-murals, graphics, travelling exhibitions, events and photographic documentation.

If art is a purveyor of meaning, then the cultural work we undertook for this campaign helped locate the meanings of this development for both local people and a wider society. More people joined the cultural events[71] than would have otherwise taken part in demonstrations, exemplified by the thousands who took to the river for the *People's Armadas to Parliament*. The imagery also gained a currency that saw it repeatedly reproduced through the media, while the artwork continues to be exhibited and published. Another outcome has been that the imagery and artefacts have served to keep the knowledge gained in that era alive. Just as shards of pots tell the stories of earlier civilisations, it is the cultural artefacts of Docklands that survive to tell the tale. Although archiving was not a priority at the time, local people were keen that events and development sites should be documented from their own perspective, not just by mainstream media. The Museum of London Docklands includes documentation of the project in its exhibit on the eighties and the negative archive we built up is apparently their only record of events from the community's point of view.

Change starts where one is, and developed from there can rival the sweeping political changes of those holding political power. This highlights the benefits of a "situated" practice that is able to engage in the politics of specific circumstance, and extend out from there. Chantal Mouffe has described how the political erupts in very different places and not only through democratic structures. With reference to Ulrich Beck's theory that society should no longer look for the political in the traditional arenas such as parliament, political parties and trades unions, she has asserted that it is necessary to stop the equation between politics and the political system. Mouffe pointed instead to a series of new resistances that are grass roots-oriented, extra parliamentary and no longer linked to classes or to political parties. She claimed that these demands have been taking place through a variety of sub-systems and concern issues, which cannot be expressed through traditional political ideologies, and are shaping society from below[72]. This can be seen in the strategies of some of the projects I have described that have taken a more oblique approach following the move away from the campaigning of the seventies and eighties. The need for a shift in emphasis onto identity and subjectivity was also expressed by Gene Ray and Gregory Sholette in their article "Whither Tactical Media", which appeared in *Third Text* in 2008. They recognised a new social order that called for a "do it yourself" form of tactics[73]. These strategies have taken two distinct, and also sometimes overlapping, forms in my work, although both were originally learned through the earlier campaigning.

The first tactic has been that of "giving voice", one of the key remits of community arts, and articulated by Sandy Fitzgerald as "the question of power and the right of people to contribute to and participate fully in culture, the right to have a voice and the right to give voice"[74]. Art offers an effective means of creating platforms in the public domain where these voices can better be heard, while targeting those who need to listen[75]. Simply being heard can have a transformative effect as noted by Paolo Freire, who referred to the inward realisation of his "educands" of their own inherent power to change both themselves and what is around them[76]. In a similar way participants in *The Young Person's Guide to the Royal Docks* found their "voice" when they were able to use their local knowledge to question a business representative in a public arena, and with that the potential to take into their future lives active participation in issues affecting their community.

When that voice is collective it can be even more powerful. Alana Jelinek has described how art becomes more politically potent when it manages to express collective plurality[77]. Collective expression offers weight and validity to anecdotal experience and, when coupled with visual resonance, is well placed to encourage an empathetic response. This is the impetus behind the emphasis on "structuring" outlined in Chapter 6, designed to bring together and combine multiple segments of individual input into a coherent whole to make a collective statement, as in *West Meets East*, *Celebrating the Difference* or the construction of a new society in *VOLCO*. The demarcation of individual and group identities by participants themselves was central to this work, and indeed underpinned all the Art of Change projects described in Chapter 3, together with the more recent *Young Person's Guide to East London*. For this work I used an approach of conceptual or physical montage to both allow for and facilitate representation of complex and overlapping spheres of interest and belonging. Nira Yuval-Davis has emphasised that the only way to approach "the truth" is through dialogue between people occupying different positions[78]. *VOLCO* set out to do this through fantasy and imagination, with participants creating online identities, then using a discussion forum to debate their ideas for the new planet before finalising and uploading them to the Volcan archives. Other projects including *Between Family Lines*, *West Meets East* and *Celebrating the Difference*, aimed for a similar outcome through visual juxtaposition. *The Infinity Story* did the same through textual narrative, while *The Young Person's Guides* explored issues of identity through narratives of place.

The second main strategy for social change employed in the work has been the creation of alternative models, which the Docklands communities found much more effective that oppositional campaigning. *The People's Plan for the Royal Docks* in 1983 put forward options significantly more beneficial to the local community than the proposed London City Airport, taking lesson from the plans drawn up a decade earlier by the shop stewards combine at Lucas Aerospace. In more recent work, the notion of alternative modelling has been embodied in *The Young Person's Guides,* which presented a view of East London not previously encountered in mainstream information, while *Active Energy* has re-focused attention on a form of sustainable energy that is both needed and appropriate for its location, despite being largely overlooked by energy providers. While these later projects have proposed practical alternatives, *VOLCO* created a model for a future society built on cooperation through the means of imagination. Freire has described how, through his re-worked education process, the peasants came to see themselves as transformers of reality, which had previously seemed a mysterious entity, through their creative labour[79]. In a similar way the social purpose of *VOLCO* was to enable participating children to glimpse the possibility of creating a new world through their own creative endeavours—a young person's version of the "dream" proposed by Freire in his later writing, who explained how "the dream makes things possible"[80].

It is always difficult to assess the social impact of arts projects. Even the most sensitive qualitative evaluation cannot account for those moments when some active involvement by a young person bears fruit in later life, or when a community in London or Brazil is inspired by learning of the experiences of the other. Proof is perhaps more the concern of academics, policy makers and funding agencies, since one can only really tell experientially how wide the ripples of a project may have spread. Catherine Wilson commented that the possibility of artists influencing wider actions and thinking is as infinite as the creative process itself, noting particularly that social outcomes rely on nodes of interaction in the wider public realm that the artist does not control[81].

If the campaigning over the London Docklands were to be judged in terms of the final redevelopment as a whole, it would not necessarily be deemed as successful[82]. Its strategy for cohesive community activism involving the arts is nevertheless one that is frequently referenced as a model, and would have certainly made impact on a much greater scale, had it not been for three successive terms of a Conservative government. A significant shift can be seen in the cultural work over this period, however. In the early days of the campaign to save Bethnal Green Hospital the video that I made with Peter appeared as the last item in the campaign's public meeting under "any other business". In contrast, the work we did in the Docklands gradually came to be regarded as a key tool in the campaigning process, and taking a cultural approach to demonstration and events became accepted as the norm. As with the Lucas Aerospace plan, the work has seemed to gain an after-life as others draw on the knowledge gained and re-use it to inform future initiatives.

The social effectiveness of later projects, with strategies more geared towards attaining "recognition" and fewer clearly identified social outcomes, is even more difficult to assess, although Nabeel Hamdi's notion of how small changes at a local level can grow to a global scale has offered some insight into how the process of change starts and spreads[83]. In these cases, external judgement of impact is even less relevant, since the work is founded on need and takes effect in its immediate enactment. Its wider repercussions are often implicit in the work but not explicit as a plan. The Geezers as participants in *Active Energy* may represent a group commonly seen as one of the least powerful in society, yet their idea of creating power for London from their local tidal river, most obvious to themselves, has global implications. The tidal turbine constructed in 2013 is already seen to have potential worldwide application, with the practical value of the project as a whole recognised through a Green Energy award from a regeneration agency[84]. The process through which it has been developed is nevertheless an artistic one, capable of "drawing out" ideas and bringing together individuals, organisations and institutions in a shared endeavour. Art cannot necessarily make change, but it can take vision to the brink of where change is possible.

Notes

1. The top-down approach was simply continued by the Coalition Government and then the Conservative government that followed, although without the social agenda.
2. Freire, op. cit. 1992, p.116.
3. Gablik, op. cit. p.20.
4. Dupré, op. cit. 2008b.
5. Ukeles, op. cit. p.295.
6. Kester, op. cit. p.79.
7. Gablik, op. cit. p.115–116.
8. Ibid p.91.
9. Alana Jelinek, *This is not Art: activism and other non-art*, London and New York: I.B. Tauris, 2013, p.161.
10. Whereas interdisciplinarity combines two or more disciplines into one activity, transdisciplinarity is seen to cross disciplinary boundaries to create a holistic approach.
11. Joseph Beuys, "I Am Searching For Field Character" in *Art Into Society, Society Into Art: Seven German Artists*, cat. London: ICA, 1974, p.48.

12. Jelinek, op. cit.
13. I currently teach undergraduate modules in Art Practice and the Community and an MA in Art and Social Practice at Middlesex University.
14. Stuart Hall, "New Ethnicities" in *Critical Dialogues in Cultural Studies*, London: Routledge, 1996, p.446.
15. Kenan Malik, "Against Multiculturalism" in *New Humanist*, Vol. 117, Issue 2, London, 2002.
16. Hall, op.cit.
17. Arun Kundnani, *The End of Tolerance: Racism in 21st Century Britain,* London and Michigan: Pluto Press, 2007, p.42.
18. Ibid p.46
19. Hall, op. cit. p.447
20. Thomas McEvilley, *Art and Otherness: Crisis in Cultural Identity*, New York: McPherson & Co.1992, p.24–25.
21. Clara Connolly, "Between Family Lines" in *Jewish Socialist*, No. 6, London, 1995, p.51.
22. Cynthia Cockburn and Lynette Hunter, "Transversal Politics and Translating Practices" in *Soundings*, London: Lawrence & Wishart, 1999.
23. Nira Yuval-Davis, "What is Transversal Politics?" in *Soundings*, London: Lawrence & Wishart, 1999.
24. Nancy Fraser and Axel Honneth, *Redistribution or Recognition*? London and New York: Verso, 2003, p.94.
25. Connolly, op. cit. p.51
26. From the mission statement of The Art of Change, 1991–2001.
27. Freire, op. cit. 1970, p.119.
28. Tom Finkelpearl, *Dialogues in Public Art*, Cambridge, MA: MIT Press, 2000.
29. Mörsch, op.cit. 2005.
30. Bernard Levin, "This Poisoning of the Wells of Art" in *The Times*, London, 1978.
31. Peter Suchin, "Mistaken as Red" in *Mute* online journal, 2007.
32. Peter was particularly responsible at that time for contributing to theoretical debates and writing about the work.
33. Another incentive for developing this project was witnessing my own children's growing boredom with learning following introduction of the National Curriculum together with increased use of testing and school inspections, which reduced the amount of creative work that even the most determined school could offer at that time.
34. Carmen Mörsch, "To take all that learning and put it together with all that art" in *Art for Change—Loraine Leeson, Works from 1975–2005*, Berlin: NGBK, 2005), p.130.
35. Manuel Castells, *The Information Age. Economy Society and Culture, Volume 1: The Rise of the Network Society*, Oxford: Blackwell, 2000), p.357.
36. The Interrupt symposia were a series of five events staged in the UK during 2003, organised by Vivienne Reiss, Head of Educational Development in the Visual Art Department of the Arts Council of England and David Butler, now Coordinator of LifeWorkArt, at the School of Arts and Cultures, University of Newcastle of Tyne. The symposia were designed to facilitate debate and discussion around the central question: "Where does socially engaged, participatory and education arts activity stand within current debates around contemporary arts practice?"
37. Walter Benjamin "The Author as Producer" in *New Left Review* 1970 (originally published 1934).
38. Ibid, p.6.
39. Turkle, op. cit. p.61.
40. Jean Baudrillard, "Simulacra and Simulations" in *Selected Writings*, Stanford: Stanford University Press, 1983, p.7.
41. Turkle, op. cit. p.268
42. Dupré, op. cit. 2008a
43. Jo Freeman, "The Tyranny of Structurelessness" in *The Second Wave*, Vol. 2. No. 1, 1970.
44. Belinda Kidd was one of the first employees of the Docklands Community Poster Project, when it began to receive financial support from the Greater London Council in the early eighties. With a background in the History of Art, hands-on experience of arts centre

management and prior knowledge of co-operative structures, she was instrumental in turning this loose group into an efficiently run organisation over nearly ten years. She later went on to hold key positions in national arts institutions.

45. Ibid.
46. I currently hold the posts of Senior Research Fellow at University of Westminster and Senior Lecturer at Middlesex University.
47. These virtual symposia were initiated in 2014 by artist Roxane Permar at Shetland College UHI, and have developed from there with input from Middlesex University. Undergraduates, graduates, artists and researchers from several universities across the UK have been able to share their work live and online, with keynotes from international speakers, who have included Greg Sholette, Pablo Helguera and Jane Trowell of Platform. https://artsocial practice.net
48. Nabeel Hamdi, *Small Change*, London and Sterling VA: Earthscan, 2004, p.xxii.
49. Tower Hamlets Arts Committee's diverse membership under a Labour administration in the seventies and eighties included representatives from tenants and community groups as well as artists and arts workers.
50. I was privileged to serve on the GLC Community Arts Sub Committee for its full term 1981–86.
51. www.creativitycultureeducation.org/our-programmes/creative-partnerships
52. As Creative Agent to Columbia Primary School in Bethnal Green, one of my main tasks was to produce six-monthly evaluation reports.
53. It has become common practice to offer artists a small research and development fee prior to the main commission; however this is rarely sufficient to cover adequate community engagement, which is a time intensive process.
54. Eleanore Belfiore and Oliver Bennett, *The Social Impact of the Arts*, Basingstoke and New York: Palgrave and MacMillan, 2008, pp.7–9.
55. The authors report how Members of Parliament Estelle Morris (2003) and Tessa Jowell (2004) both spoke on the negative impact of evidence based policy-making on the arts.
56. Fraser, op. cit. p.75.
57. From a presentation given on December 10, 2016 at the Policy Forum for London Keynote Seminar on Priorities for arts and culture in London by Hadrian Garrard, Director of Create London.
58. As Head of Young Visitors' Programmes at Tate Millbank in 1995, Colin Grigg commissioned *Awakening* as one of the first Tate supported projects to encompass community involvement.
59. In 1999 Clare Connor, Education Officer and later Director of Stratford Circus, offered £1000 for a pre-programming event prior to the inauguration of that venue, and was open to this being the start of a larger project.
60. SPACE managed three artist commissions that concluded the Democratising Democracy research project by Queen Mary University London. The commissioning process was conducted by Head of Learning and Participation Fiona Fieber, which was so successful that it led to further collaborative working.
61. Hamdi, op. cit. p.17
62. *VOLCO* was not commissioned by the NDC, however. It had already been developed as a project and the NDC funding enabled it to be further improved and trialled in its schools.
63. Lorna Dargan, "Participation and Local Urban Regeneration: The Case of the New Deal for Communities (NDC) in the UK" in *Regional Studies*, Vol. 43, Issue 2, London: Routledge, 2009, pp. 305–317.
64. John Cockram and Loraine Leeson, "Re-generation" in *Engage* 17, London, 2005, p.17.
65. Policy Action Team 10 and 17 other Policy Action Teams were set up by the Labour government in 1998 to look in an integrated way at the problems of poor neighbourhoods. Each team was made up of officials from Government Departments, experienced practitioners and academics. PAT10 focused on the contribution that sport and the arts could potentially make toward neighbourhood renewal.
66. Belfiore and Bennett, op. cit. p.7
67. Cultural Policy Collective, *Towards Cultural Democracy*, Scotland, 2003, p.11.

68. It was possible to use regeneration income alongside other funds to develop *VOLCO*, which had a wider social aim, while the piecing together of finance from a variety of sources actually helped to retain the original project aims and avoid it becoming subsumed into another agenda.
69. Hamdi, op. cit. p.xviii.
70. The London Docklands Development Corporation (LDDC) was appointed to oversee the re-development of the London Docklands by the 1979 Conservative government, to which it was directly answerable. Under a new act of parliament the land was transferred to their control from the Labour controlled local authorities, which received no recompense.
71. The cultural work for this campaign was not just carried out by the Docklands Community Poster Project. Other individuals and organisations produced songs, poems and theatrical performances, took photographs and turned political rallies into community festivals.
72. Chantal Mouffe, *On the Political*, Routledge: Oxford and New York: Routledge, 2005, p.39.
73. Gene Ray and Gregory Sholette, "Whither Tactical Media" in *Third Text*, London: Routledge, 2008.
74. Fitzgerald, op. cit. p.79.
75. It has been argued that "giving voice" is somewhat of a misnomer, since communities are often very clear about what they want, it is rather if or how they are listened to that is more the issue.
76 Freire, op. cit. 1970, p.119.
77. Jelinek, op. cit. p.160.
78. Yuval-Davis, op. cit. p.95.
79. Freire, op. cit. 1970, p.155.
80. Freire, op. cit. 1992, p.181.
81. Wilson, op. cit. p.6.
82. Despite falling short of its main objectives, the Docklands campaigning achieved a number of small but significant victories including preventing destruction of the heart of Wapping by a trunk road, achieving housing for rent along the riverside at Cherry Gardens in Southwark, saving the Mudchute City Farm from destruction and forcing the issue of the proposed airport to public enquiry through production of the Peoples Plan for the Royal Docks.
83. Hamdi, op. cit. p.xviii.
84. In 2016 *Active Energy* received an award from RegenSW, a regeneration agency that offers annual awards for advances in the development of green energy. This was the first that recognised the role of the arts as playing a potential key role in this.

References

Jean Baudrillard, "Simulacra and Simulations" in *Selected Writings* (Stanford: Stanford University Press, 1983).

Eleanore Belfiore and Oliver Bennett, *The Social Impact of the Arts* (Basingstoke and New York: Palgrave and MacMillan, 2008).

Walter Benjamin "The Author as Producer" in *New Left Review* (1970, originally published 1934).

Joseph Beuys "I Am Searching For Field Character" in *Art Into Society, Society Into Art: Seven German Artists*, cat. (London: ICA, 1974).

Manuel Castells, *The Information Age. Economy Society and Culture, Volume 1: The Rise of the Network Society* (Oxford: Blackwell, 2000).

Cynthia Cockburn and Lynette Hunter, "Transversal Politics and Translating Practices" in *Soundings* (London: Lawrence & Wishart, 1999).

John Cockram and Loraine Leeson, "Re-generation" in *Engage 17* (London, 2005).

Clara Connolly, "Between Family Lines" in *Jewish Socialist*, Journal no.6 (London, 1995).

Brett Cook and Mierle Laderman Ukeles "Unburning Freedom Hall and the Packer School Project" (interview) in *What We Made: Conversations on Art and Social Cooperation,* Ed. Tom Finkelpearl (Durham and London: Duke University Press, 2013).

Cultural Policy Collective, *Towards Cultural Democracy* (Scotland, 2003).

Lorna Dargan, "Participation and Local Urban Regeneration: The Case of the New Deal for Communities (NDC) in the UK" in *Regional Studies*, Vol. 43, No. 2, (London: Routledge, 2009).

Francoise Dupré, "Making Stuff" in *Axis* online journal (2008a).

Francoise Dupré, "Complex Relations" in *Axis* online forum (2008b).

Tom Finkelpearl, *Dialogues in Public Art* (Cambridge, MA: MIT Press, 2000).

Sandy Fitzgerald (ed.), *An Outburst of Frankness* (Dublin: Tasc at New Island, 2004).

Nancy Fraser and Axel Honneth, *Redistribution or Recognition?* (London and New York: Verso, 2003).

Jo Freeman, "The Tyranny of Structurelessness" in *The Second Wave*, Vol. 2. No. 1 (1970).

Paolo Freire, *Pedagogy of the Oppressed* (London: Penguin, 1970).

Paolo Freire, *Pedagogy of Hope: Reliving Pedagogy of the Oppressed* (London: Continuum, 1992).

Suzi Gablik, *Conversations before the End of Time*, (London: Thames and Hudson, 1997).

Stuart Hall, "New Ethnicities" in *Critical Dialogues in Cultural Studies,* (London: Routledge, 1996).

Nabeel Hamdi, *Small Change* (London and Sterling VA: Earthscan, 2004).

Alana Jelinek *This is not Art: activism and other non-art* (London and New York: I.B. Tauris, 2013).

Grant Kester, *Conversation Pieces: Community and Communication in Modern Art (*Berkeley, Los Angeles and London: University of California Press, 2004).

Arun Kundnani, *The End of Tolerance: Racism in 21st Century Britain* (London and Michigan: Pluto Press, 2007).

Kenan Malik, "Against Multiculturalism" in *New Humanist*, Vol. 117, No. 2 (London, 2002).

François Matarasso, *Did it make a difference? Evaluating community-based arts and business partnerships* (London: Arts and Business, 2001).

Thomas McEvilley, *Art and Otherness: Crisis in Cultural Identity* (New York: McPherson & Co., 1992).

Carmen Mörsch, "To take all that learning and put it together with all that art" in *Art for Change—Loraine Leeson, Works from 1975–2005* (Berlin: NGBK, 2005).

Chantal Mouffe, *On the Political* (Oxford and New York: Routledge, 2005).

Gene Ray and Gregory Sholette, "Whither Tactical Media" in *Third Text* (London: Routledge, 2008).

Peter Suchin, "Mistaken as Red" in *Mute* (online, 2007).

Sherry Turkle, *Life on the Screen* (New York: Phoenix, 1995).

Hilary Wainwright and Dave Elliott, *The Lucas Plan: A New Trade Unionism in the Making?* (London: Allison and Busby, 1983).

Catherine Wilson, "Community Engagement" in *Collections* (Newcastle upon Tyne: a-n The Artists Information Company, 2008).

Nira Yuval-Davis, "What is Transversal Politics?" in *Soundings* (London: Lawrence & Wishart, 1999).

8 Situating the Practice

Since embarking on our quest to find a way to realise our work outside of the gallery system, Peter and I were clear that what we were doing remained art, despite the fact that it often seemed at odds with the mainstream. Our training in Fine Art and all that we did pertaining to that discipline, together with our knowledge of its history, informed us that an important next step for art was to re-discover its social roots. A longer view of the development of arts and culture demonstrated that it had only been for a period of less than five hundred years that art had followed the culture and economy of the West in embracing individualism, and then capitalism, to come to be regarded as a saleable commodity. It was clear to us that since the beginning of civilisation artists had worked with others, often in teams, to capture and communicate the meanings of their societies. In exploring a new kind of art, or at least re-discovering former cultural roots, it therefore became necessary to address and question many of the *a priori* assumptions that underpinned contemporary artistic practice. This chapter explores some of those key questions, which include aesthetics, the function of art and what constitutes an artwork. It also addresses some of the dilemmas that have arisen from the unprecedented acceptability of socially engaged art in recent years, which has led in part to both "trendiness" and institutionalisation. From the perspective of my own practice I will then look again at where we are now with an art of change.

Locating the Aesthetic

> Whatever knowledge may be contained in a poetic work, it must be completely converted into poetry.
>
> Bertholt Brecht[1]

According to *Collins English Dictionary*, one meaning of "aesthetics" is the "study of the rules and principles of art". In this sense the purpose of this written exploration has been to discover the rules and principles of socially engaged art as experienced in my practice. Within this the notion of aesthetics has repeatedly asserted itself as a challenging issue for politically oriented and community based art practice. It has been a concept historically dominated by an "art for art's sake" approach originating with the Enlightenment of the eighteenth century and developed through the nineteenth century in France, England and Germany, eventually coming to underpin the priorities of twentieth and twenty-first century art institutions. The apparent dichotomy between ethics and aesthetics has been the bane of community arts since the seventies, ranging from accusations of badly painted but "worthy" murals of the earlier eighties, to more recent concerns, voiced most emphatically by Claire Bishop in her articles and *Artificial Hells* of 2012 that ethics rather than aesthetics have come to determine artistic quality in this field.

The relevance of visual quality to socially based work was first recognised by Peter and myself during the making of the *Emergency* video for the campaign to save Bethnal Green Hospital, when we encountered the value of bringing our visual and imaginative skills as artists to bear on collaboration with activists. In order to be effective in this work it was clear that the impact of the creative outputs was of central importance. This was borne out through all the campaigning work, even the *People's Armadas to Parliament*, an event orchestrated by activists. However, while this was the case, it was also clear that the resonance of the work did not only derive from the visuals, but the total experience of the creative actions.

Grant Kester, through his first book *Conversation Pieces* of 2004, made a significant intervention in this thinking through identifying an aesthetics embedded in the quality of the dialogue and communication of an interactive work. The concept of "dialogical aesthetics", which he has traced as a movement with its own historical roots, he sees as underscoring the importance of the collaborative element, and has reminded us of how the "dematerialisation" of the art object described by Lucy Lippard several decades earlier paved the way to greater collaborative interaction. For him this aesthetic is defined in terms of the openness and quality of listening and the dynamic set up between artist, collaborator and viewer[2].

Is this process of interaction an adequate platform from which the effectiveness of an artwork may be judged, however? At the other end of the spectrum from Kester and others who have welcomed dialogic processes for their ability to produce meaningful form and value, stands Nicolas Bourriaud. His concept of "relational aesthetics" expounded in his book of that name in 2002 regarded the social interaction as sufficient in itself, treating it as simply another constructional constituent of an artwork[3]. This thinking fitted squarely into the avant-garde tradition of challenging art world boundaries, and wholly relied on them. His argument was unashamedly formalist—in his world-view people interact as elements of an artwork and without their own autonomy.

The relevance of Bourriaud's concepts to my own consideration of aesthetics lies in the impact they made on the field of socially engaged practice and the institutions supporting this work. The kind of social interaction he proposed was easily subsumed into the art establishment, where it became a theoretical underpinning for artists seeking to work in any way with people. The concept of relational aesthetics has ultimately provided a depoliticised and sanitised affirmation that social engagement can fit neatly into artistic practice without disrupting the autonomy of the work.

From her perspective as a practicing artist Francoise Dupré, in an article for *Axis* published in 2008, identified that missing from Bourriaud's theory was a meaningful developmental process for all concerned. This position she has found at odds with her own person-centred intentions where participants' experience and history have central importance and play an active role in the project. Dupré nevertheless also values the materiality of the art process[4]. On the surface this might seem to align her views with those of Claire Bishop. However, Bishop has been keen to retain the aesthetics/ ethics division, and identified "a present-day standoff between the nonbelievers (aesthetes who reject this work as marginal, misguided, and lacking artistic interest of any kind) and the believers (activists who reject aesthetic questions as synonymous with cultural hierarchy and the market)"[5].

Bishop saw the former at worst producing "irrelevant" art for art's sake, and the latter as "self-marginalising" to the extent that they simply reinforced the status quo. In this sense she has assumed that, for those more concerned with the social engagement than the art, aesthetics becomes automatically collapsed into ethics, sacrificing the former. She has gone so far as to refer on a number of occasions to the "self-sacrificial" approach of those with a social agenda, as if the politics annihilates the artistic quality. Some artists, she felt, have escaped this trap by choosing not to align themselves with activism, but instead work in a way more akin to the avant-garde, which she has correlated with greater artistic value.

Bishop's re-focusing of attention on the role of aesthetics beyond that of the interactive process itself is to be welcomed. Her proposition, however, that loss of the aesthetic is necessarily a casualty of a political or social agenda fails to take into account the range of practices and criteria used by artists in this field, a point reinforced in a response by Kester to her article later that year[6]. While Bishop provided examples of projects to support her view, it was not clear why she should extrapolate from this that artists with a primary commitment to social change would automatically forfeit one of the most powerful aspects of their discipline. It was precisely the recognition of what we as artists could bring to the social causes we supported that led Peter and me to put all we had learned about art into the service of the campaign to save Bethnal Green Hospital and subsequent projects. Artist Ailbhe Murphy has in fact elevated that proposition by saying how important it is that socially engaged art brings "the entire history of art production to bear on the collective endeavours of a modest group of individuals"[7]. At the same time Paolo Freire has reminded us that "it would be an absurdity for there to be, or seem to have to be, some necessary association between ugliness and scientific rigour"[8] and Kester has warned that "aesthetic discrimination" cannot be made in isolation from the broader social and political context within which the work is experienced[9]. There are indeed multiple locations of the aesthetic to be considered and in my experience it has been essential that all parts, including any tangible outputs, function at their optimum if they are to have any wider effect.

A Question of Function

> Utility is the great idol of our age, to which all powers are in thrall.
>
> Friedrich Schiller[10]

The industrial revolution that followed the Enlightenment saw a move from hand production methods to new manufacturing processes. As industry and commerce took hold it was important to protect the aesthetic from utility. Belfiore and Bennett have described the independence of the aesthetic sphere from moral and didactic considerations epitomised in eighteenth-century discourse, when Kant reputedly asserted that beautiful objects should affect us as if they had a purpose, but with no particular purpose to be found. They have indicated how, in the early twentieth century, uselessness was seen as a trademark and also an aesthetic moral and political asset for artists, serving to prove a higher ethical ground[11].

The notion of the "uselessness" of art still prevailed when I commenced my own practice. This was despite the fact that the twentieth century had already been significantly intersected by cultural approaches to political activism, not least through the revolutionary art of Russia, China and the May 1968 student uprising in France. I had already been introduced to a potential convergence for art and education through the work of Joseph Beuys, and was beginning to recognise the possibility of art as a means rather than an end. While functionality in my early practice remained political, opportunities for other social "uses" increasingly presented themselves in later work. *VOLCO,* for example, stepped beyond a simple linking of education and art through its ability to also act as a stand-alone learning resource for schools. *The Young Person's Guide to East London* functioned as an online source of information and free newspaper for visitors to the city, while the central practical concern of *Active Energy* has been to promote the development of renewable energy as a sustainable power source for London. These social uses are not bi-products, but rather central aims within these projects, existing alongside creative purpose, with practical functionality often underpinning the facilitation of the social engagement itself. When I approached groups of disaffected young people to invite them to contribute to *The Young Person's Guide to East London,* it was the prospect of collaboration in the making of a professional product with global access that most interested them rather than it also being an art project. In these instances the aesthetic principle resided in the resonance of the imaginative construct to which all contributed, perhaps most clearly seen in *VOLCO* where the perceived shared goal was to create a virtual society. Similarly, during introductory workshop sessions for *The Young Person's Guide to East London,* questions from participants reflected their nodes of interest. I frequently found myself answering, "Yes, it will be a professional product and accessible to all. Yes, it will be completely based on content produced by yourselves. Yes, it will actually be used by visitors to the London Olympics". The excitement generated was for a useable product, while the overall purpose and processes through which it came to fruition were creative. Similarly, in the case of *Active Energy,* the initial question to the group was not about art but technology. The fact that the resulting work was also shown in galleries and that artefacts were produced along the way did not detract from the group's own practical mission.

These projects have all included a social functionality that persisted beyond the moment of artistic framing, as distinct to artworks that encompass a usefulness realised solely within an art event or installation. It is clear that the "art" of these projects is not only located in the visual or even the dialogic work surrounding the *Active Energy* installations for example, but must also reside in the imaginative construct envisioned by the group. Does this mean that such work shares a place under the same theoretical umbrella as conceptual art with its origins in Duchamp's urinal? Although holding in common a similar emphasis on quality of intentionality, the two types of practice differ in distinct ways. First, the intentions of the socially engaged projects are tangibly realised through products that may not have been created or even proposed as an artwork. Second, their conceptual element operates within a social rather than art institutional framework. That is, the work's key constituency judges its value in societal rather than artistic terms.

The issue of social functionality nevertheless takes on a different complexion when it is driven by an outside agenda. The social inclusion policies implemented in the UK at the turn of the millennium, together with the financial mechanisms through which they were delivered, created a scenario whereby artistic autonomy was subsumed into an imposed ethical framework. When artists are hired solely to deliver social outcomes, the question of their cultural role sometimes hardly enters the frame. It was in this way that public agencies and institutions began to offer opportunities for art practice with social purpose. Not only was creativity neutralised through the imposition of pre-determined target outcomes, as indicated in the last chapter, but the values of a practice rooted in community were turned on their head.

At the other end of the spectrum, a change in artistic practice was also developing in art institutions in a way that none concerned with community-based practice could have previously envisaged. Function ceased to be an anathema to mainstream art, partially assured by Bourriaud's alignment of process with avant-garde boundary breaking, and also in response to shifts in artists' own processes and practice. These new forms became closely aligned with art world trends, leading to a flood of work with practical process or outcomes, but no real social function. Early examples of this were Francis Alÿs' *When Faith Moves Mountains*, commissioned for the 2002 Lima Biennial, where hundreds of volunteers moved a large sand dune the distance of one foot, or Santiago Sierra's projects in which people were paid to undertake everyday, uncomfortable or humiliating tasks within a gallery setting. Other artists nevertheless engaged with art institutions to put together this new acceptability of function with the opportunities offered by commissions, for wider social purpose. The artist group Wochenklausur, for example, has instituted a range of socially useful resources and activities including a shelter for drug-addicted prostitutes, cinema for immigrants, and medical care for the homeless. All these the group aimed to embed in local provision as a means of initiating ongoing resources. Artist Tania Bruguera spent ten years researching *Arte Útil*[12], from which she created an online museum to bring together new uses for art within society. Its aim has been to challenge art's social and cultural context, promote its ability to respond to urgent social issues, forge a direct relationship with audience (who she sees as both users and beneficiaries), pursue sustainability and re-establish aesthetics as a system of transformation.

At an event held bi-annually since 2011, the Visible Award has been proffered by Cittadellarte to an artist or arts group voted to have best engaged with the social sphere "to make visible other fields and issues"[13]. The 2015 shortlist included projects such as *Conflict Kitchen*, a Pittsburgh restaurant that serves cuisine from countries in conflict with the US and makes use of creative devices to promote discussion. Also listed were *Ecoart Uganda,* which constructs children's play equipment from recycled materials, *Editorial Movement*, a community print shop in Mexico, and *Convention on the Use of Space-White Paper: The Law* from The Netherlands, which has held public meetings to support squatting through the production of a legally binding convention. The criteria used by the audience gathered at a Liverpool Biennial event to judge the winner of the 2015 award clearly favoured projects led by, and of benefit to, community participants. Although the initiative itself seemed to offer support rather than direction, it also became clear that many of the shortlisted projects had in fact resulted from curated biennial commissions. The hand of the institution seems never too far away in the present time.

After many decades of controversy, social function is now embedded in the domain of the art world. On the one hand, this is good news and something that many of us have worked towards. On the other hand, artists whose outputs are rooted in social process need to be wary of institutional co-option, of where other agendas rule, and of the new ways in which the art market is now making its influence felt.

Rebuilding the Cultural Frame

> The square confines creativity
> Art activity must be framed by a context
> The square is now to be orientated towards a wider context
> Art activity must explode its frame in order to become creative within society
>
> Dunn and Leeson[14]

In the mid-seventies Peter and I used these four assertions in the *London/Berlin Series* of performances and installations in recognition of the need for art to begin to move out of institutional control if it was to take a greater role in social transformation. While the work at that time was still conceived and situated entirely within art institutions, it was one of our last projects to come out of this context, with subsequent work progressively exploring practice within the wider social sphere. This re-framing called for new procedures including a re-working of our previous notions of aesthetics as described above. In retrospect, this desire for change was also connected to the ongoing shift towards post-modernism. We were already in the wake of Lucy Lippard's *Six years: the dematerialisation of the art object*, followed in the next decade by Hal Foster's 1983 collection of essays *The Anti-Aesthetic,* which addressed postmodern culture. It seemed that implicit in the move away from modernism was a rejection of the notion of the autonomous work of art. A re-worked notion of aesthetics was thereafter to go hand in hand with a new working praxis linked to political and social issues in ways not previously envisaged. With a greater focus on transformation through practice Owen Kelly's *Community, Art and the State* professed that, "The truth is that the citadels need to be taken down, brick by brick, so that we can use the bricks to build a whole collection of new buildings"[15]. Such revolutionary overthrow was not to be, however. Instead, these new constructs found themselves sitting alongside the mainstream in a problematic alignment. Both power and value remained in the citadels, despite the steps towards a legitimising art historical framework to support this new aesthetic. Paulo Freire put that stalemate down to lack of political development on the Left following the turn to the right after the radicalism of the seventies and eighties and the need for a real "reinvention of power" as opposed to its mere acquisition, as had been the case with modernity[16].

For a long time community orientated art took a marginalised position without a political power base as it emerged from the seventies and eighties. Few other than Owen Kelly, Su Braden in *Committing Photography* and artist David Harding[17] produced commentary on this field of practice during this era. Visual arts beyond the gallery in the nineties became rather dominated by public art, with some opportunity for community involvement opened up by National Lottery funding. At the same time persuasive arguments such as Sarah Selwood's *The Benefits of Public Art* of 1995 were made about its social value, to be taken up by the New Labour agenda of "social inclusion". As this took hold, funding became more bureaucratised, and increasingly reached artists via arts agencies or institutions. The New Labour government under which this took place was succeeded by a Conservative dominated Coalition, and then by a Conservative government, initially with no discernable arts policy beyond a paragraph in the manifesto covering heritage, creativity and sport[18]. This was followed in their second administration by a white paper[19] focusing mainly on access, geographical parity, international standing and investment. Over recent decades the Arts Council has experienced significant changes of responsibility, with several re-organisations leading to the division of its offices into national regions, which now follow separate policies[20]. Since 2014 Creative Scotland[21] has included the creation of space for debate, critical thinking, risk and experimentation in its plans, together with encouragement of socially engaged practice. The Arts Council of Northern Ireland[22] includes participatory arts as one of its categories for support, while the goals of Arts Council England[23] focus mainly on excellence, access, sustainability, skills and young people. A single open-access funding stream allows for any sort of proposal. However, the application process is onerous, even for those experienced in these matters and also highly directive in terms of the questions through which a project has to be proposed. While the fact that the UK still has public funding for the arts is to be applauded, its systems have proved rather too intrusive for my own purposes. I have preferred instead to finance most of my projects through National Lottery or charitable funds that focus on community rather than artistic value, which has at least enabled the work to avoid creative judgement by officers who are likely to have little experiential understanding of this kind of work.

A reorganisation of the UK Labour party under its new leader Jeremy Corbyn has recently addressed the dearth of political development on the Left as lamented by Freire. Its plan to place arts and culture at the heart of government harks back to a similar valuing of the social role of art by the Greater London Council in the eighties, although its proposed arts policy at the time of writing is less radical. The strategies proposed for the visual arts by Conrad Atkinson and Margaret Harrison in *The State of the Art or the Art of the State,* produced at the demise of the Greater London Council in 1985, went significantly further. They additionally addressed provision for artists' studios and housing, strengthening of links with the trades union movement, and an arts interface with education, the voluntary sector, local government and industry. At the time of writing the Labour party is still in opposition and open to consultation, so there remains opportunity for a much fuller policy to be developed. Whatever happens in the future, its new leadership has achieved a reinstatement of socialism on the Labour agenda that encompasses in its vision a role for the arts, and has opened up debate and possibilities for an upcoming generation that is increasingly embracing collective voice through activism.

Across the Atlantic, the nineties in the US saw the beginning of an increase in activity and writing on art in the social domain that began to fill the publication gap and inform practice in the UK. The "spirit of art as activism" was a phrase first coined by Nina Felshin to document art in North America that was agitating for progressive social change. Her 1995 book *But is it Art?* recorded longstanding practices such as the work of Carole Condé and Karl Beveridge with Canada's labour movement, the Guerilla Girls' *exposés* of sexism, racism and corruption in politics and across cultural forms, and Group Material's dismantling of art's identity and function within the social order. At around the same time Suzanne Lacy's *Mapping the Terrain* identified "new genre" public art that brought artists into direct engagement with audiences, a cause taken up some years later by Miwon Kwon in *One Place after Another*, who considered site specificity and locational identity, including projects that engaged their audience as active participants. Kwon developed the debate by considering the different forms that collaborative relationships could take, and the issues and contradictions caused by uneven power relations. Grant Kester's *Conversation Pieces* then offered a new historical perspective, differentiation of intention between socially engaged art and that of the longstanding avant-garde, and the new concept of "dialogic aesthetics" that took into account the totality of the social process involved. His subsequent *The One and the Many* of 2011 looked at socially engaged projects in a global arena. This overview of how these practices had continued elsewhere in the world during a period when the UK and US had experienced a turn to the right, both in government and the arts, was particularly helpful for artists such as myself, who had felt very much in a vacuum during that time.

One of the few books to appear on this subject in the UK was *The Art of Negotiation* in 2007, which contained a series of interviews looking at the intentions and methodologies of artists who had undertaken commissioned participatory projects. Its editors were David Butler and Vivienne Reiss, who in 2003 had together organised the influential *Interrupt* series of symposia to explore socially engaged, participatory and education arts activity in relation to debates around contemporary arts practice. Back in the US in 2009 Beverley Naidus' *Arts for Change* traced the development of social practice in relation to pedagogy at a time when many of us were trying to introduce these practices into our teaching. She later offered me the privilege of developing a new course on community-based practice in the US through a Fulbright residency, which I took up in 2011. That year also saw the publication of Greg Sholette's *Dark Matter* that addressed from a practitioner's perspective the behaviours of collectives dedicated to cultural resistance, followed in 2016 by *Delirium and Resistance* where he specifically addresses the link between activist art and the crisis of capitalism. In 2012 Claire Bishop's *Artificial Hells* offered a historical and theoretical overview of participatory art and the challenges it raised regarding issues of ethics. The same year in New York the exhibition and publication *Living as Form,* accompanied by a *Creative Time* summit, examined the intersection of art and social justice during twenty years of practice in this field. Tom Finkelpearl's collection of interviews in *What We Made: conversations on Art and Social Co-operation* in 2013 next explored artists' experience of social co-operation through a series of artist interviews. More recently *FIELD*, the first major journal for socially engaged art criticism, was launched by Grant Kester in 2015, offering opportunity to hear a range of voices on these issues.

While the developing public attention in the US helped to establish social practice as a force to be reckoned with in art circles, political activism and street protest were on the rise across the world. The Occupy Movement, Movement of the Squares in Greece and the Arab Spring have all been symptomatic of a new sense of what can be achieved through collective campaigning, and each also encompassed a cultural dimension. During this period Alana Jelinek's *This is not Art: activism and other non-art* of 2013 also offered a timely reminder of the very specific role of art in activist struggles. This not only resonated with my own experience, but has been a useful teaching tool for working with students who often struggle with the overlap of social and artistic roles in outreach projects.

The world is changing again and with it the way that wider humanity is using culture as a means of expression. Has the "social turn" of recent years then led to the re-framing of art practice that Peter and I had hoped for in the seventies? The net is certainly now cast wider; art initiatives with social purpose are at last acknowledged within the cultural sphere and also attracting funding. Artists with social integrity can nevertheless find themselves on a knife-edge when it comes to negotiating sufficient resources to practise, survive and disseminate the work in a situation where art world success is more often than not accompanied by institutional strings or co-option. What is needed, then, to encourage work that sets out to make a difference while preventing even greater institutional control? Here are a few suggestions:

Some reversal of current target-driven, commission-led funding for the arts is required to better allow new ideas and ways of working to emerge. The Greater London Council demonstrated how, with political will and policies that embraced diversity, equality and inclusivity, it was possible to offer support to help develop initiatives that had started from the ground up, and where there was need. Rather than issuing directives, financial support enabled projects to grow and develop in ways that had effect and meaning for a wider public. The now widespread attempt among arts funders and agencies to distil "good practice" and impose it on others not only does not work but is counter-productive to innovation in both ideas and methods.

Arts practitioners should be involved in judgements about creative worth. In my own working experience peer assessment was tried and tested in the seventies and eighties through advisory panels at the Arts Council, Greater London Arts Association and The Greater London Council. It is also common practice in publishing and academic research. When creative judgements are made by those most qualified to do so, this can both help diffuse the power of the institution and serve to disseminate knowledge among peers.

If greater value is placed on knowledge and experience held by the wider public, with support to bring this into the public domain, this will help throw light on social and environmental issues in need of attention as well as uncovering paths to new solutions. Recognition that many artists are adept at combining knowledge of creative process and outcome with skills in social interaction should help ensure the place of art on the political agenda, not only in terms of "access for all", but also through drawing a wider section of the public into creative production for social benefit.

It is important that diversity is not only valued in terms of equality and human rights, but recognised as the foundation on which a positive and inclusive culture is formed and developed. In recent years Arts Council England has developed a Creative Case for Diversity[24], addressing how it can underpin everyday practice through production, presentation and distribution, and offer a useful way forward.

Opportunities for debate, critical thinking, risk and experimentation should accompany development of policy through local, national and international networking, exchange and collaboration, and involve practitioners.

The importance of culture and creativity within education as well as through extra curricular activities cannot be overstated. Ken Robinson's 1999 report *All Our Futures—Creativity and Culture in Education,* commissioned by the Department for Education and Schools, made an excellent case for this nearly twenty years ago, but it has not been realised. The same government department is now attempting to impose as the preferred sixth form qualification the English Baccalaureate, which excludes creative subjects.

Lastly, I hope we can see an end to exploitative practices in the arts. Proper fees should be paid to artists across the creative disciplines, as proposed under current Labour arts policy. This is already the practice in other countries such as Canada thanks to a longstanding and active artists' union.

Although by no means a definitive list, this outlines the support ideally required for the kind of "cultural frame" required to help bring art's creativity more effectively into society, as Peter and I envisaged so many years ago. Recent shifts in political power at the time of writing, however, threaten to eclipse an approach that assumes a continuation of liberal democracies. The result of the UK's referendum to leave the European Union, the election of Trump in the US and the rise of right wing populism across Europe are threatening to take the western world into unchartered territory. The support required to develop the current trajectory of socially engaged art practice in a more positive direction may indeed not be forthcoming, and in the longer term the way forward might have to be more radical or subversive than anticipated. Reflecting on my own practice has revealed the extent to which wider social and economic conditions have shaped the work, and the effect of these seismic political shifts should not be underestimated. Altered circumstances will call for new strategies and "exploding the frame" of institutional control will have to take on contemporary meaning. The experience of stepping out of the frame, or at least straddling the artistic and social spheres, has nevertheless brought about recognition and experience of different ways of working, which can serve to inform a situation where greater challenges are accruing. One particularly pertinent lesson from the practice that is now called for is the way that art can help enable people to move beyond their differences and fear of the "other". A re-imagining of identity within the current situation of retrenchment is urgently needed if the world is not to become increasingly fragmented.

Although the art world has been widening its boundaries, the political sphere has begun to narrow and it has to be seen what kind of institutional foundations it is now possible to lay that can support and encourage rather than channel and control creative practitioners, or indeed whether neither remains an option. In the meantime we should share the creative processes that can support change, because a time may be coming when they are required more than ever. It is a moment to exchange strategies, pass on knowledge, and work both inside and outside the citadels to prepare ourselves. Those who have been interested to read this book will already have a sense of the power of art to support change, and may soon find a situation where there is both need and opportunity to put this into practice.

Notes

1. Bertholt Brecht 1901, cited in Belfiore and Bennett 2008, p.186.
2. Kester, op. cit. 2004.
3. Nicolas Bourriaud, Relational Aesthetics, Dijon: Les Presses du Réel, 2002.
4. Dupré, op. cit. 2008.
5. Claire Bishop, "The Social Turn: Collaboration and Its Discontents" in Artforum, February, 2006.
6. Grant Kester, Letter to the Editor, Artforum, March 2006.
7. Murphy, op. cit. p.188
8. Freire, op. cit. 1992, p.72.
9. Kester, op. cit. p.83.
10. Friedrich Schiller, On the Aesthetic Education of Man, 1794.

11. Belfiore and Bennett, op. cit. p.183).
12. www.arte-util.org
13. www.visibleproject.org/blog/award
14. Peter Dunn and Loraine Leeson, *London/Berlin Series*, unpublished, 1976.
15. Kelly, op. cit. p.92.
16. Freire, op. cit. p.198.
17. www.davidharding.net
18. https://s3-eu-west-1.amazonaws.com/manifesto2015/ConservativeManifesto2015.pdf
19. www.gov.uk/government/publications/culture-white-paper
20. In my own working lifetime in London, state funding for the arts has been through the Arts Council of Great Britain, with regional funding dispensed through the Greater London Arts Association, Greater London Arts and London Arts Board. In 1994 the Arts Council of Great Britain was divided into separate national arts funding bodies for each of the countries of the UK, which now follow separate policies. In 2002, the funding structure in England changed again, with the merger of the national Arts Council and the Regional Arts Boards to create Arts Council England, providing a unified funding structure for England.
21. www.creativescotland.com/__data/assets/pdf_file/0012/25500/Creative-Scotland-10-Year-Plan-2014-2024-v1-2.pdf
22. www.artscouncil-ni.org/the-arts
23. www.artscouncil.org.uk/great-art-and-culture-everyone
24. www.artscouncil.org.uk/diversity-and-equality/creative-case-diversity

References

Eleanore Belfiore and Oliver Bennett, *The Social Impact of the Arts* (Basingstoke and New York: Palgrave and MacMillan, 2008).

Claire Bishop, "The Social Turn: Collaboration and Its Discontents" in *Artforum* (February, 2006).

Claire Bishop, *Artificial Hells: Participatory Art and the Politics of Spectatorship* (London and Brooklyn: Verso, 2012).

Nicolas Bourriaud, *Relational Aesthetics* (Dijon: Les Presses du Réel, 2002).

Su Braden, *Committing Photography* (London: Pluto Press, 1983).

Tania Bruguera, *Reflexions on Arte Útil* (Madrid, 2012).

David Butler and Vivienne Reiss, *Art of Negotiation* (Manchester: Arts Council England and Cornerhouse, 2007).

Francoise Dupré, "Making Stuff" in *Axis* online journal (2008).

Nina Felshin, *But is it Art? The Spirit of Art as Activism* (Seattle: Bay Press,1995).

Tom Finkelpearl, *What We Made: Conversations on Art and Social Co-operation* (Durham and London: Duke University Press, 2013).

Hal Foster, Ed. *The Anti-Aesthetic: Essays on Postmodern Culture (*Port Townsend, WA: Bay Press, 1983).

Paolo Freire, *Pedagogy of Hope: Reliving Pedagogy of the Oppressed* (London: Continuum, 1992).

Greater London Council, *The State of the Art or the Art of the State* (London, 1985).

Alana Jelinek, *This is not Art: activism and other non-art* (London and New York: I.B. Tauris, 2013).

Owen Kelly, *Community Art and the State* (London: Comedia, 1984).

Grant Kester, *Conversation Pieces: Community and Communication in Modern Art* (Berkely, Los Angeles and London: University of California Press, 2004).

Grant Kester, Letter to the Editor, *Artforum* (March 2006).

Grant Kester, *The One and the Many: Contemporary Collaborative Art in a Global Context (*Durham and London: Duke University Press, 2011).

Mwon Kwon, *One Place after Another*: *site specific art and locational identity* (Cambridge, MA: MIT Press, 2004).

Suzanne Lacy, *Mapping the Terrain: New Genre Public Art* (Seattle: Bay Press,1995).
Lucy Lippard, *Six years: the dematerialisation of the art object from 1966 to 1972; a cross-reference book of information on some esthetic boundaries* (London: Studio Vista,1973).
Ailbhe Murphy, "The Fine Art of Floating Horses" in *An Outburst of Frankness* (Dublin: Tasc at New Island, 2004).
Beverly Naidus, *Arts for Change: Teaching Outside the Frame* (Oakland, CA: New Village Press, 2009).
Ken Robinson, *All Our Futures—Creativity and Culture in Education* (Suffolk: DFeS, 1999).
Sara Selwood, *The Benefits of Public Art: The Polemics of Permanent Art in Public Places* (London: Policy Studies Institute, 1995).
Greg Sholette, *Dark Matter: Art and Politics in the Age of Enterprise Culture* (London and New York: Pluto Press, 2011).
Greg Sholette, *Delirium and Resistance: Activist Art and the Crisis of Capitalism* (London and New York: Pluto Press, 2016).
Nato Thompson, *Living as Form: Socially Engaged Art from 1991–2011* (Massachusetts and London: MIT Press, 2012).

Appendix

Summary of Projects 1975–2016

1975–76 London Berlin Series

Performances, video and installations between London and Berlin, questioning the context of art and role of the artist. Collaboration with Peter Dunn.

1976–77 The Present Day Creates History

Photo/text exhibition, exploring lessons learned from the concurrent development of two towns with very different histories. Collaboration with Peter Dunn.

1977–78 Campaign to save Bethnal Green Hospital

Exhibition posters and video produced and distributed in association with the hospital campaign committee. Collaboration with Peter Dunn.

1978–80 East London Health Project

Posters produced with East London Trades Councils. Collaboration with Peter Dunn.

1981–91 Docklands Community Poster Project

Ten years of cultural campaigning with the communities of East London around issues arising from the development of the London Docklands. Collaboration with Peter Dunn and others.

1991 Digital Highways, Local Narratives

Multimedia installation at Agnes Etherington Gallery, Kingston, Ontario. Collaboration with Peter Dunn, Karl Beveridge and Carole Condé.

1992 West Meets East

Photo-mural and touring exhibition with teacher and pupils from Central Foundation School for Girls in Bow, East London, that explored the young people's experience of living in two cultures.

1993–94 Celebrating the Difference

Photo-mural produced with teachers and pupils from George Green's School, Isle of Dogs, East London, addressing issues of culture and identity, commonality and difference in an inner city area fraught with racial tension.

1994 Between Family Lines

Four-projector tape slide production and exhibition made with women from five cultures who had suffered under fundamentalism or orthodoxy. Collaboration with Karen Merkel and Women Against Fundamentalism.

1995 The Green Chain

Public Art Strategy for Lee Valley Park proposing participatory projects, and artworks using technology, post-industrial and natural materials found in the park. Process led by Peter Dunn.

1995–96 Awakenings, after Stanley Spencer's Resurrection

Large-scale digital montage commissioned and exhibited at Tate Britain, following a year's production with pupils from George Green's School. Collaboration with Peter Dunn.

1996 Putting Ourselves in the Picture

Alpona panels and beadwork hangings created with women and children at Thomas Buxton School, East London, combining traditional Bangladeshi skills with digital processes.

1996 Beyond the Classroom

Co-ordination of a project to support schools in the commissioning of public artworks for their premises. Instigated and funded by the Lee Valley Park Authority with London Arts Board.

1996–97 Through Our Own Eyes

An "artists in schools" residency programme offering training and support to six graduates to develop their art practice within an educational context. Collaboration with University of East London and Tate Gallery, Millbank.

1997 A Welcoming Change

Commission by the Royal London Hospital for proposed refurbishment of its main entrance to create a welcoming environment reflecting the needs and cultures of the hospital's main users and communities. Collaboration with Anne Thorne Architects.

1997 The Infinity Story

Interactive illustrated story produced with three hundred children at Godwin Junior School, East London. Collaboration with Camille Dorney.

1998 Forging a Gateway

Input to a strategy by a multicultural artist team for refurbishment of the Aldgate subways complex. Commissioned by by Anne Thorne Architects.

1998–99 I.D

Tate Gallery commission to create a web site project with pupils from George Green's and Langdon Park secondary schools, taking inspiration from the John Singer Sargent exhibition. Collaboration with Henry Iles.

1999 Momentos

Commission by the Art Gallery of Ontario to create a web site project with four Toronto high schools, taking inspiration from their Cornelius Krieghoff exhibition. Resulted in an online resource and set of virtual postcards. Collaboration with Peter Dunn.

1999–2001 Widening Participation

A partnership initiative with Chelsea College of Art and Design, incorporating undergraduate involvement in projects, establishment of a higher education mentoring scheme for young people, and a postgraduate placement with The Art of Change.

1998–2002 The Catch

Public artwork for Barking town centre incorporating workshops with local children through the *Cascade* mentoring scheme. Commission by LB Barking and Dagenham produced in collaboration with Anne Thorne Architects.

1999–2002 Unlocking the Grid

Consultation report resulting from an approach to Arts Council England to fund research into the creation of content for the National Grid for Learning in schools in a way that would incorporate the arts across the curriculum.

1999–2009 VOLCO

Evolving planet in cyberspace constructed by over a thousand young people interacting online with others of different cultures and life experiences that used collective imagination to create a new world based on principles of co-operation.

2002–07 Cascade

Placements and mentoring around projects in the community focused on local regeneration issues, involving children, young people and university graduates.

2005–07 The Young Person's Guide to the Royal Docks

Online guide created with young people from The Royal Docks Community School and incorporating the *Cascade* mentoring scheme that addressed issues of heritage and regeneration in London Thames Gateway.

2007–09 Precious Places

A series of twelve commemorative plaques, exhibition and online trail produced with communities in South Newham to mark places of importance to them in this neighbourhood. www.portsofcall.org.uk/precious.html

2008–12 The Young Person's Guide to East London

Online guide and free newspaper produced with four hundred East London teenagers prior to the London 2012 Olympics. Received Media Trust Inspiring Voices award and Olympic Inspire Mark. www.ypg2el.co.uk

2014–15 Lambeth Floating Marsh

Art/science initiative addressing issues of biodiversity through construction of a floating reed bed on the River Thames and images of river micro-organisms projected along the embankment. Collaboration with scientist Nithin Rai. http://lambethfloatingmarsh.org.uk

2008–ongoing Active Energy

Interdisciplinary project in collaboration with The Geezers seniors group and engineer Toby Borland. Outputs include design of a low cost tidal turbine for the River Thames, a floating water wheel to drive an aerator for fish in the River Lea, a lightwork for AgeUK, and exhibitions in the UK and US. Partner organizations have included SPACE, Bow Boys School, Mattress Factory museum of installation Pittsburgh, the Hydrocitizenship research project (via Middlesex University), House Mill and Thames21. Received the 2016 RegenSW Best Arts and Green Energy award. www.active-energy-london.org

Index